THE MEDIC

A World War II Story of Imprisonment, Hope, and Survival

CLAIRE E. SWEDBERG

STACKPOLE
BOOKS
Guilford, Connecticut

Published by Stackpole Books
An imprint of The Rowman & Littlefield Publishing Group, Inc.
4501 Forbes Blvd., Ste. 200
Lanham, MD 20706
www.rowman.com

Distributed by NATIONAL BOOK NETWORK

British Library Cataloguing in Publication Information Available

Library of Congress Cataloging-in-Publication Data

Names: Swedberg, Claire E., author.
Title: The medic : a World War II story of imprisonment, hope, and survival /
    Claire E. Swedberg.
Description: Guilford, Connecticut : Stackpole Books, [2021] | Includes
    bibliographical references and index. | Summary: "From the Bataan Death
    March to Japanese prison camp to a "hell ship" and forced labor, American
    medic Henry Chamberlain survived the horrors of three and a half years of
    imprisonment during WW II. Claire Swedberg tells his story of excruciating
    hardship, abiding endurance, and transcendent courage beautifully, with great
    style and deep pathos"— Provided by publisher.
Identifiers: LCCN 2020057891 (print) | LCCN 2020057892 (ebook) | ISBN
    9780811739955 (cloth) | ISBN 9780811769839 (ebook)
Subjects: LCSH: Chamberlain, Henry Tilden, 1922- | World War, 1939-1945—
    Prisoners and prisons, Japanese. | Prisoners of war—Philippines—Biography.
    | Prisoners of war—United States—Biography. | World War, 1939-1945—
    Concentration camps—Philippines. | World War, 1939-1945—Medical care—
    Philippines. World War, 1939-1945—Concentration camps—Japan. | World
    War, 1939-1945—Medical care—Japan. | Bataan Death March, Philippines,
    1942. | United States. Army—Medical personnel—Biography.
Classification: LCC D805.P6 S94 2021 (print) | LCC D805.P6 (ebook) | DDC
    940.54/7252092 [B]—dc23
LC record available at https://lccn.loc.gov/2020057891
LC ebook record available at https://lccn.loc.gov/2020057892

I dedicate my story to those former American prisoners of war who gave their lives to protect their families, friends, and our country.

—Henry T. Chamberlain, Staff Sergeant, USAF (ret.)

CONTENTS

AUTHOR'S NOTE

This story is based on the life and recollections of World War II US Army Medic and surgical technician, Henry T. Chamberlain. The events here are true and based on his personal accounts, as well as corroborative research. Several names have been changed to protect the privacy of the individuals' families.

ACKNOWLEDGMENTS

A project such as this relies on the support of innumerable, international researchers, historians, authors, and witnesses to these events. Throughout the entire process of collecting and writing Henry Chamberlain's stories, I was assisted by a knowledgeable team of historians from Japan, the Philippines, and the United States who supported the writing process by providing context, background, and fact-checking. I'm especially grateful to all the POWs and veterans who published or otherwise shared their stories. Each individual's experience is both personal and universal and I'm grateful for every story I had access to. Special appreciation must be mentioned to historians Desiree Benipayo, Cecilia Gaerlan, James Zobel, The MacArthur Museum, Bob Hudson, Mine Takada, Sanders W. Marble, and the US Army Medical Department Museum. Thanks go to the American Defenders of Bataan and Corregidor and its dedicated members and officers for keeping history alive. Thanks to Joe Brown who shared the story of his father Charles Brown, a POW of Cabanatuan. My gratitude also goes to the Chamberlain family, all of whom supported Hank in retelling his story and ensured we had space, time, and support to carry on our unending conversations. Editorial and personal support came from my family and most especially my husband, Michael Wirth.

Finally, I thank Henry Chamberlain for having the gracious generosity to tell his story without hesitation and without filters. He proved throughout this process to have patience, humility, and patriotism. Through telling his story I have learned that he has lived his life and especially his war years with bravery, selflessness, and nobility. "I am no hero," he often declared.

Ultimately, I leave it to the readers to make their own conclusions. I hope those who read this story gain an appreciation for this history, find the spirit of survival embraced by these POWs, and can share Hank's goal that nothing such as this ever happens again.

INTRODUCTION

2017, SENDAI, JAPAN

Seventy-five years had passed since Henry Chamberlain last laid his eyes on the "mine god" that presided over the shaft of the Mitsubishi lead and zinc mine. The contrast between that time—World War II—and today couldn't have been more striking. Now, as a ninety-six-year-old, he rested between the support of his daughter on his right and his Japanese interpreter on his left. The rain fell softly on the small huddle of dignitaries around him—Mitsubishi executives, as well as a group of historians and diplomats, none born yet when he'd left this place. One member of the delegation raised a wide umbrella over Chamberlain's head.

The former POW gazed at the empty frame that had once contained a shiny, towering Japanese deity, guarding the entrance, installed to ensure good fortune for the mine and the men working inside. Chamberlain had cursed that symbol, day after day.

"What are you remembering?" his guide asked through an interpreter. He pointed.

"We had to bow to a figure there," his voice was calm and steady, no anger left in him. "Every day we bowed on our way in, and then we turned and bowed again on our way out," he said. The interpreter repeated his words in Japanese. The group listened with sober expressions, a few nodding their heads. Chamberlain was staggered by the contrast between his considerate hosts and the barbarism of his past. So he told them the rest, the part he hadn't mentioned for decades: about the last time he had seen the figure, on liberation day. He described the way he glared at that silent figure consumed with rage of the past war's injustice. At that time, in 1945, he had lifted his middle finger high over his head "I shouted, 'F-you!'" his eyes shone with the memory of that triumph. This too was interpreted to his hosts, and no flash of anger, no objections arose. This was history now.

The mine was now in disuse but tidy, silent, while the mountainous landscape loomed around, lush in its greenery. But memories clamored around Hank. He could feel, he could see, the presence of several hundred men, all dead now, but standing there beside him, some Americans, some British, in various stages of starvation and sickness, all faces raised to the god.

Those prisoners' spirits around him were dressed in the ragged remains of what had once been starched Army uniforms, now just a few scraps knotted around their waists to cover their privates. Some wore clogs they'd hammered out of discarded chunks of wood, others stood on their bare, calloused, or bleeding feet. Their hollow eyes seemed to consider another twelve hours in an endless litany of long days' labor underground. Chamberlain, the only medic working the mine, was there to help those who collapsed, if they were still alive.

Each day had started that way. Often Chamberlain had nothing to eat, but he chewed on a glob of coal tar he had scraped from the walls of the barracks. He and his fellow prisoners stuffed the thick black wads of tar in their mouths, kneading it between their loosening teeth. Chamberlain found the juice tasted sickening at first, but it eventually offered comfort to his empty stomach. Sometimes tar was all there was to keep them occupied until they ate the balls of maggot-infested rice at the end of a day's work.

While the mine had swarmed with Japanese, American, British, and Chinese miners during the war, now it was silent. The area was pastoral, the mine entrance was barred shut, the smelter that had burned day and night, now idle. As he looked around him, at the hill where his barracks had stood, at the path that had led to the crematorium, he began sinking to his knees.

His action sparked a flurry of worried responses from those around him. "No, Mr. Chamberlain, please wait." It was a matter of seconds before a chair was delivered in front of him, and they lowered him onto it. He had insisted on walking to this site. He folded at the waist and rested his head in his hands.

He might have looked like he was overcome, but he wasn't. He was praying, he told his daughter Rebecca that night in the hotel. He wasn't usually a church man, but this time, "I felt it was right, I had to say two prayers."

"What were they Dad?" she asked.

"I prayed for the men who were in that mine. I prayed for the POWs that lost their lives there."

He thought about those whom he saw enter the mine in the morning knowing, by the look of defeat in their eyes, the hopeless set of their shoulders, that they would not survive the day. They took up a pick and lantern in the morning and by afternoon Chamberlain might be carrying their bodies to the cremation site. Those were the men he couldn't help.

He prayed for them, but his second prayer was for the guards—the men—some military, some civilians, the ones with bamboo canes they struck on the shoulders and backs of prisoners, the ones with bayonets, the ones who were most severe and the ones who were treated as badly by their superiors. He prayed for their forgiveness, for those men, every one of them, were gone now as well.

I

COMBAT MEDICINE

1

MONDAY, DECEMBER 8, 1941

FORT WILLIAM MCKINLEY, THE PHILIPPINES

First it was just a sound: the drone of approaching planes, and Private Henry (Hank) Chamberlain glanced at the window. It was close to noon and he and his friend Earl Wilson had been whiling away their Sunday morning in the medics' barracks, keeping cool as the sun climbed high in the tropical sky.

It was the first day they had to take it easy after a week attending patients in the Fort McKinley Hospital Clinic. The clinic he was assigned to—just outside the teeming city of Manila—served military patients as well as their family members and local civil servants. Fresh out of training in the States, he'd spent the last few months assisting with routine surgeries, suturing cuts, and wrapping sprains.

On this December Sunday the barracks bunks were empty and made, most of the men had gone off to church service at the Fort McKinley chapel, or were at the PX (post exchange store), the laundry, or in town. It was already a warm day and the few who were still in the barracks—Hank and Earl Wilson—were still in their shorts and t-shirts.

As the hum of plane engines approached, Chamberlain stood up to see out the window. Air flight overhead was just part of the routine sounds of life in the Philippines, planes passed over regularly from Clark Airfield, Nielson Airport, and Nichols Fields, but this was different. It sounded like the engines were whistling, instead of the deep throaty rumble of the US Army planes they were used to. He and Earl exchanged a glance.

Two deafening explosions shook the barracks, shattering the afternoon calm. The concussion knocked Hank off his bed. The two army medics were racing for the door before they had time to think. On the barrack's

3

front porch they froze; smoke poured skyward several blocks to the south where Fort William McKinley's warehouses stored army supplies. Flames flashed through the trees, and a Manila air-raid siren suddenly wailed. Then Chamberlain saw the fighter planes, several of them, barreling in his direction.

It was nine hours since 353 Imperial Japanese aircraft had decimated the US Naval fleet at Pearl Harbor, Hawaii, but none of the privates in this army barracks had heard of that yet. In fact, the soldiers and medics, and all of Fort McKinley, were caught utterly by surprise. Hank and Earl may have been the only ones standing on the porch that morning, gaping south as the planes approached low: five hundred feet—then even lower. They couldn't see the markings as the plane seemed to hone in on his position.

The two medics could have ducked back into the barracks but Chamberlain thought better of that, and they stood rooted to the porch floor, watching one of the planes drop closer, just fifty feet above the trees, plowing on toward them. Then it opened fire.

Terror sent the two medics leaping over the railing—two more steps in their bare feet and they were hunched behind a mahogany tree that grew in front of the barracks, eight feet wide at the base.

Bullets sliced the ground toward them and then caught the trunk of the tree with a deep, thunk, thunk, thunk. Hank felt each shot's impact in the woody flesh as he pressed against it. The bullets slammed on past them, spraying dirt and rocks as they rained over the barracks and beyond. And then the plane lifted and swung to the right, displaying large red circles on the wings. Then it was gone.

Bombs exploded in the distance, their sights set on Nichols Field, and smoke rose skyward. In the adjacent field, two Filipino infantry regiments opened with return fire bullets from machine guns and any other weapon available, ripping into the sky at any remaining enemy planes.

While the air-raid sirens blared, the two medics huddled in their spot, hearts hammering, bodies trembling, clutching the tree that had saved their lives. Flames rose behind the forest where the warehouses had been, and they could hear the crackling of bursting wood. Once they were convinced no more planes were coming, Hank stood. His ears were ringing and sweat soaked his t-shirt. He learned that day that terror releases the bowels, every time.

"God damn." They stared in the direction the planes had traveled, "What the hell is this? What are they shooting at us for?"

Earl shook his head, his hands on his head, his face reflecting Hank's fear, "Was that the Japs?"

Just as Hank and Earl had taken cover from the planes' strafing, about sixty miles away Clark Airfield was under attack. The Japanese assault on the United States—beginning in Pearl Harbor—was just getting started. Its navy sent two hundred Mitsubishi bombers from Formosa (today known as Taiwan), two hundred miles away, to take out US equipment and planes, followed by fighters targeting American and Filipino military sites. In fact, for Japan, the Philippines represented the key that unlocked the door to the Pacific.

The attack was a resounding success for the Japanese. At Clark Airfield, the planes had been neatly parked in a row, wing tip to wing tip, and within minutes most of the local American air power, including fighters and B-17 Flying Fortress bombers, were wiped out. Half of the Filipino air fleet was gone as well. By the time the air assault on the Philippines was over, Japan's control of the skies would deliver a major advantage over the tropical islands that had served the United States as a strategic base of operations. Now, Japan commenced its land invasion.

It was the first time Hank had been shot at, but it would hardly be the last. He didn't know it yet, but America's war with Japan was underway and he was trapped on an island where the enemy would soon take charge. He had started on a hellish path through what would be four years of war and three-and-a-half years of captivity in the hands of the Japanese.

2

1940

FORT CROOK, NEBRASKA

Hank felt the full assault of his sergeant's glare as he stood at attention in the man's office. His eyes fixed on the American flag hanging beside the desk, while his sergeant leaned over that desk toward him, his outrage palpable.

"What did you just tell me, Private?"

"I don't want to be a rifleman. Sir!"

"You're the best sharpshooter in your class, this is the Army, Private Chamberlain. What do you expect to be doing here? We're going to be fighting a war and I need shooters. What Goddamn reason do you have not to be a rifleman?"

Hank took a deep breath before answering with the force of a lifelong conviction. "I don't want to kill people, sir." The sergeant let out a breath that could have been exasperation or a laugh.

"Don't call me sir, call me Sergeant. Go await your orders, Private, I'm not done with you yet. Now get the hell out of my office before I do something I'll regret."

"Yes-Sergeant!" he couldn't get out of the office fast enough, but he measured his pace, stepping out into the summer Nebraska sun and taking a long breath as the door slammed shut behind him. Now what? He had signed up for the army on his eighteenth birthday, on the advice of his friends—volunteer before they draft you into a service you'll hate. He hadn't put much thought into the moral collision course ahead. Life had made him an excellent sharpshooter. He had grown up in Omaha with a rifle in his hands—he had needed it to feed himself and his single mother. Often his rifle was the only thing between him and a night's sleep on an empty stomach. Day by day he had been building his skills as a sharp-shooter. But he wasn't going to kill a fellow man. Somewhere in those Sunday mornings in church, and in his own young life, he had learned a conviction. "I thought it was wrong to kill somebody. Somewhere in my religious training I'd learned that much." Never. It wasn't right. Now it looked like he had made himself an enemy in the last place he needed one—his own regiment in the form of his sergeant.

★ ★ ★

Henry Tilden Chamberlain, Jr., (always known as Hank) was born on June 6, 1922, one of a few hundred residents of Morse Bluff, Nebraska, a farming village overlooking the Platt River, near Omaha. His father provided farm labor, but he left Hank's mother Alvina to raise their only child on her own. So the boy grew up with a single mother, then for about six years with George Morgan—the man his mother married—an electrician who had worked for Ringling Bros. and Barnum & Bailey circuses. Hank never found a way to get along with his stepfather.

Alvina Louise Soper worked in Omaha repairing broken film for a film exchange. Sliding her hand along the film edges she could feel out the start of a break and then splice and repair the film with a liquid brush. It paid enough to manage many of the bills, with no husband in the picture, but for most of his life, they'd relied on Hank's odd jobs, or support from George, during the six years that he was in their lives.

Small game was hard to come by during the Great Depression when Nebraska's open land had been picked over by several generations of hungry pioneers. Large game was almost nonexistent. So, when he was lucky enough to spot a rabbit or bird, he could take it down with one clean shot. Even though he became a marksman to shoot animals for food, or to protect the farm, he also knew the fragility of life.

Just once Hank had seen a gun aimed and fired at another person. It happened while the family was eating supper in the early 1930s. His stepfather George Morgan was especially proud of a Chrysler Imperial he had purchased off the showroom floor. He parked it in front of their two-bedroom house on North 41st Street in Omaha, and often stepped out front to look at it, polishing it off each time it rained. As usual one evening, as they ate their supper, George and Hank had nothing civil to say to each other, and Hank was hurrying to leave the table. He didn't notice the sound in front of his house, but George's head shot up, on alert, straining to hear. "What was that?" He dropped his fork and went to the side window, pushing the curtain aside. Then he leaped back. "Holy Goddamn hell where's my gun?" Within seconds he was running through the front door with his .44 Magnum hogleg pistol, peering down the steep hill of their front yard at the street. He trained his sites, then fired several times. Alvina let out a shriek. Hank heard the anguished cries of a man hit. "What did you do?" Alvina screamed, putting one hand out to grab her husband's arm. George pulled it away and ran to the street calling, "He was stealing my car! Call the cops!" Hank followed his stepfather but paused when Alvina called to him, "Don't you go out there, you don't want any part in that. You stay right here." So Hank listened to the man's screams from the kitchen, while Alvina picked up the phone and ordered the neighbors off the party line so that she could call for help. After an interminable wait of just a few minutes, police arrived. The man would be arrested and treated for the gunshot wound to his leg. Hank watched the police lift the would-be thief into the back of their car, as he was still crying out in pain. George was unconcerned with the man's suffering, much more distressed to realize he'd shot his own car through the hood and destroyed its distributor. Hank's feelings for his stepfather hardened into a deep contempt.

★ ★ ★

Now, in late 1940 in Fort Crook, as war stormed across Europe, and the US military ramped up to meet the threat, US Army private Hank Chamberlain's sergeant fumed. He didn't need an infantry man who wouldn't shoot a gun, and he wasn't having it.

Knowing his Sergeant's wrath was coming, Hank paid a visit to the medical unit on base where his own childhood doctor was stationed. He found Dr. Dahl in his office treating minor training injuries and illnesses among the new recruits. Hank told Dr. Dahl his dilemma. He didn't want to be a rifleman. "I want to help people, not kill people. I want to serve my country without killing."

A few days later, after revelry, the sergeant came into the barracks. Before the men could stand at attention he stooped over Hank's bed and gave it a hearty kick. "Get up and pack your shit, you're coming with me." They drove in silence to the train station. "You have anyone you want to talk to before leaving town? You've got an hour." He handed a fistful of coins to the young private. Hank called his mother to say goodbye. It would be the last time he would hear her voice for four years.

His sergeant delivered him to the train platform, pushed him toward the arriving train, and then handed an envelope to the conductor, "Don't open this until you're sixty miles out of town." Hank seated himself at a window and watched the prairie slide past as he headed west. An hour later the conductor stood at his seat and opened the envelope. It contained meal tickets and the name of his destination: McChord Field in Washington State. His assignment—medical training. He was elated. Even as a boy he'd thought of working as a doctor, helping people out of their pain or their sickness. His first job on the base was driving the ambulance. Before being sent out on his first run, the sergeant had a question for him. "How do you handle the sight of blood?" Hank shrugged, "Not a problem, sir. I've been a hunter all my life, I've seen a lot of blood." That announcement must have been good news for his new sergeant, and it led to his assignment as surgical assistant.

As a boy Hank's aspiration was in medicine. He spent several weeks in the hospital with diphtheria, and he knew that the pain in his throat, the miserable headache, fever, the gasping for a breath of air, were relieved with the help of the fleet of nurses and doctors who attended to him. He wanted to help others the way they had helped him. That's what it came down to. But there was no money even for the next meal, let alone medical school. The army had been the obvious choice. The fact that he would be expected to do the opposite of helping people, to actually kill people, hadn't come fully into focus until boot camp.

Now at this cloudy airbase in the northwest reaches of the country, he was entering the best time of his life. He formed a tight group of friends all training as medics, including recent Utah high school graduate Earl Wilson and Everett Schneeweiss from California who he referred to as "Sneezy." Bill Holt was the fourth member of their group, from a more affluent background, and a likely candidate to make a career out of medicine.

For the first time, Hank had three square meals every day, a good job, and strapping good health. At five feet ten inches, 165 pounds, he was strong and happy. The sandy-haired private was quick with an infectious smile and twinkling eyes and soon earned the attention of a new girlfriend in Spokane named Cathy. He had the world ahead.

3

OCTOBER 1941

MANILA, THE PHILIPPINES

When Hank, Earl, Bill, and Sneezy were assigned overseas Hank had never heard of the Philippines. He went looking for a map and then pored over the picture of an archipelago, smoothing down the folds that separated the Southeast Asian islands. "That little bitty place?" They were destined for a land of warm breezes and tropical foods; in fact the four friends marveled at their good luck. They weren't going anywhere near Europe where news reports described Germany's methodical aggressions.

Instead, traveling to the other side of the world, they were stationed at Fort William McKinley—not far from Manila—where American and Filipino forces were training and medics practiced on the injured and sick. Hank and his three closest friends worked hard under the supervision of Dr. Harry Brown at the fort hospital in its Spanish style stucco building, with a red-tiled roof, covered in ivy and shaded by native flame trees.

They spent their evenings enjoying the unfamiliar seafood and tropical fruits, warm weather, and unending social scene of Manila. The city streets were chaotic with pedestrians, bicycles, and carabao pulling carts laden with produce. Vendors hawked local fruits and vegetables, as well as fabric and baskets made by the indigenous people in the mountains. The streets were flanked by open sewage trenches, with the rank smell of human waste. But the warm humid breeze also delivered the perfume of tropical plants. Wild poinsettias flowering well ahead of Christmas decorated the verdant hills.

The four medics ate the local food, flirted, and drank. They rented bicycles from a middle-aged Japanese merchant and rode around the city streets. Earl, a devout Mormon, avoided the troubles related to drinking and women but enjoyed the nightlife escapades. Bill was a thinking man, with college in his future and the most affluent of the group. Sneezy played baseball in the States and here in Manila he attended baseball games among the servicemen and brought Hank along for fun. Of the four, Hank had seen the hardest side of life. He'd lived on the streets, knew poverty and mental and physical illness. When life was going his way he appreciated it, because he knew all too well that comfort and ease could be fleeting. Of the four, he was the least disturbed, or surprised, by the illnesses and injuries coming into the Fort McKinley hospital—tropical diseases and malnutrition, along with the injuries the Philippine Scouts and US Army soldiers suffered in training.

There were surprises for Hank too though. He'd known few Asians back in Omaha. He might have walked past a Japanese spy, helping prepared the Japanese Imperial Army for its invasion, but he wouldn't have known the difference. The Filipinos for the most part greeted him on the streets with a "Hi, Joe," and he felt at ease there. Hank had little sense of the tension rising around the Pacific, or the conflict homing in on the tropical archipelago he now called home.

Harry Brown appreciated Hank's background. He too had grown up without many luxuries. The doctor was about a decade his senior, had recently married, and he treated Hank like a younger brother. He brought the young medic into the surgical procedures, counseled him through the setting of broken bones, stitching of wounds, and a childbirth or two. Hank, who had lacked father figures, appreciated a doctor who entered medicine to heal those in need. Children willingly came for their treatments or vaccinations, and the stick of candy Brown would find for them in a glass jar on his desk.

While the medics learned their trade at Fort McKinley's hospital, General Douglas MacArthur had been called out of retirement to oversee the Philippine military training of its army and those Filipino soldiers too, often ended up in the Fort McKinley clinic. Hank paid little attention to rumors related to Japanese aggression in the Pacific.

4

DECEMBER 1941

FORT WILLIAM MCKINLEY, THE PHILIPPINES

Japan's unexpected assault on Pearl Harbor began at 3 a.m. Philippines time. That gave the US military ten hours before about two hundred Mitsubishi bombers and Zero fighters streamed over the Philippine Islands from Formosa, two hundred miles away. The aerial bombardment still caught the US Armed Forces by surprise. While bombers dropped their explosives on Fort McKinley's air installations at Nichols Field, about sixty miles away Clark Airfield was also getting hammered. Rows of planes were still parked wing tip to wing tip making an easy target for the Japanese bombers. Within minutes the American airpower was devastated, including a squadron of US Boeing four-engine B-17 "Flying Fortress" bombers. Half of the Philippine air fleet was gone. It wasn't just the bombers either, the Japanese aircraft destroyed American Curtis P-40E fighter plane interceptors and P-35A fighter aircraft at Clark and Iba fields. The former airfield also saw its radar units put out of action. Now, with sirens still blaring and firefighters racing to the bomb sites, there was widespread confusion among the enlisted men in Fort McKinley.

In the hour following the attack, medics hurried to the barracks, to the hospital, and some back to the barracks, were ordered to stay put, to pack, then to stay put again. Chamberlain was among the first group assigned to the two-story hospital that had served as Hank's training ground as he helped treat everything from sprains and broken bones to malaria.

Now he skirted the side of the building that separated the clinic from the barracks, casting wary looks at the sky and toward the clinic's front door. By the time he reached the entrance, a jeep had screeched to a stop before him and two soldiers unloaded several injured patients. One patient stared listlessly, silent with numb shock, the end of his leg a bloody stump, a blood-soaked pant leg where his foot should have been. These were the soldiers who had been in harm's way when the Japanese bombed Fort McKinley's warehouses.

Inside the hospital, there was no sign of that calm, casual, clinical efficiency that Hank was used to. Patients lined the entrance way, doctors and nurses raced from one to another. Dr. Brown stood near the door, meeting each victim as he was carried inside. His face was uncharacteristically grim. He glanced up to see Hank's arrival and his expression showed a flash of relief.

"Chamberlain, stabilize that patient for surgery," Brown gestured to the man with the blown off foot. Hank followed the men carrying his gurney into surgery. As they lowered the patient onto the nearest table, however, a shout caught them all by surprise. "Where are you putting that patient? God damn it! Over here, set him over here, there's more coming!"

Once the patient was secured against the far surgery wall, Chamberlain fought past his trepidation and nausea. He'd never seen an injury like this.

"What do I do?" He didn't know if he asked the question aloud until Dr. Brown shouted out, "Take off that tourniquet, clamp the bleeder."

Chamberlain put a stabilizing hand on the patient's shoulder. "Hold on, and try to stay quiet now," he said. "You're going to be fine." He gripped a sterile set of scissors and cut away the pant leg, exposing the raw flesh and bone of his ankle. He untied the makeshift tourniquet that had been applied below the knee by another soldier in the field, and the vein began to pump out the man's blood until Hank could get a clamp over the broken arteries still trying to supply the missing foot. Before he could consider the results, Brown shouted "Chamberlain, we need you over here."

Injuries kept pouring in all afternoon: soldiers, civil servants, and even some civilians. He scrubbed wounds cut in jagged gore, wiped away dirt and grease, washed wounds with saline. He joined the surgeons to help with suturing.

"Stop the bleeding" was the number one priority. Broken bones were splinted. If the doctor ordered it, Hank administered pain medication to the victims in the most distress, many already came in with a morphine drip.

As fast as he could serve one man, another was ready to take his place. Nothing he did that day had been covered in his training, and every patient brought a new frightening challenge. Hank's only thought was to help the next patient and the next, and not to make any mistakes that would do more damage to those already suffering.

By Monday, twenty-four hours after the initial attack, the clinic, like other parts of the base, was getting fired on from the sky. The neighborhoods around it were too. Several times a day Zero planes roared overhead, opening fire at anything they saw moving, and then sweeping away. With their red dots emblazoned on the plane wings, the medics referred to them as the "Flaming Assholes." More patients flowed into the clinic, many were the results of these aerial attacks. There was both American and Filipino personnel; the Japanese fire power didn't discriminate.

By the end of Monday, the clinic was running short on supplies, so Brown sent Chamberlain to the warehouse that had been struck during the bombing, to salvage any medical equipment he could find—bandages, gauze, stretchers, splints, sulfa, medicine of any kind. He walked to the explosion site, where the air was still thick with the smell of smoldering ash.

The site was devastated. The warehouse where the medical supplies were stored was just splinters now. Fragments of the building and the goods stored inside were scattered hundreds of feet in every direction. He stopped to consider the immensity of this damage, the odor of burning waste, the smoke still rising from places in the pelted earth. Dashing from one pile of wreckage to another he located a half-burned carton of cleaning supplies, put it under his arm, and deposited it on the side of the road. Always with one eye turned toward the sky, he searched further and found sterilizing equipment, then surgical tools and shoved them in his pockets. Everything he couldn't carry went into his roadside pile to be collected by a jeep later. That would supply them for a few more days at the clinic.

At nights he returned to his barracks, still exhausted and confused. The medics, along with other privates listened to the radio, trying to make sense of their new reality. But with their limited understanding of the broadcasted Filipino language—Tagalog—most were able only to pick out a few familiar terms.

One order was clear: stay in the barracks, no more visits to the PX or gym or laundry without an escort. There were other orders too: to stay out of the way of Japanese firepower. They would no longer be fraternizing in town with the Filipinos. They would turn out the lights at night, after which Chamberlain and his friends lay in their bunks staring into the dark. Hank's body was stiff with tension, his nerves ragged. He heard men shouting in the distance at times, the barking of dogs, and though he listened for the Japanese planes, they didn't seem to approach after dark. Despite that, no sleep would come. "Bill, you awake?" He heard Bill turning on his bunk and his friend sat up, his silhouette facing him. "Wide awake."

"When do you think they're going to put a stop to these Jap planes?" They both lay in the dark with no answer. They couldn't believe the war would last long, America couldn't be outmaneuvered by Japan. For Hank, it was just the beginning. He wouldn't rest well again for years.

During the day Japanese planes were relentless. They often attacked nearby Manila, and Chamberlain could see the action from the base. Air-raid sirens moaned with or without the planes, fanning a sense of panic for the Filipino population. At the clinic the doctors and medics could no longer rely on the power: it flashed off, stayed out for hours, was restored, only to go back out. That meant the loss of light and heat for sterilization of tools. And medical supplies needed to be closely managed. Whenever something could be reused, it was.

On his way to the hospital, Chamberlain heard the familiar whine of the Zeros' guidewires vibrating in the wind. As it grew louder, he dove for cover behind the nearest structure. Some of the medics with him, who couldn't reach cover, took the next best strategy and rolled into a ball. The planes swept like lawnmowers, back and forth, fixing their sights on men as well as the buildings the men were in. He watched in horror. It seemed as if the planes were in slow motion, machine-gunning his friend.

When the planes passed, he leaped to his feet, rushing to the closest prone figure.

"Okay, where are you hurt?"

He turned the man over and looked at the swelling patch of blood soaking the man's pants. He was crying out from the pain. Chamberlain had seen enough in four days to know what to do. He pulled out the blade he had carried with him since the age of eight, a gift his grandfather had presented to him, declaring "every boy needs his own knife."

Folding out the blade, he grabbed hold of the man's pant leg and sliced it along the seam, tearing and cutting himself a long piece of fabric. He then cinched it around the leg, above the gaping wound.

"Stretcher, I need a stretcher!" he shouted, His voice was hoarse from four days of shouting. It was likely, he knew, that this friend was going to make it. But would he be able to leave the Philippines?

5

DECEMBER 13, 1941

STERNBERG HOSPITAL, MANILA

By the end of the week his commanding officer, Colonel Duckworth, told Chamberlain and his comrades to pack their bags. He had no idea, when he climbed into the back of an Army truck, on December 13, 1941, where he was going. The men were being mobilized in different directions throughout the Manila area. Hank sat in the truck pulling out through the base's Carabao Gate, and away from the only place he'd known in the Philippines, away from his friend Sneezy, from Earl and Bill, and from Dr. Brown. He had no idea if or when he would be seeing his mentor or friends again.

The truck jostled its load of medics through the muddy streets of Manila and stopped in a crowded barrio, not far from the Pasig River, where the busiest US Army hospital in the city stood. In fact, Sternberg General Hospital was the largest and best-equipped medical facility in the Philippines, and now, with the war on, it was transformed into a central receiving point for casualties, American and Filipino, military and civilian alike.

"All right men, fall out."

Chamberlain stepped out of his truck and into chaos. Here he would be working with ten times the number of patients he had seen at the base. People of all walks of life rushed around him here—Filipino workers recruited to manage cleaning, cooking, and transportation. Before the war Sternberg Hospital had served civilians with diseases such as leprosy, tuberculosis, and amoebic dysentery.[1] Now nearly every patient suffered war-related injuries, some devastating.

The injured came in in spurts: victims of gunfire, bombings, or fire. The stench of burning flesh was nauseating, as was the sight of mangled

17

bodies—slick with dirt and blood—arms and legs at weird angles, some dangling by a shred, others only jagged stumps.

Orders were fired at him the minute he reported for duty. His first patient was stunned from shock and pain, his arm hung unnaturally loose from the socket, a bone protruding through the skin. Like the others, Chamberlain began shouting: Where were the splints, the gloves, anti-septics? He lifted the arm as gently as he could, while the man let out a whimper.

The next patient had an abdominal injury, intestines exposed in the deep gash of his belly. "You're going to be okay," he reassured, but worried that this one, he already knew from a week's experience, probably wasn't going to make it.

Before the war, Sternberg General Hospital had a capacity of about 450 patients, about one thousand were onsite after the war began. Doctors and medics accommodated patients anywhere they could find space. Hank helped doctors shove desks together in offices to make room for the next injured soldier. When they ran out of stretchers, men lay on the floor, and then the steps in front of the building. Hank learned to step over those who still awaited a table to lie on.

When patients died, their bodies were covered with a sheet, and Chamberlain, other medics, or civilian Filipino workers carried the dead up a flight of stairs into a storage room. They stacked the bodies there, covered with a blanket or sheet, one, two, three high until someone came to pick them up. In the tropical heat of Manila, this improvised morgue was stifling and the stench of decay filled the air around it.

★ ★ ★

Hank's first experience with death came unexpectedly in the mid-1930s on one of Omaha's most unforgivingly cold nights. Life at his mother's house had become leaner since George Morgan had been thrown out of the family house. They were living on Alvina's limited income and it wasn't enough to pay all the bills. So he took a job as a Western Union delivery boy, riding around town, skidding over ice and snow, blowing on his chapped hands. The sun had gone down and the streets were dark as he cycled past parked cars on his way home for supper. When he saw a dark shape slumped in front of a sedan on the side of the road, he hit the brakes. Was that a dog? Someone sitting, or even a stranger, lying on the side of the road in these frigid temperatures? He climbed off his bike to get a closer look and found a man in a thin overcoat, slumped on his side.

When he touched the figure's shoulder it was rigid, cold, dead. He turned the man onto his back and saw that his mouth hung slightly open, his eyes clouded. "Sir? Mister? Are you okay?" He shook the man, thought maybe he'd shown a glimmer of life, then wondered what he could do now. "Stay there, just hold on, Mister," he stood, started to run away, turned back. "You'll be okay, just hang on!" he shouted over his shoulder before cycling to a payphone. He had to dial and redial with frozen fingers, but got the call out, and returned to the man's side. He sat on the curb, waiting until a police car arrived. Instincts told him the man was dead, but he held out hope, even as the stiff body was placed in the car, that this man might survive.

★ ★ ★

At times Chamberlain was so tired he lost track of the work in front of him, and by then, the surgeon on duty told him to lie down. He and a handful of medics and doctors would find an office in the hospital to try catching snatches of sleep, but no rest came. Instead he stared up at the ceiling, listening to the voices from the surgical rooms, with images of the bleeding bodies burned into his brain, along with the calls of fear and pain from the patients. And he waited until the door burst back open and the next instruction came: "Wake up crew, we need your help,"

Hank resorted to more basic lifelines for his patients, an alcohol rub on a hot rash or injection, ice to cool infections. He pressed a needle into the vein of those going into surgery to provide the plasma needed for the procedure until there was no plasma left. Hospital staff doled out iced tea for patients and staff alike. Food came while he was working, a sandwich or bowl of rice pressed into his hand while one patient was being removed, and before the next was deposited on the blood-soaked bed. They had run out of clean linens.

As food supplies fell short, the patients were given priority, and the meals for medics, nurses, and doctors got smaller. They all complained, Hank remembered, but some complained more than others. He had grown up knowing the raw ache of an empty stomach. He'd always outlasted hunger as a boy, and he could meet hunger head-on now. That wasn't true for them all. Some of them he found so spoiled when he arrived at Fort McKinley, he referred to them as the Candy Ass Kids—the group of medics who complained about army food and preferred to buy candy at the PX. That was when they could get their hands on candy, but those days were over now.

It was the fear and confusion that overcame him though. The bombings, the gunfire from planes flying over the streets of Manila were becoming more frequent and it seemed likely now that the Japanese were going to take control of the city. Without a moment to wonder what was coming, he simply turned to the next patient in the unending stream of the sick and wounded.

6

CHRISTMAS 1941

BATAAN, THE PHILIPPINES

By late December the fight for the Philippines seemed as if it had been raging for months, a lifetime. But the direction the war was taking in Manila was unmistakable. Japanese bombing raids had been relentless, sirens called mournfully at all hours, the streets were empty. By Christmas Eve American tanks and heavy artillery were pulling out. Hank could hear them rumbling down the street past Sternberg General Hospital. The battle line was shifting, and the US Army was preparing to withdraw American medical staff from Manila. With heavy fighting in the Peninsula of Bataan, these doctors, medics, and nurses would work in several field hospitals or forward aid stations near the battlefield.[1]

The Japanese attacked aggressively and on December 23, General Douglas MacArthur, US commander in the Philippines, withdrew all American and Philippine forces to the Bataan Peninsula. The plan was to dig in and await reinforcements, but most of the food, ammunition, and other supplies that were supposed to be moved to Bataan never got there. MacArthur in the meantime moved his headquarters to Corregidor.

So that night, on a Christmas that would be like no other, Hank and the other medical staff gathered in front of the hospital headquarters in a gloomy and dispirited group. The medics, doctors, and nurses were led by Lieutenant Colonel William Craig. As Hank watched the sway of palm fronds against the dark sky, he felt the fatigue of one sleepless night after another. His head ached and he shivered in the cool breeze. He had contracted malaria from the mosquitoes that swarmed the hospital. The quinine a doctor administered him the day before had helped, but not enough.

Now standing at the hospital gate, he had the name of his destination: Bataan, but had no idea what to expect there. He summoned the patience of an enlisted man, waiting for the next directive. He knew Bataan was under siege, there was heavy fighting there, in the jungle at the foot of steep mountains. Philippine Scouts, newly trained Philippine troops, and the American military were defending the Island of Luzon against the onslaught of Japanese invaders. Already many of the injured he'd seen in recent days at Sternberg had come from this peninsula across the Manila Bay from their city. It seemed their injuries were the worst Hank had seen yet.

Hank carried his musette bag over his shoulder; loaded with all his supplies including extra clothing, blanket, mosquito netting, canteen, cup, razor, toothbrush, and the knife his grandfather gave him. He brought a picture of his mother and another of his brunette girlfriend Cathy. The truck was loaded with bags of medicine: morphine, sulfa, iodine, and bandages.

Their ride to the Manila port came in the form of a convoy of American jeeps and trucks, where they sat in the beds as the vehicles wound through the solemn, empty streets of Manila to the port, where the expanse of water shone before them, lit by moonlight.

As they climbed out of the trucks, Hank considered the scene before him. For the first time he laid his eyes on the wreckage the Japanese had already inflicted on Manila. Ships and much of the port had fallen to the heavy bombardment of Nippon bombs. Their transportation came in the form of a medical ship they loaded with the medical supplies that would help create two field hospitals and their supporting stations.

The boat slipped through Manila Bay westward through the night, silent but for the lapping of the waves against the vessel's flanks. They moved slowly and it was morning before they reached their destination, the barrio of Cabcaben. From here, Hank was headed to a combat-area medical unit near a town called Limay, hunkered at the base of Mount Mariveles.

The sun rose as doctors, medics, and nurses hurriedly disembarked. Their destinations varied. Nurses climbed directly onto waiting buses headed for the two new field hospitals. Hospital 1 would serve the most severely injured and provide extensive surgical support, while Hospital 2 would support Hospital 1 and would soon become the largest military hospital in history.

The medics helped off-load supplies from the ship. As they worked, Japanese bombers appeared like wasps over a cookout, circling overhead. The planes started dropping bombs one after another, none quite hitting the medical team's ship—the supposed target—as if the Japanese weren't serious about their attack. Although the men watched the sky nervously, it didn't amount to anything more than a "lot of noise," Hank recalled. Colonel Craig in the meantime stood on the boat deck giving orders as it was unloaded, ignoring the bombers entirely.[2]

Chamberlain was selected with a small group of about fifteen men (including five physicians, with Chamberlain the only surgical technician) and they made their way by jeep to their new worksite: providing infantry and artillery support. Each was assigned a sidearm—protection he would use if anyone threatened a patient. They would not be at one of the new hospitals but would make up a small mobile unit serving injured soldiers as soon as they could be rescued from the battlefield.

The jeep pushed north into deep jungle, grown dark with thickets of bamboo and large trees looming above their small vehicle, adorned in a heaving growth of vines, their roots deep in thick undergrowth.

Hank watched the jungle grow even thicker on one side, the coast rolled out into the distance on the other as they hugged the shoreline. The sun peeked down over the canopy and the jeep turned into the jungle's heart, away from the shore. What started as a dirt road dwindled to a wagon- and carabao-worn path where rocks and roots rattled the jeep's journey, slowing its progress to a crawl.

To describe it later, Hank recalled this part of Bataan as "a mess." Small villages, referred to as barrios, dotted the jungle they now penetrated. Gunfire could be heard in the distance and planes buzzed over their heads, firing into the trees around them. The men crouched in the jeep, arms over their helmets: they'd been in Bataan only a few hours and already they had been under attack for most of that time. "Nobody knew what was going on and we were not being told." They stopped and unloaded at a site near a stream pouring down from Mount Natib, which towered above the jungle canopy, and set up a tent that would serve as triage. They could sleep on the ground outside.

The forward aid station where they would work was located within a few miles of the two key facilities: Hospital 1 and Hospital 2. Before they had unloaded all their gear, the sick and wounded were trickling into their midst. Hank would soon learn that this flow of men in need would be unending. "We were the first to see the wounded and first to put dressings on."

When battle injured men and the sick came into the unit, Hank's responsibility was stabilizing these patients. They wouldn't stay long, but what happened at the medical unit could mean the difference between survival or death.

The Battle for Bataan began in earnest on January 9, 1942, with the Japanese bombarding the Philippine and American forces with artillery. Numerous assaults followed, repulsed again and again by the defenders. The Japanese paused their assault in late February until one hundred thousand replacements were delivered along with 150 heavy guns brought in from Hong Kong. Help for the defenders, however, never would come. Philippine President Manuel L. Quezon agonized, "America writhes in anguish as the fate of a distant cousin, Europe, while a daughter in the Philippines is being raped in the back room." In fact, soldiers fought in isolation, their food dwindling and short on ammunition. Reinforcement or rescue wasn't coming.

In their first night after fighting began, the station's medical staff got a taste of what was to come. Firefights erupted in bursts around them, some distant, some close enough to make the men flinch. The lights of jeeps flashed against the canopy as the vehicles rumbled into the site with US or Filipino soldiers in the back, shot, injured, or sick. Many of the Filipino soldiers lacked shoes or even uniforms, and they seemed to have already lost strength and weight. American soldiers weren't faring much better.

With a small generator, the next day they set up lights and collected water from the stream while vehicles continued coming and going from the site. Filipino residents from neighboring barrios came to provide help cooking, washing clothes, and carrying patients. It didn't take long for the Japanese soldiers to recognize the operation there, and Hank developed a habit of preparing to drop to the ground whenever he heard firepower of any kind. All the men adopted a hunched stance, whether walking, running, or standing over a patient. They had all seen how fast a bullet could find the head of a man who wasn't paying attention.

This was nothing like the battle lines Hank had heard about from the World War I vets in Omaha. Every place he looked could be a combat area, there was no line to get behind. The Japanese seemed to be everywhere around them.

With only one doctor at the hospital, Hank assumed second-in-command status as a surgical technician. It was a role he felt uncomfortable with. By this time he had heavy experience in medical procedures and surgical assistance but it dated back just a month. Now the doctor was putting more faith in him than he felt he was ready for.

Some days saw dozens of men brought in, sometimes all in critical need of care. The first step was to break the injured into categories. The ones who weren't going to make it were lined up on the ground, some unconscious, some crying out in pain and more alert than their injuries should have allowed. When time allowed Hank went to sit with these men, offering some comfort in their final minutes or hours.

Those who couldn't speak for themselves and were critically wounded but still had a chance for survival got seen first, while those who could sit up, talk, or drink water had to wait. Most of the injuries involved bullets or shrapnel—in the extremities, in the gut, neck, or face. Some had multiple bullets in them. In some cases, the bullet had hit an artery.

Civilians came in as well, carried in, by other villagers. Anyone bayonetted in the abdomen was the hardest to treat. They bled hard, they suffered, and there was little that could be done to staunch the free flow of blood. If they suffered a puncture of the lungs the labored breathing meant they weren't going to last long. It was unlikely such patients would survive the trip to the hospital.

Hank dreaded the abdominal injuries because of the misery they caused, and the bleeding out of a life. Typically he stood by the doctor providing support as the man tried to stanch the blood flow enough to transport him to surgery at the hospital. One afternoon a single delivery of the injured included several men in need of immediate attention. One young Filipino was hemorrhaging blood from a gut wound. As the doctor raised the man's shirt, he called out to Hank. "Chamberlain, I need you to stop this man's bleeding." It was a familiar refrain, but in this case the man's situation was dire. He was semiconscious but stoically silent, his shirt was saturated and blood bubbled down his sides. He would never survive the trip to Hospital 1. Hank nodded, "Yes, sir," because that was the only option.

He didn't need to put the man back together, but he needed to staunch the bleeding. That required cutting through the flesh of his gut to get at the artery. The patient's silence gave way to screaming which made Hank pause, nauseated. He couldn't stop now. He pressed deeper, cut into the abdomen until he could see the spray of blood from the artery, then he pinched shut the wound, waiting for tools a medic handed him that would clamp the bleeder closed. They would need that clamp again, but for now, he had slowed the bleeding. He brushed sweat off his shoulder and swallowed hard while he waited for the spinning to stop. "I didn't like that because I didn't know what I was doing. I may have thrown up, I probably did," Hank recalled.

That patient might survive. What he couldn't know yet was that every patient they saved would go on to be a POW, in the hands of the very men who had injured them in the first place.

That night Hank took watch duty. Before the doctor lay down for a few hours of sleep he patted the medic on the back. "You did good work today, I couldn't have managed without you," he said.

Hank nodded appreciation and took to his next assignment: watching for infiltration. He kept his pistol drawn as he sat by the fire watching the golden light from the flames flash against the tangle of trees and vines. The jungle itself was quiet, the birds had all gone with the fighting. He imagined how nice it would be to take flight and leave this place when you wanted. As he sat low to the ground, a rock between him and much of the wilder part of the jungle, he watched and listened. Occasionally he heard the rattle of gunfire. He also heard a sound that raised goosebumps on his flesh. Footsteps? Coming their way?

He drew his gun and waited, holding his breath, his heart hammering. The steps seemed to draw louder, closer. Then they were drowned out by the bursting clamor of monkeys brawling in the trees. He let out a deep breath and chambered his gun. Another night brought more steps. This time human, he was sure of it. He fired into the jungle, bullets slicing into foliage and tree trunks. All was silent. He would never know if he had frightened off wildlife or Japanese soldiers preparing an ambush.

Continually the jungle station hummed with the sound of the small generator used to supply the power for medical equipment, drills, and lighting as they worked into the latest hours. Beyond that hum, the days and nights were filled with sounds of the jungle: insects buzzed from the trees, monkeys called from the canopy while the scent of jasmine drifted around them.

By the second week, fighting was getting closer and Chamberlain and other medics went directly into the battlefield to remove or treat the injured. It was at those times that he never knew whether he was living his final day, whether Cathy and his mother would see him again, whether he would have a chance to write them each one more letter to say goodbye.

Medics didn't travel alone. Together in pairs or small groups they crawled out to a patient, a bright red cross emblazoned on their helmets, as well as bicep-level bands on the left arm. As Hank ran in a crouch to a man on the ground a bullet fired past his right shoulder and he dropped flat, raised himself up, and started running again. He grasped the injured soldier under the arms and tugged, another medic joining him, they pulled the man across the field. Another bullet shot passed his right shoulder, too close, but still missed him, and Hank found new speed as they made their way to safety.

He took off his helmet and looked at the cross, then dropped it back on his sweat-soaked head. Not only did the snipers seem to ignore the universal symbol of the Red Cross, but they also seemed to be attracted to it. Hank could taste blood in his mouth from hitting the ground hard. He couldn't believe he wasn't hit.

Back at the medical station the patients were laid out in a row on canvas sheets in front of the surgical tent. Those with life-threatening injuries were again pushed ahead of the others.

Hank looked up from his patient at Earl and he removed his helmet again. "I could swear those bastards are aiming at my Red Cross,"

Earl shrugged and nodded, "We're target practice for those bastards, we might as well wear a bulls-eye," his friend agreed. Hank recalled the Japanese bombers that had toyed with the medics and doctors as they unloaded supplies from the freight ship weeks before, what seemed like a lifetime ago. The Red Cross seemed to mean nothing to the Japanese Imperial Army.

In fact, a day later one of the medics returned from the battlefield with a bullet wound in his shoulder, not far from the Red Cross patch. That settled it. The Japanese were using the symbol for bullet practice. As he helped the doctor pull the bullet out of his friend's shoulder, Hank thought of a solution.

"We need to cover the Red Cross," he said. Before returning to the field he visited the streambed where he collected water to smear mud over the cross on his helmet and on the patch on his shoulder. Now he was just another American soldier.

★ ★ ★

Hank's stepfather George had served in the army during World War I, had seen action in Italy, and was on two separate sinking ships shot through by German subs. Hank was familiar with hearing the war stories of the elder generation, and although George rarely spoke about his experience, it was apparent that the war had affected him. They called it "shell shock." One Fourth of July Hank and a cousin bought penny firecrackers and were throwing them in the street in the heat of the afternoon. Hank thought about the way George avoided the evening fireworks shows, always staying home, in the quietest part of the house.

"These firecrackers would just about make George jump out of his skin," Hank laughed and the two boys, about twelve years old, started planning. Hank discovered that George was in the bathroom with a window open to the backyard, drawing in as much fresh air as the summer afternoon could offer. He couldn't be in a better position for their attack. Hank lit the end with a match, dropped it in the grass under the open window and he and his cousin bolted, just far enough away to witness the results. The shouts of terror from George were more extreme than he expected, and he'd never heard his stepfather sound so frightened. The screaming went on after the firecracker fell silent and Hank and his cousin exchanged a look. George's voice tapered down to a whimper then stopped. Hank busted out laughing, "That was hilarious!"

He thought now that he owed his stepfather an apology.

7

JANUARY 1942

BATAAN, THE PHILIPPINES

The number of patients grew while supplies dwindled. With the chaos of injured soldiers flowing in, waiting for rudimentary, sometimes life-saving treatment before being transported to a hospital, organization was makeshift at best. Necessity led doctors and medics to stopgap solutions to ensure they never wasted supplies. One of the most precious medications, to ease suffering, was morphine which they used sparingly. There was no way to know how long they would be out there in the field, without replacement medicines. Fighting was furious and no deliveries were coming. So only those in the worst condition got the injection that meant relief from the worst pain of their lives, if only for a few hours. Furthering the confusion was the language barrier—many of their patients were Filipino soldiers and few spoke English. That meant that simple communication was even harder, and evenly dispensing morphine was almost impossible. In a hospital the medics could have recorded—on paper—the time and dosage of medication administered to each patient and kept those records at his bedside. Here, patients lay on the jungle floor of a warzone, were moved as others came and went, and often couldn't even provide their names in a language the medics understood. The station needed a more rudimentary solution.

It came in the form of a stick and a bottle of iodine. If no doctor was available, Hank made the agonizing decision as to whether a patient warranted some of the precious remaining morphine. If he did, Hank injected the pain killer, then dipped a stick into the iodine and brushed an X on the patient's forehead.

There was no way to indicate the time or the dosage, but at least it provided a prevention of double-dosing. The patients then lay in their rows, some marked with an X. These X-marked patients were typically quieter as medication numbed their pain.

The last cloth mask had been used by now, so there was nothing left for surgical procedures, some men wrapped a piece of their own clothing around their faces, but they eventually dropped away.

The number of Filipino patients streaming into the mobile unit took Hank by surprise. So many teenagers, or older men, taking up arms, only to find themselves here on the floor of the jungle waiting for treatment. Despite language barriers, he tried to talk to them and found that with hand gestures they understood—where are you hurt? He pointed over their body and waited. Sometimes they were just sick, other times no one needed to ask, the injury was obvious. If it was bad enough the patient only cried and Hank used the morphine when he could, patted the man on the hand or arm, talking soothingly. "No more of that crying now. You be still, it's okay, it's alright."

Once bleeding stopped, splints were applied, or open wounds covered, patients flowed out of the mobile station destined either to Hospital 1 for surgery or critical care, or to Hospital 2 for recuperation. As soon as a vehicle was available, medics loaded it with patients to be delivered to the hospitals. Those who died were stacked near the tented compound, just far enough away that they wouldn't interfere with the medical work and would not be ravaged by wild animals. That didn't help prevent insects however. Flies blackened the corpses. Both insects and the odor of rotting flesh rose day and night from the bodies. The smell was overwhelming.

The flies and mosquitoes were relentless and voracious as they fed on the injured as well. When a wound opened, the flies found it. They gnawed at bloody flesh and then they laid their eggs. An injury, uncovered for any significant time, ended up flyblown—eggs hatched maggots that would soon be eating the exposed tissue.

Mosquitos covered the living, and many could do little to brush them away. If he had both hands occupied with treating a patient, Hank just let them take the blood they wanted, unable to swat.

That meant a heightened risk of malaria which was now making its rounds through the patients and the medics. The quinine Hank had taken to beat back his first bout with malaria had worked its way through his system and the disease now returned with a vengeance.

Not far away was a small village consisting of grass and bamboo huts that housed large families. Here Hank and the other members of the station could sometimes find shelter with a Filipino family, to treat a patient or conduct surgery under cover. The roofs of bamboo and straw provided some protection from the insects as well as the afternoon rain squalls and the gunfire.

By this time the men didn't know where the next meal was coming from. Bataan was held by sixty-five thousand Filipino troops, fifteen thousand American ones, and populated by another ten thousand Filipino civilians, and the available food was finite and growing more meager as the fighting went on. Everyone was hungry. Hank and his fellow medics and doctors relied on donations from Filipinos and scavenged food to supplement the shrinking rations of rice. "We never knew when we were going to get our next meal," he recalled. "There were cooks but they were no longer cooking, we did whatever we could." He noticed by now that his clothes were hanging looser on his body, so he tightened his belt. Soon they would need to find other sources of food.

Soldiers were faring even worse. They were reliant on two small rations of rice per day by now, slept in foxholes, often without the benefit of mosquito nets, so that by the time they ended up in the care of Hank and other medical personnel they suffered from malaria and its related chills and fever, not to mention malnutrition-based illnesses, in addition to the injury that brought them to seek medical attention—often a shrapnel or bullet wound. A few who hadn't had access to water for a day or two or three could be out of their wits with thirst.

It was impossible to imagine how they could go on this way. Hank befriended a Filipino civilian from the neighboring barrio who pointed out some edibles in the jungle. The man, who spoke only Tagalog, handed Hank a fistful of greenery and gestured to him to deliver it to the camp. Hank turned the leaves over in his own hand and the man pointed to several of the trees in the area where leaves of the same variety were growing.

Hank recalled times in his own childhood when he'd relied on the greenery around him to stave off malnutrition, and he saw the value of it now. He smiled and gestured his thanks.

★ ★ ★

As a boy, after his mother threw George out of the family house, Hank found his financial security slipping away. They couldn't afford the house without George's income, so they moved into a modest apartment until a fire destroyed all they had. Then they were on the streets, without enough money to find a new home. Like many of the newly destitute, they took up camping on the grounds of the Nebraska Territory Capitol

Building in the center of Omaha. They had nothing, and Hank learned that even with nothing, there were ways to survive. One of the men cohabitating this public space showed Hank that nutrition was possible even with the humble yellow weeds that sprung up around them. They picked dandelion leaves and boiled them, and Hank ate this little morsel of nourishment with gratitude. In fact he took to scouring lawns for these valuable little plants and eating the leaves raw. It was enough to stop the cramps of hunger.

★ ★ ★

Here in the jungles of Bataan, Hank gazed up at the trees and considered the wealth of leaves growing overhead—deep green, tropical plants with water-engorged flesh. They tasted alright and after serving them with their cooked rice, the men took turns climbing the trees and cutting down the greenery until the tree branches were nearly bare.

For meat Hank took up hunting with his .45. While birds were gone, there were some options including wild carabao and pigs. When they brought an animal down, it was dragged into camp and eaten as fast as they could cook the meat. It would rot soon in that temperature.

Nearly all day and night Hank could hear the crackle of machine guns and bursts of rifle fire. The shelling in the jungle was a constant din around them. Hank learned to hear the difference between the sound of Japanese and American artillery—different pitch—while he could also differentiate between Japanese plane engines and the American versions.

At night Hank closed his eyes but sleep didn't come easily. When he did sleep he heard the bullets flying, saw the splatter of blood, exposed ragged bones, torn up flesh, and jolted awake to realize it had been a dream, but one that foretold the next day and the next.

Circling their battery-powered radio at night, the medical staff heard some bad news that partially explained the growing flow of injuries just as their supplies and food dwindled. The Japanese had seized most of Luzon Province, Bataan was heavily under threat, and the increasing firepower coming from the Japanese was shrinking the area Americans and Filipinos protected.

One evening the doctor asked Hank to drive a load of patients to Hospital 2. There was no driver, and the flow of new patients had slowed, so they could afford to let Hank go for a night. Deliveries of the wounded were usually scheduled after dark to avoid daytime traffic and reduce the risk of enemy air attack.

Once the vehicle was loaded with the injured, many silent and stoic, Hank stepped into the army jeep and turned over the engine. Several

Filipino civilians climbed in to help him see the road ahead. The jeep had suffered a lot of abuse since the Japanese invasion, bearing bullet holes in its flanks and a windshield shot out from the last time it had been on the road.

Hank inched along the dirt path, about six injured men in the back while several of the Filipino civilians walked ahead of him watching the ground and listening for planes. He moved at a crawl not only because he couldn't see, but to limit the impact from ruts and holes rising ahead. Occasionally he could not help hitting a pothole hard, and the jeep bounced violently, summoning feeble cries of pain from the patients. Typically this ride took about eight hours to get a casualty from the battlefield to the hospital just a few miles away.[1] Sometimes it could be even longer.

When the rain came he stopped to wait it out, about ten minutes, and they continued. The first gunshot that cracked in Hank's ear sent him careening off the road and he pulled the jeep into the brush for cover. They didn't try to return fire or run from the vehicle; no one was in condition for heavy running. It was better to hunker by the jeep and wait it out. The patients had to wait too, and another hour later during a lull in the shooting, Hank took off as fast as they could get the tires back on the path.

The sun was rising when Hank pulled in front of the sprawling field facility that was General Hospital 2. Two posts stood at the end of a dirt road, with signage warning drivers to stop and identify themselves.

Lt. Col. Jack William Schwartz, chief of surgical service at the hospital, met the jeep at the makeshift gate and told Chamberlain to hold on, as Hospital 2 staff shuttled the patients in on stretchers. Col. Schwartz lit the saved butt of a cigarette as the last patient went inside and he nodded at Hank.

"Good to see you again, Private Chamberlain. Where are you coming from?"

Chamberlain identified his field camp.

"Well, you're not going back there. I really need you here."

Chamberlain looked at the officer in surprise, then his face broke out into a grin. "Thank you, Colonel, thank you." He didn't know much about this hospital, but it couldn't be worse than the life he was living in the mobile unit.

When the war was over, Hank would receive a combat medical badge for his efforts there on the front lines, followed by two Bronze Stars from General MacArthur.

8

LATE JANUARY 1942

GENERAL HOSPITAL 2, BATAAN

Hospital 2 amounted to a swath of jungle, hacked clear of brush along the south bank of the Real River. It offered no permanent structures, no running water, no fence or gate. When Hank carried his patients inside, he looked over this open-air hospital where rows of patients extended as far as his eyes could see. A hastily erected wooden platform and roof for surgery and recovery was the center point, surrounded by tents, and occasional cots on which various levels of the convalescing reclined, some sleeping, some seated, some wandering or limping around the area on braced legs or peering through the bandages shrouding their heads.

Every open square foot of this riverside space was the result of hours of hacking away at bushes, creeping vines, and clumps of bamboo.[1] Over time Hank would help the men hack the jungle back further, foot by foot, to provide space for more injured soldiers.

A team of nurses worked here, as well as dozens of medics and doctors, each of whom had brought their tents in the form of half-shells shared with another soldier to create a city of pup tents. Most patients lay open to the air, their half-shell laid out beneath them as the only barrier between them and the ants and biting insects inhabiting the bare ground.

The Real River provided the site with freshwater, while trees towered around them providing shade from the heat and some protection from the afternoon or evening rains. The river poured down from Mt. Bataan while capillary streams flowing into the river offered potential areas for semiprivate bathing, often dedicated for use by the nurses. One kilometer to the south was the city of Cabcaben.

The hospital was intended to serve about a thousand patients, but by the time Hank arrived as many as six thousand patients were being served in eighteen wards. The river was a shallow twelve-foot wide waterway but enough water could be drawn from the river to be chlorinated and stored in a three-thousand-gallon tank as long as the chlorine lasted.[2] Headquarters was at the center, among a thicket of banyan trees.

The nurses' quarters was a roofless structure of burlap walls across the river, where they had a modicum of privacy. Burlap bags had been sewn together to create those walls. Some nurses also slept in several large, abandoned buses on the compound.[3]

As Hank walked among the patients, he discovered two old friends— Earl and Bill. When they recognized Hank, they hurried to his side and he was so relieved to see them he reached to hug them both. They looked well, although they, like Hank, were using their belts to support shorts that hung off their skinny waists. Earl's fair, freckled skin was burnt brown from the sun. Bill's once neatly cut dark hair hung into his eyes. They too would have noticed changes in Hank. Life in the mobile unit had meant little bathing, his clothes now tattered, pieces of clothing torn off to bandage patients, mud smeared over the red cross on his sleeve, and a .45 sidearm on his hip. Bill and Earl had their weapons in the form of bolos—large, straight knives—strapped to their sides with hand-made holsters. The bolos were scavenged from Filipino patients who hadn't survived their injuries. However, rather than using them as weapons, the men employed them to hack through brush. Hank knew right away he needed a tool like that himself. There was no time for reunions though. Hank reported to headquarters and was assigned work assisting in the surgical area.

As he approached that tented area, he passed between long trenches dug next to patients. A few months ago, he would have wondered what their purpose was, but he knew all too well now that they could be the only form of defense for some of the thousands onsite if Japanese fighter planes passed over. The planes came regularly, Earl and Bill told him, strafing at the airfield on the other side of a hill, a quarter mile away. And occasionally shelling intended for the airfield ended up in the hospital. Since there were several small barrios on that side of the hill, locals living in these barrios sometimes offered support with food or medical supplies.

So when bombers or fighter planes swept low in search of targets, the patients knew what to do—drop off the cot if they had one, roll down into the trench, and bring the half sheet with them. They wait and pray. When the damage was done, and the planes had continued, the hospital personnel would appraise the damage. The patients who didn't have the strength to climb out of the trench—which was most of them—lay on their army-issued half-shelter pup tent until medics came by and lifted them out by tugging on both ends of the canvas.

As he walked through the hospital grounds Hank could hear the ceaseless racket of artillery fire from battles raging nearby, just as he had in the mobile unit. He entered the tented surgical area and found some familiar faces among the doctors and medics as well as the nurses. Hank grinned at their greetings, "Well look who it is! Where you been, Chamberlain?" The area where they worked was fifty or sixty feet long and twenty feet wide, amounting to a stilted platform to keep it out of the water when heavy rains created floods, with a rough grass roof overhead. A row of beds held patients who required surgery, but either couldn't wait for transport to Hospital 1 or needed a relatively basic procedure.

Hank would soon learn that the hospital operation ran as well as it did in part due to the nurses. Many of the same military nurses, all officers who outranked Hank, had been at Sternberg, at that time wearing starched white nurse uniforms. Now they were in khakis like the men, and they too relied on belts to hold their loose-fitting clothes in place.

Overseeing the nurses was Josephine May Nesbit, who Hank had met at Sternberg Hospital. At Sternberg, Nesbit served as acting chief nurse. Hank had come to like and depend on her during those early chaotic days. He and Nesbit formed a friendship early on. Working under chief nurse Captain Maude Davison, Nesbit was a motherly presence for the nurses as well as the medics at Sternberg as well as Hospital 2, and Hank was glad to be working with her again. He referred to her as Ma Nesbit, while Filipina colleagues called her "Mama Josie." She in turn affectionately called her nursing staff "my girls."

"She mothered everybody, including the medics," Hank recalled. Nesbit grew up in rural Missouri as part of a large family with nine siblings. Born in 1894 she was middle age by the time of the war, and old enough to be the mother of most of those in the camp. Despite their age difference though, Hank and Josephine had a common childhood experience that connected them. Both had lacked most of the childhood comforts—a stable home, reliable meals, and idle time for play. She worked on the family farm all day and lost both her parents by the age of twelve. She then grew up at a grandparent's home and then a cousin's. So the two shared a rootless childhood that gave them both a degree of grit in the jungle war hospital.

Neither tended to complain. In fact, they simply moved to the next patient and provided any comfort when basic medicine wasn't available.

In surgery, Hank took to aiding with painful procedures that should have included anesthetics and hygienic conditions but instead took place in a hurry as flies bombarded the patient and physicians alike. Hank quickly took to providing the bandaging, lifting, stitching, and comforting of patients the first day he arrived. "You're okay, it's over now," he comforted one patient when the stitches were in place, and he felt a warm hand on his shoulder. He turned to see Nesbit, smiling as she patted his shoulder.

"I think all Americans cared about each other," Hank recalled.

For the next few weeks Hank served as a surgical technician where those in need of extractions, sutures, or amputations were attended to. That meant removing shrapnel and mending broken bones. Each surgical team consisted of a doctor, nurse, and medic as well as any necessary helpers to hold the patient still or fetch the tools needed on short notice. Often a patient came in infected from a long-untended wound, and the fastest solution—the one most likely to save a life—was draining the infected area. "A lot of the pain came from the gas created by the infection," Hank said, a condition known as "gas gangrene." "Sometimes we could stick a surgical needle in," he said, or slice open the swollen tissue, and the gas was released with a whoosh. The air clouding the wound then reeked of rotting flesh, the kind of smell that could have made him vomit, but he had trained himself to keep his senses. If he gave in to nausea, and if he vomited, that was food and liquid he needed. He didn't know when food rations would increase but he didn't dare assume there would be more food coming. So instead he held his breath, cleaned out the wound as best he could, raising his face skyward to take deep drinks of cleaner air before hunkering down over the rotting wound. "Some of those guys survived, some didn't."

If a shell fragment embedded itself in bone, Hank used a mallet to help hammer it out.

Since nearly all pain medication has been exhausted, patients were left to contend with their own suffering. Most soldiers—fighting and dying—were Filipinos, and they also represented the majority of patients. Most had been rice farmers, hastily trained for war, if they were trained at all. They had little by way of equipment and those admitted into the hospital wore civilian clothes, their feet bare, often with a bolo as their weapon. Whether they were well-armed or not, every man being admitted had to relinquish his weapon, something they bitterly resisted. Names were attached to the weapons, which were locked into a storage area until the soldier recovered or died.

A stench hung over the hospital—burnt skin, gangrenous flesh, and death. The smell of malarial diarrhea and vomit was inescapable. And the clamor of doctors, nurses, medics, patients, talking, shouting, crying, and trying to be heard, all working, recuperating or dying in chaos. It never really stopped, even at night.

The supply of sulfa drugs for external use was still available, but most medicines were dwindling to nothing, and soon they would all be gone. Wounds healed slowly because of the weakened condition of the men, and the period of hospitalization was normally longer than might otherwise have been the case if there had been enough food for a proper diet.[4] Fewer battle casualties were coming in between February 15 and April 3, and the beds ordinarily used by the wounded could be given to the starved and malaria-ridden soldiers.[5]

As surgeries became rarer with each day, Hank's tasks included cleaning out sore or infected wounds. In some cases, malnutrition, the depth of the wound, or the severity of illness overcame the weaker of the men, the younger men, or those who were just too severely damaged to go on. Schwartz watched Hank set to work on one patient before commenting, "Leave him lay, Hank, he's dead." The man still had breath in him though, and that was something Hank couldn't do. When possible, he sat with the dying just as he had done in the mobile unit, even for five minutes if that was all he had, comforting them if they were suffering or afraid. For the Filipinos who didn't understand English, even a pat on the shoulder and smile helped.

Woodfires burned at the hospital, and caldrons of river water boiled above them for sterilization. For the first few weeks Hank was there, Bunsen burners had enough fuel to boil water for forceps and needles, scalpels and saws. Hank dipped some reused dressings in river water to clean for the men who wanted it and found this too boosted their spirits. Some of these soldiers had marched up and down dirt roads, crawled through mud avoiding enemy fire, slept in the brush without a bath and hadn't eaten a decent meal since December. Often, they were covered in blood, their own or that of a fellow soldier; excrement; and the dirt of the jungle.

Hank tried to collect the names of those who came in, but not only did many not speak English, when Hank held up a pencil and paper, gesturing for them to write their names, he found they were illiterate. He was surrounded by unfamiliar dialects as well as cultures and religions. He saw prayers whispered on the lips of the sick and injured: Catholics, Presbyterians, Methodists, as well as the religions of the local Filipinos. Several American military chaplains took care of religious matters any way they could, Hank recalled.

Near the hospital men had dug out holes to serve as graves for the men who didn't make it. In some cases, holes from bombs dropped by the

Japanese made their task easier, and they simply deposited bodies in these newly dug cavities in the soil and covered the men. They fashioned grave markers out of sticks, cut in the shape of crosses, or tied together with twine or vines.

They often tried to tie dog tags or other forms of identification on the cross to memorialize the deceased. The many who were Filipinos often went into the ground anonymously since Hank and the other medics had been unable to learn their names.

As time passed Hank started to recognize where the hospital's greatest threats lurked. Occasionally a Japanese soldier or two would infiltrate the space and fire on patients or workers, killing several Americans this way, although Hank was never there when it happened. In each case, the Japanese soldier was killed as fast as he could be taken down. Hank took to carrying a bolo like his friends were, one used to whack down the jungle growth to allow for more patients, but he also kept his hand close to the handle whenever he sensed an ambush.

The greatest threat continued to come from the sky, however. When Japanese planes flew over, sometimes they opened fire on the sprawling mass of humanity in the hospital itself. The trenches patients and personnel dove into when under fire could save lives, but they also could cause injuries for those negotiating the hospital after dark. If it was a cloudless night and the moon was out—even a crescent moon—the entire hospital was illuminated, but on a cloudy night the hospital was as dark as the grave. Hank could make out no more than outlines, shadows, recognizable shapes. They had no flashlights—they were long gone—Hank sometimes carried a stick and tapped it ahead of himself so he wouldn't stumble into a trench.

One early morning in April Hank was roused by the familiar sound of the plane engines, and he realized Japanese bombers were flying directly above the hospital. When the bombs rained down, patients, doctors, nurses, and medics all dove for the nearest shelter. Patients who might not have been able to move just an hour earlier found the strength to jump out of their beds into the trenches. But there was nowhere to fully escape the devastation. When the bombing was over the night air was filled with the anguish of the injured. The pharmacy and its scant supply of drugs were demolished, one ward was flattened, and Hank reviewed the full impact by the morning light. At least seventy-three men were killed, mostly patients, and more than one hundred injured.[6] Dust floated over the grounds, where the ward had been. Patients who'd had no chance to hide had been blown out of their beds. Bodies and severed limbs hung from the tree branches.

There was no time to consider any of this, the damage to human flesh, the broken bones, burns, and dismembered limbs all required help, and he spent days running from one to the next, trying to ignore the frustration of working without proper supplies.

After sixteen hours this way, once the heat subsided with the dropping sun, Hank went to the riverside to wash. He had a friend that often awaited him there. The first time he had visited the river for washing, he'd noticed a monkey drop from the canopy to stand watching Hank as he undressed, washed, and pulled his clothes back on. Even though he had little by way of food to offer, Hank took to bringing a spoonful of rice or other edibles, holding it out for the little primate. Even if he had nothing to offer, the monkey came closer, sat nearly at his feet. So now the monkey came to recognize him when he approached the river, and he had even coaxed it to sit on his shoulder. He found solace in his new friend.

★ ★ ★

As a teenager Hank spent many nights in Omaha with no home to return to after the sunset. Homelife with his mother was volatile and unpredictable, and money was tight. So Hank worked during the day when he could find jobs. A city fruit stand employed him to sweep the sidewalk in exchange for an apple. A farmer paid him to shoot the coyotes that were preying on livestock. But on a cold January night he found himself with no money and no place to go. He walked through a residential neighborhood where warm, inviting lights glowed in windows and he imagined the heat inside, the hearty meal that might be on the family table. As a light rain opened out of the dark sky he shivered and looked around him for shelter. He spotted a gap under the porch of a house across the street and he ran for it, climbing underneath. There he discovered a considerable cavernous space and peered through the dark for the most comfortable position to rest his head until morning. He realized he wasn't alone. Something was breathing. He saw a dark lump just ten feet away and then he held his breath as two eyes looked at him. "Hello?" When he got no response his slid closer and then let out a chuckle; it was a dog, a Saint Bernard, and its tail was thumping against the ground with a steady beat. Hank crawled over to the animal, reached out, and petted its matted fur. He'd found a companion for the night. He curled up with the dog, his arm over its beefy neck, and the two kept each other warm until the thin light of morning shone under the porch. Hank walked away grateful to have made it through a cold night, as he scratched at flea bites.

★ ★ ★

When Hank returned to the hospital camp with his newfound pet clinging to his shoulders, the medics and nurses alike laughed. The little monkey became a common site, entering the hospital to search for Hank. At times the primate jumped on the medic's back when he was working on a patient and grinned its teeth at those around them.

The Real River provided bathing and water for the entire hospital. When the nurses used the river water, they were afforded some privacy by the men. Beyond bathing and private sleeping quarters, however, the nurses were treated as just another soldier. One incident required some support from the medics, however. On an early morning Hank recalled hearing women shouting from the river. While they usually bathed free from male eyes, this time they spotted a Filipino civilian watching them furtively from the other bank. Their screams brought several medics who fired their weapons at the man. He disappeared into the brush.

The stream of patients continued to rise by the day. While the number of patients has been estimated at around six thousand, Hank recalled just how hard it was to get a headcount. No one had the time or resources to count. "We couldn't even admit them, no pencil and paper left to admit them. There was such a tremendous amount of injured, or sick—dysentery, malaria—and there was also the shelling and bombing. We had no transportation by that time, and they carried them in by hand, sometimes it took days and days."

Eventually one morning Hank went to the river in search of his pet monkey and his friend didn't drop out of the tree. He called and whistled but the cry of distant birds was the only reply. He returned to the camp and called around, then asked Bill if he'd seen him. "I did he was wandering around here yesterday, haven't seen him since." Hank took his search to another group of medics he didn't know as well and was delivered crushing news.

"Oh, that old monkey? We ate him."

Monkey meat was not a favorite among POWs who spoke about it later, but it provided the protein and fat that men craved. According to one statement from a POW, "that monkey meat is all right until the animal's hands turn up on a plate."[7]

With no new supplies coming to the hospital, officers began decreasing daily rations. By February the original ration of two thousand calories a day was cut in half. Medical supplies were saved for the most badly injured or sickest.

The rice now had been in storage for months and came peppered with insect infestations and rat droppings. To supplement the rice the men were occasionally fed meat from a butchered carabao. There were no fruits or vegetables. By March the supply of quinine was gone and malaria raged through the camp.

Dysentery was equally cruel. Those with dysentery often had little warning before they had to run to the latrine and would soil themselves before ever reaching the slit trench toilets that lined the perimeter of the hospital. The path to the latrines was lined and dotted with liquid feces.[8] The men periodically swept the path clean by flicking away as much excrement as they could with long sticks.

Contaminated drinking water was a source for dysentery whether from the streams and river, while big blue flies and mosquitoes were carriers of malaria and other diseases. Hank found that many Americans had contracted several different types of malaria. One deadly version, known as blackwater fever, caused jaundice, dark urine, convulsive chills, and fever after which many patients simply collapsed. These patients rarely recovered. Eventually all suffered in varying degrees from chills, aches, cramps, and diarrhea.

Anyone able to began looking for their own food. Hank's hunger helped him recover from the loss of his pet monkey. He understood just how dangerous it was for any animal around these hungry souls. Ever the skilled subsistence hunter, he could bring down iguanas with his sidearm, although bullets weren't always necessary and a tap on the head could kill them.

By spring a new phase of the war commenced, and it was an ominous one. At night Hank heard the explosions in the jungle, unlike anything he'd heard yet throughout this war. He was told they were demolishing all the American arms that were left to keep them out of enemy hands.

In April 1942, with the enemy less than two miles away and defeat inevitable, the American nurses were ordered to evacuate. The hospital also employed twenty-six Filipino nurses and Nesbit demanded that all nurses leave together or all stay, refusing to leave the Filipino nurses to fate.

They then were all approved to evacuate, traveling to the Malinta Tunnel hospital on the island of Corregidor—an underground bunker where the fetid air and concussive bombing took their toll. They left one day ahead of the Japanese arrival in the hospital.

They did not, however, avoid capture. In May, Nesbit was invited to join the last escaping parties on the last submarine to defy the Japanese blockade. She and the Band of Angels opted to remain; they became prisoners of war, along with the remaining foreign nationals of Manila, and from August 1942 until the beginning of 1945 she and her former superior, Maude Davison, ran the Santo Tomas Internment Camp Hospital.

With the nurses gone, and the Japanese closing in, morale at the hospital plummeted. There was little question anymore that the war was going to be over for them soon, but what the Japanese would do with them was in doubt. No training had ever included what to do as a prisoner of war. Now Chamberlain found himself considering this unimaginable future, surrendering to the enemy who had killed so many around him. The same enemy that had opened fire on him at the start of this ordeal, which seemed like a lifetime ago now.

When a patient died, he had to be buried at the site, as there was nowhere else for the bodies to go. Hank was among those assigned to dig holes to serve as graves. In some cases the shelling created holes for them, and the bodies were deposited there. Hank tried to lay them down gently, and he said a silent prayer. But then he had more living patients waiting for him back in the hospital.

By this time, as the hospital had been focused on repairing damaged soldiers, the war had become a losing effort for the American and Philippine forces. On March 12 General MacArthur, his family, and several United States Army Forces in the Far East (USAFFE) staff officers had left Corregidor aboard patrol torpedo (PT) boats, leaving the battle in the hands of other officers.

The Japanese controlled most of Southeast Asia, while the Bataan Peninsula and the island of Corregidor were the only strongholds left for the Allies in the eastern Pacific. Despite the lack of supplies, American and Filipino forces had managed to fight the Japanese for three months and provided a strategic advantage, delaying the Japanese conquests across the Pacific.

By April 9, 1942, General King met with Japan's Major General Kameichiro Nagano and agreed to a surrender. The defenders of the Bataan Peninsula, starving and exhausted, lay down their arms. The Allied surrender consisted of seventy-six thousand soldiers. By the time Corregidor was overcome, on May 6, 1942, virtually all Philippine Scout soldiers and officers, as well as all Americans, became prisoners of the Japanese.

For months Hank and his comrades had been hearing conflicting news about what was taking place around them. Supposedly thousands of American soldiers were on the way to support them. They didn't come. There was no talk about being a POW; the army would have discouraged that kind of thinking. "We knew it wasn't going well. We knew we were probably in trouble but didn't know what kind. None of us had ever experienced things like that," Hank recalled. What Hank did know was that POWs had been taken in World War I, that some of those men were shot on the spot, by the Germans, "so we were concerned the Japanese would execute us."

The soldiers who regained some health were staying—there was nowhere for them to go. Those who could stand and walk were set to work with chores, helping dig latrines, bury the dead, or hunt for meat.

Japanese guns were now firing almost directly over their heads at Corregidor. It was time to prepare for what was coming. Hank started by hiding his valuables. Pictures of his mother and girlfriend went into the lining of his musette bag. He shoved his grandfather's knife into the seam at the bottom of the bag.

A team of medics and patients then went to the weapons storage, where every patient's gun had been safeguarded, and they went to work destroying them. They unloaded them, disassembled them, broke them when possible. They put the barrels in the crotch of a tree and bent them, until there was none left that would ever fire again.

The last to go would be Hank's pistol. By the time he knew there was no escape, he headed into the overgrowth of the jungle. He took his .45 apart and tossed its pieces as deep into the jungle as he could, where they were covered by foliage as soon as they landed. It was the hardest thing he'd done yet, defying one of the first principles of a soldier: never separate from your weapon. Now he was throwing his fate into the hands of the enemy. He shoved wet dirt over any exposed pieces as an afternoon rain splashed the first drops over his small grave. He patted the dirt down firm and walked back to camp, unarmed.

He was at the mercy of the Japanese and there was no way to know what that was going to mean. He was not alone, the hospital had a record-high number of patients. When Bataan surrendered on April 9, an estimate of over nine thousand were on the roster at Hospital 2. According to some accounts, it had served as many as twenty thousand patients from all over the Philippines.

Tomorrow, he thought, could be the last day for them all.

II

CAPTIVITY

9

APRIL 1942

GENERAL HOSPITAL 2, BATAAN CAPTURED

During the night doctors, medics, and patients lay awake listening to the impact of heavy explosions within short range, the retreating Americans were blowing the ammunition dumps. The heavy 155-millimeter and some 75-millimeter shells lay in storage in corrugated sheet metal bodegas. They were all that had remained in munitions stores for the army and they were not going to let them fall into the hands of the enemy.[1] Since the night of the invasion Hank had begun saying a nightly prayer for an end to this conflict. Now his prayers carried him in and out of fitful sleep and he woke up with no idea what to expect.

The sun rose on Thursday, April 9 with the sound of fighting still crackling in the distance. As it shone pale light over the jungle hospital the firing came to an eerie stop. Those awaiting their fate included 7,000 patients, 67 officers, 200 civilian employees, and 250 enlisted men, one of whom was Henry Chamberlain. He was told to expect the Japanese Imperial Army to arrive upon their hospital at any time. At 1100 hours an alert came that all Luzon forces were surrendering the Bataan Peninsula. Hank helped his fellow medics stitch together Red Cross banners of scraps of fabric and some needle and thread. They raised large white sheets that flapped mournfully in the breeze. Hank could hardly look at them.

The sound of bombing and strafing churned on around them, but it was scattered as opposed to the constant drone of artillery they'd experienced for the past days and weeks.

Their food was almost gone, no new rations would arrive, and it was time to find out what their fate would be. They waited. At 1700 hours the first Japanese infantrymen drove into the hospital, followed by two officers and twenty enlisted men. The group met with hospital commander Lieutenant Colonel William North. The message was simple, the Imperial Army had taken control of the hospital, staff, and patients, all of whom were Japanese prisoners of war.[2]

The Japanese soldiers then dispersed throughout the patients, the beds, the medics, and doctors, one stepping into the ward where Hank sat with a patient, and announced, "Who is number one man, who rank?" When Lt. Col Schwartz stepped forward, as the chief of surgical service,[3] the soldier shouted an unintelligible verbal assault, then swung back his arm and slapped Schwartz across the face. The Americans stood watching in silence. "That's when I knew this wasn't going to be good," Hank recalled.

Major Segeguchi, the senior Japanese surgeon on Luzon, seemed to be tasked with dismantling Hospital 2 and mobilizing the patients and medical practitioners. Since the battle for Corregidor was raging on, that mobilization would have to be done gradually. The middle-aged man strode around the facility, eyeing the patients through his glasses, stroking his mustache. Segeguchi (also spelled Sekiguchi) was a medical corps officer who had initially been delegated to plan the removal of prisoners, but until then he was in charge of Hospital 2.[4] The Japanese seized both Hospital 1 and Hospital 2, but the experiences contrasted distinctly. Those at Hospital 1 found that Japanese soldiers treated them reasonably well. A Japanese soldier had been treated for injuries at Hospital 1, vouched for the kindness of the American medical staff, and the hospital was rewarded with notable respect from the Japanese.

The seizure of Hospital 2 could not have been more different. Segeguchi took a hands-off approach when it came to his troops who were assigned to guarding the hospital. If they were not encouraged to loot and steal from the patients and staff, they were more or less sanctioned, and the troops were hungry for food, goods, and revenge after months of hard fighting. The Japanese seized and removed all medical equipment, medicine, and supplies.

While Segeguchi and other Japanese leadership met with Schwartz and hospital surgeons, the Japanese troops roamed among the patients, medics, and doctors. Their goal was to collect anything of value and to demonstrate their loathing of these new captives. The Japanese hatred for their prisoners was multifaceted and never entirely understood by the men who were on the receiving end. Many of the Japanese soldiers had undergone brutal training themselves, frequently beaten by their commanders, with little provocation. In one incident Japanese Army officer Masanobu Tsuji was said to have packed thousands of Japanese soldiers into cramped, hot ship holds and kept them there for a week with little water to see how well they could fight after this endurance test.[5] He also was known to force officers who had been taken prisoner to commit suicide after being repatriated, echoing as well as exaggerating a cultural shame around being taken alive by the enemy. With this message as part of their training, the Japanese soldiers were intent on demonstrating to their new prisoners just how worthless their lives were.

As they assessed this field hospital, Japanese troops roamed through the cots and the sick and injured, looting any remaining medicines, medical equipment, as well as doctors' and patients' personal belongings. They burned or otherwise destroyed medical records. Hank watched uneasily, standing over his patients. Their new captors pocketed watches, rings, any kind of food they could locate. The last treasured items of canned sardines, condensed milk, or juice were all collected by the Japanese.

The first and most common sign of brutality came by way of slaps across the face. The Japanese slapped doctors, medics, and even the patients as Hank and his fellow medics stood by and watched their new guards go through their musette bags and pockets. The guards would give them a crack across the face if anything was found of value, and they got a crack across the face if nothing of value could be found.

When a Japanese soldier—now captor—approached Hank, he held out his hand, gestured impatiently, and barked at him in Japanese. Hank handed over his musette bag. His knife was in the lining. He had stashed photos of his mother and Cathy in his pocket. He didn't have much else of value. The man shook the bag's contents on the ground and rifled through them. He paused when he noticed Hank's toothbrush. The man picked it up by the handle and looked up at Hank with a grin, then shoved the brush in his mouth. He dropped the prisoner's bag on the ground and walked away looking for better goods, the brush handle sticking out of his mouth like a cigarette. Hank hoped any bacteria from his various ailments would now invade their new host.

In the meantime, the leadership meeting was a matter of laying down the rules. Through an interpreter, the Japanese informed the men that the hospital and all the property in it now belonged to the Imperial Army of Japan. A list of rules was laid out which included forbidding any men from leaving the camp. They would no longer use the water supply of the camp except for necessary drinking purposes. And violators of any of the list of rules would be shot dead.

The next objective seemed to be to clear out the hospital. The first to go would be the Filipinos who represented the vast majority of the population. One guard approached the first Filipino patient in Hank's ward and struck him with the side of his bayonet.

The patient, who was suffering from a gangrenous wound on his knee, struggled to understand as the guard shouted at him in Japanese, then two words in English, "You go!" He raised his rifle and pointed, ready to fire, and the patient jumped, struggling to pull himself out of bed. This seemed to be what the guard wanted. "You go!" he repeated. "Go home!" The patient stumbled off the cot, hopping on one good leg as fast as he could go. He fell, pulled himself up, and kept moving. The guard walked to the next bed, another Filipino, with the same orders and threats. All the Filipino patients were on alert now. It became clear that no one was going to be staying.

Hank objected when they began prodding one of his most feeble patients though. The man was barely conscious and unlikely to survive any effort to flee. He recalled later that most of the Filipinos with leg amputations were put in trucks rather than marched out when the Japanese came in. "I saw those men leaving and they were in pretty bad shape. Those who could, left walking."

Within the next twenty-four hours, 5,500 of the hospital's patients were gone. That included the postoperative cases, men with fractures, gaping wounds, and unfinished amputations. They limped, crawled, and stumbled in a miserable parade through the hospital gate with the Japanese prodding them on their way. Hank would learn later that most of these individuals never made it home and instead would die in the Death March out of Bataan.

One woman remained, the American wife of a Filipino soldier. A day after surrender she was raped by two Japanese soldiers in the officers' ward of the hospital. This incident was reported to Major Segeguchi, but no action was ever taken.

Within the first few days of seizing the hospital, the Japanese began installing heavy artillery in the form of cannons circling the hospital and aimed at Corregidor. Corregidor was only a few miles as the crow flies to the hospital and it was a good location from which to launch artillery, close enough, Hank recalled, that a good swimmer could cross over to the island in a short time. The Americans would then be reluctant to respond, with its massive army hospital the sure recipient of their firepower.

Hank and Dr. Brown watched the weapons being deployed, pointing their firepower south. Hank realized, watching the installation of these weapons, that they were aimed at Corregidor and would ensure that the hospital would be in the firing line, the hapless targets of friendly fire.

Japanese military vandals began taking what they could of the hospital for their purposes. That meant they took apart the generator and the power source was disabled. There would be no more light for the operating room, and with no way to light the room after dark, operations dropped off.

Those in Corregidor probably were unaware that Hospital 2 was still active with American POWs and medical patients being held captive there. Corregidor's defenders had likely spotted the exit of thousands of Filipino patients, and there was little reason for them to believe any patients were left behind. And so the United States responded by firing at the Japanese vigorously. They sent ten-inch shells hurtling into and around the hospital, big enough to blow giant holes in the ground and toss any structure in its path into the air. Some of these shells exploded in the trees above the hospital and Hank scrambled for cover along with everyone else in the hospital, as shrapnel in the form of shell shards and chunks of the trees towering around them shot around the facility.

Once a single shell landed, unexploded, in the hospital. They looked at the menacing and volatile munition embedded in the ground near their tents. "Anyone know how to take it apart?" The medics, ambulatory patients, and officers all shook their heads. No one had training in live ammunition, and it wasn't worth the risk to try. So instead a group of men gingerly built a small structure out of sticks tented around the weapon, alerting people to give it a wide berth.

For the following month, the hospital was in range of a barrage of shelling, with fragments spraying patients and medics. Most of the shells were "over" or "short" of the target, but there were several casualties from the shell fragments that sprayed the hospital area.

One day the shelling brought real devastation to its target. On April 29, 1942, a salvo of six-inch shells from Corregidor landed in Ward 14 of the hospital, killing five patients and wounding another dozen men. When the onslaught was over, Hank stood from a muddy trench, his hearing gone, his muscles tight with shock. He ran to the first downed man he saw. In addition to locating the injured on the ground, the medics had to comb the trenches and help tug patients back out of their holes. That process required four or six men, in their weakened condition, to lift one man out. At the sound of "Medic! I need you here!" he realized his hearing had returned.

As weeks passed, Hank and his fellow clinicians continued to serve patients in diminishing numbers. Now some of the medics themselves were patients, and everyone suffered from diarrhea that doubled them over with cramps and left them lethargic, nauseated, and weak. It seemed many men were going to succumb to diseases or friendly fire; they just didn't know which would take their lives first.

Following the American attacks, several prisoners pieced together fabric fragments and then painted on the words in English—"Don't fire, Hospital #2 still operating." They took the sign and laid it out on a hill behind the hospital, visible to those on Corregidor.

The Japanese guards had nothing but disdain for the patients and medical staff. Hank heard that some of the Filipino patients had been shot. He had feared the same for some of his patients.

For a Japanese soldier being captured was highly dishonorable—a fate worse than death. It left shame not only on the soldier but also on his entire family. That concept dates back in Japanese history to the Tokugawa Shogunate (1603–1868). And during the interwar years between World War I and World War II, Japanese Army leaders saw an advantage in having every soldier fight to the death. With that in mind, the soldiers were instilled with the value that there was great shamefulness in being captured, something out of what the Japanese Army called the *Senjin Kun* (Ethics in Battle) manual. That manual had been issued to most Japanese soldiers, beginning in January 1941, although some troops didn't see a copy until as late as 1943.

This perspective had to have become starker when they seized thousands of American POWs and discovered that these troops didn't exhibit the deep shame of being captured that they expected—making them even more reprehensible from the Japanese viewpoint.

The second aspect of the Japanese Army culture that would lead to untold suffering for Allied prisoners was its atrocious treatment of its soldiers. A Japanese enlisted man was accustomed to being hit, slapped, kicked, and insulted as a routine, and a kind of resentment and callousness must have resulted.

Hank found it hard to settle down. Sleep didn't come at night and when he worked on patients, he developed a new gesture of glancing around him, turning frequently, every few seconds to see if anyone was coming, looking over his shoulder for a guard with his gun drawn, or a club raised over the medic and patient, preparing to strike. Punishments came unexpectedly and often seemingly unprovoked, he could never feel safe, and he kept his guard up even when lying down at night.

The Japanese provided some rice, but not enough to reverse the wasting away that every prisoner's body was experiencing. So the men began using a desperate kind of ingenuity just to stay alive.

Since no food was forthcoming, or water, a few men started to venture away from the hospital when the opportunity arose. The hospital sprawled for more than a mile, and there weren't enough guards to watch every prisoner at every second. No fences enclosed the hospital, so there was nothing but fear that kept the men restricted. Within the first few days Hank saw men attempt to leave, only to be shot dead on the spot, their bodies left where they lay in the heat for several days as a reminder of the penalty that awaited anyone who ventured out. Their broken bodies eventually were carried to the burial area now overflowing with the dead.

Hank, Earl, and Bill talked about leaving the hospital only to sneak back with whatever provisions they were able to scrounge. The first time Hank ducked out of the camp Earl joined him. They ran toward the barrios, the road, looking for anything they could possibly eat.

Initially, they found nothing and snuck back in twilight disappointed, but undiscovered. Hank still slept with the terror of a Japanese guard coming to his bunk, dragging him outside, shooting him down, or beating him. On another excursion he got very lucky. He found a sock filled with raw rice lying abandoned, or overlooked, on the jungle floor. Hank, Bill, Earl, and a few of the patients ate well that night.

Each Japanese guard carried a rifle with the bayonet fixed and ready to go. Hank soon witnessed the bayonet use for stabbing prisoners. It was a slow and deliberate death. He knew all too well what the blade did to the vital organs, the way they would bleed out, and the suffering involved in the gradual process. Death might take minutes or more than an hour. If the injured person was fortunate he would pass out and die peacefully.

Several medics slipped out of the hospital early one morning and returned in the heat of the afternoon, their movement as they slipped in through the jungle underbrush caught the eye of a guard. The two were seized and held until more guards arrived, shouting their indignation at the two hapless medics who kneeled where they were directed. Chamberlain and the other staff were organized in a lineup to witness what happened to those who left the hospital. He looked away rather than watch the men's suffering and was grateful when they lost consciousness. After they died he helped carry them to the burial site.

Terror could not master hunger, however, and Hank soon went on another excursion. He made his way south toward the beach where a road from Manila hugged the coastline and small coastal barrios stood within rifle shot of the roadway. Hank had to be especially careful here, where the road often was passed by Japanese troops driving wagons, Filipino vehicles, or American military trucks, sometimes using American prisoners as drivers.

In his exploration he spotted smoke hanging mournfully behind a rise in the jungle floor. It hovered over a barrio Hank had visited just weeks before, where a small community grew corn and other vegetables and had shared chickens and a carabao with the hospital workers. He crawled on his belly up the hill to look over the top.

What he saw froze him to his spot. The scene below was a burning hellscape of flames, ash, and bodies, surrounded by the wailing of the living. Japanese soldiers walked among the ruins looking for metal or other salvageable materials. The bodies themselves had been there long enough to bloat from the tropical heat. From his vantage point Hank could have thought they were still alive, for the bodies seemed to be moving, but they were covered with insects squirming over the dead flesh. They looked like giants, swollen in the sun. Several were being attended to by loved ones. One woman rocked back and forth as she sat next to a body, which could not be possible to tell if it was child or adult, male or female, only that it was someone who had been precious to her. She held the body's hand. Another Filipino was preparing to lift a body and then dropped it as a Japanese guard fired his weapon in the man's direction. They shouted at the man in Japanese, several moved toward him with guns drawn and he hurried away.

The Japanese had now put some Filipino prisoners to work helping scavenge metal pieces, and Hank watched them being hefted onto the back of trucks for the Japanese, some of those vehicles being captured American trucks. The metal was being sent back to Japan to help with the war effort.

When Hank returned to the hospital he lay in his bunk with the images of those bodies, the anguish of the crying survivors haunting him all night. Days later he snuck out again, and this time he was lucky, he found a discarded sock near the burned barrio, now smoldering and empty, the sock bulged and at first he stood back, poked it with his foot, then reached down, weighed it in the palm of his hand where it sank round, soft, and heavy like a tennis ball. He peered down inside and then reached in. Rice! He shoved the treasure into his pocket and ran with a lighter step back to the hospital, later sharing the raw rice, swallowed dry in handfuls by his friends Earl and Bill, and himself.

By now Hank and his comrades had been POWs for several weeks, and he was no more accustomed to it than the first day they were detained. Nothing in training had prepared him for this.

Whenever the captors could cause pain they seemed to enjoy it. If a prisoner didn't understand an instruction it was followed with a crack to the head. If a prisoner walked too fast, too slow, or wore a facial expression that the guards didn't like, they would be struck. If the infraction seemed more serious—such as hoarding or stealing a morsel of food, it could be worse. Hank was stunned at the first execution, then less so the second and third time. One of the greatest surprises was the cavalier attitude toward causing pain or death. While beating, torturing, or harassing a prisoner, the Japanese soldiers laughed. The Japanese seemed to joke, chatter among each other, and laugh more vigorously, pointing at the suffering of a prisoner.

Despite this, Hank continued to take chances. In the second week of April 1942, Hank and Earl escaped one last time from the hospital but would regret what they were about to see. They had learned that skirting the road near the coastline a mile or so from the hospital could yield food, the occasional Filipino farmer might have a piece of food for them or would conduct a trade. This time though, as they climbed over the two-lane highway that skirted the Manila Bay, they heard ungodly sounds. Shouting and intermittent gunfire, as well as cries of anguish, punctuated a dull roar of footfalls. The march of prisoners to their encampments had begun.

Mystified by the sounds, Hank and his friend dropped to their bellies and crawled over the rise, peering down at the road.

The prisoners appeared to be Filipinos, marched in groups of one hundred, some stumbling rather than walking, some being helped along by two others. The men in the back of the group were the ones receiving abuse from a half-dozen furious guards. Hank watched a man who had fallen to his knees be struck through the belly with a guard's bayonet. The group didn't hesitate to continue without him.

It was spring in the tropics and heat radiated from the road. The Japanese carried water canteens they paused to drink from and the prisoners appeared to have nothing. Most wore no shoes, and the guards were routing them off the road to walk over crushed rocks that were clearly slashing their bare soles. The parade went on and on, and those who were dying or left for dead lingered in their suffering where the two medics alone stared at them in stunned silence. Dread fell over Hank and he glanced at Earl. "That's going to be us next," Earl whispered. Hank knew his friend was probably right.

The Death March that they were witnessing would altogether amount to more than sixty thousand prisoners, marching down a sunbaked, dusty road, sixty-five miles to Camp O'Donnell. About 650 Americans are said to have died during the march, while the number of Filipino dead is estimated between five thousand and eighteen thousand.

Hank and Earl remained, motionless after the group had passed, and they saw another was coming to play out the same miserable scene before them. They had been there about fifteen minutes. The two medics nodded wordlessly to each other and slunk back away from the road and straight to the hospital. Bill was relieved to see them return but grew somber when they shared what they had seen.

"They're marching the prisoners out?"

"They're marching them, they're torturing them, they're killing them," Hank said, his voice weary from the thought of their miserable future.

10

MAY 1942

BILIBID PRISON, MANILA

On May 11, 1942, Major Segeguchi announced that Hospital 2 was closing, and the Japanese began mobilizing its patients and personnel. All American medical staff and those patients who had recovered enough to walk were heading out. The Americans had spent one month in captivity and most were weaker—from hunger and illness—than they had been before their capture. As they saw the announcement printed in Japanese and English on the hospital bulletin board, Henry Chamberlain and his fellow medics were confused. If the officers knew what was happening, they weren't sharing that information.

What Hank would soon learn, however, was that the US Army had lost its battle in Corregidor against the 14th Japanese Imperial Army on May 6. The Philippines was entirely in the hands of the Japanese. The hospital no longer served a purpose; neither to treat casualties nor serve as a Japanese decoy. The battle for Manila was over, no more patients were coming in, and all men onsite—whether personnel or patients—were just prisoners now. Japan intended them to join those thousands of American POWs and tens of thousands of Filipinos already mobilizing to incarceration at two sprawling former military compounds: Camp O'Donnell and Cabanatuan.

As they processed this news, Hank exchanged a glance with Earl. It was early morning but the sun already beat down on their bare heads. The day's chorus of insects had started its performance from the jungle overstory, while flies circled their heads, landing, biting, and landing again. Hank couldn't help feeling relieved to be going from this place. But he and Earl both considered the miserable parade of prisoners they'd seen walking down the road days before—the Death March. Had their time come for the same ordeal?

Within hours about six hundred ambulatory staff members and patients were marching out of the hospital that day, starting early and walking to Hospital 1 in Little Baguio. Among them were most of the medics, Col. Schwartz, and other doctors. Hank watched them go, waving goodbye to Earl and Bill. His friends wished him well, but none knew if they would see each other again. The large exodus consisted of a bedraggled group, marching, limping, staggering out the gates. Both Bill and Earl had their musette bags slung over their shoulders. Bill no longer wore shoes, having lost them to a Japanese guard. Hank recalled the way the Death March POWs had been forced over sharp rocks and he worried about his friend. Meanwhile Hank had been ordered to stay where he was. When the group had gone, what remained was a fraction of the guards and the prisoners who were unable to march out due to overall weakness or the gravity of their injuries. Hank and a small group of fellow medics would now be left to care for these remaining prisoners.

Those hundreds of men who'd left on foot marched to Hospital 1 and spent several weeks there before being delivered to Bilibid prison in Manila along with Hospital 1's staff. Hank soon learned that he and his group, including his patients, would be taking a direct route to this notorious penitentiary, by truck. Not many days after his friends and patients had left, Hank was roused early in the morning to prepare the patients for transport. He was feeling worse than usual and dragged himself to his feet despite a retching feeling in his gut. He packed his few belongings—his canteen and mess kit, blanket, and most importantly the pictures of Cathy and his mother. He slid his grandfather's knife into its protective pocket in the bag's lining. The bag itself was stiff from mud, sweat, and heavy use, but it was a precious possession for Hank.

Then he and his few fellow medics started lifting patients onto litters, one after another. The average patient weighed no more than 120 pounds, but the medics were weakened by malnutrition and a task that would have been easy weeks ago was now impossible. With four men per patient, they carried these loaded litters to trucks, hefted them into the back, and laid them out on the floor as gently as their aching arms would allow.

Chamberlain went about his work in a fog. His arms ached and trembled. Multiple illnesses had invaded his body by now, and this morning he was especially miserable—aching, feverish, nauseous with diarrhea. With quinine long ago exhausted at the hospital, malaria was sweeping through the compound. The highly contagious, tropical disease can enlarge the liver, cause yellowed, jaundiced skin, high fever and chills, and nausea and vomiting. Dysentery adds gastric distress, diarrhea, and cramps. Fighting such diseases is harder when compounded by malnutrition. Hank hefted another litter on the truck and knelt on the ground to catch his breath. Fear crept into his thoughts about his condition—how much longer would it be before he was one of the men on the litters. Another medic offered him an outstretched hand and he took it. Not today. He would not get that sick today. He turned to fetch the next patient.

Once all the patients were secured, the guards yelled, shoved, and gestured to the medics to climb in after them, and they crowded in so tight that Hank had to hold on to those beside him to prevent falling onto patients.

One American POW was singled out to drive each of the trucks, with a Japanese guard seated beside each one and his bayonet between his knees. The Japanese were not familiar with driving American vehicles and put the prisoners in charge of operating them. As the prisoners put the trucks into gear, they began pulling out the gate of the hospital. The sides of the guards' Japanese hats flapping in the breeze as they picked up speed.

It was going to be a hot day, but in the early morning the breeze still offered relief. It was good to be out of the hospital, and Hank inhaled the scent of the jungle overstory growing along the dirt road. But the truck soon brought them onto the thoroughfare that had been the site of the Bataan Death March throughout April, just weeks and days before. The stench told the story of what had happened there. Before they had even reached the site of this miserable trek, they caught waves of rotten human flesh in the streams of air. Hank knew the smell but had never been exposed to something this intense. It wafted into the truck and clouded around them, under the dark canopy: the smell of death and suffering. The redolent still air was nauseating. Already malarial, some of the men vomited.

Once they reached the road they could see why the smell was so strong. Bodies filled the trenches, and some lay crushed on the road, run over with heavy machinery like roadkill. Insects were doing their part in breaking down the bloated dead. Men run through with bayonets, lay in their own pooled, coagulated blood, rotting. Men shot, decapitated, run down with machinery, nothing but dark stains of gore that had days before been living men.

The violence these men had experienced, as well as the bloating, left the bodies almost indistinguishable. Without seeing the US Army uniform they wouldn't be able to tell if it was one of their men.

The Filipino victims far outnumbered the Americans, however, their retched bodies were more typically clad in civilian clothes, nearly all had bare feet, some lay in pools of blood. No matter the nationality, all were flyblown and crawling with maggots, swarmed by flies. Some were women, and Hank recalled seeing the Death March as it took place with the young girls and women who had tried to relieve the POWs' suffering with a bit of food or water and were killed when caught. Hank noticed little bottles or cans, kicked over by the side of the road, most likely relief for the prisoners who had been turned over by the Japanese. The guards had no sympathy for civilians who tried to help the prisoners.

Hank and those other medics who had a view out the truck side and back were silent in their shock. He didn't speak out loud but in his head he would ask a question that would stay with him for the rest of his life: "How could anybody treat another human being that way?" These young men who had so recently been full of life "were such a slimy mess, and there were no recognizable features about their bodies. Nothing."

The patients were his best and only distraction. The heat under the truck canopy and the jostling on the rutted road meant the men at his feet cried out, cursed, and whimpered. Hank did what he could to comfort them, although he had none of the life-saving sustenance they needed—water, food, cool air.

"You do what you can for others, we were taught that during the Depression years," he recalled. A few of the injured still had pieces of shrapnel lodged in their wounds. Doctors had opted against surgical removal, concerned that the surgery would be harder on the body than leaving the metal where it was embedded. Now each time the truck lurched over ruts, rocks, and potholes those patients cried out in pain, and all Hank and the other medics could do was try to hold them steady during the worst impacts.

The men watched warily when a guard shouted a command, peering at the front of the truck. The driver continued, either not hearing or not comprehending what was said. The guard repeated, louder this time, slapping his open hand against the vehicle's flank. After the guard seated in the front shoved at the driver, the point was made, and he pulled the truck to a stop. Other vehicles in the lumbering caravan slowed, then maneuvered around them. The guard in the back climbed out and stepped to the side, opened his pants, and relieved himself, and another guard stepped down to do the same. Other trucks in the caravan drove around them bouncing over the ruts in the ditch that edged the road. The POWs sat in the idled truck under the searing sun, dust from the ride caked with sweat on their sunburned skin. Cicadas rattled loudly from the trees.

While the guards zipped up their pants with some satisfaction, many of the POWs had been forced to soil or wet their pants in the long ride.

After the first guard climbed back in, the American driver hit the accelerator. His visibility couldn't have been good, and the men were packed so densely in the back that it was impossible to see what was happening directly behind them. This was bad for the second guard who was preparing, at that moment, to climb in. As the truck pulled away he stumbled backward and landed on his back with a shout.

Chamberlain watched the guard rise to his feet call out, and then break into a run after the truck. The guards watched their comrade's plight as the truck picked up speed and they waved their arms furiously at the driver, even as the guard got smaller behind them. Once those in the cab of the truck grasped what had happened, the driver got a knock on the head, "Stop!"

It was one of a handful of common English words the guards often used. The brakes hit hard and every passenger—medic, patient, or guard—lurched in the back. The abandoned guard picked up his speed and scampered to the truck, climbing up with help. Hank avoided eye contact with anyone. Guards didn't like to be looked at, let alone laughed at. POWs were beaten for smiles, frowns, rolled eyes. They had all learned the fine art of an expressionless face. Hank knew he'd burst out laughing if his eyes caught a glance with any fellow American. And he knew better than to do that. The truck continued to crawl along making slow progress while men who needed to step off the truck to relieve themselves got more distressed.

One patient, lying on the truck bed floor put his hand on Hank's leg, groaning, "You got to help me with this diarrhea Hank, I can't hold it. They've got to let us stop."

Hank shook his head. He knew that wasn't going to happen. "Let 'er fly, you can wash up later." He looked up at the passing canopy of trees marveling how low he had come, how little he could do. He had joined the army to save lives. He was rendered useless now.

By nightfall they still hadn't reached Manila and the truck stopped. Those who could clambered off the truck and then lifted the others down onto a meager strip of flat land between the road and a carabao wallow the water buffalo had dug out by scraping, rolling, and hoofing at the ground until they reached mud that cooled their thick hides. The men now eyed the mud wondering if that was their only option for drinking water. Instead a bucket of warm water was placed in front of the men, with a dipper. Those who had a canteen could fill it, and the others made do with a cup or their hands. They were handed a ball of rice.

The guards seated themselves under the cover of the truck canopy for the night. When the rain cascaded out of an evening storm cloud, the prisoners sat in the downpour. Their cold bodies were soaked in rain and their excrement, their meager clothing chafing against their skin, but they raised their faces and opened their mouths to collect every drop they could. Hank curled up on the ground and listened to the sounds around him, both his head and his guts on fire.

The next day the journey continued until the convoy of trucks finally pulled into the outlying shacks that signaled Manila. The city had been pummeled for weeks by bombing, strafing, and fires, and the place was barely recognizable. As they reached the center of the city of Manila, the trucks got ensnared in the heavy traffic of rickshaws, carabao, donkeys, pony-pulled carts, jeeps, and trucks. Shouts from a male Japanese voice didn't break him out of his thoughts, but the frantic shrieks of a female caught his attention.

Two soldiers stood over a woman seated in the dirt behind a small table with sundry wares for sale, and one had leaned down and snatched a baby from her lap. There was no way to know how she had attracted the attention of these soldiers, but their hatred for her was apparent.

The way they grabbed the baby, swinging it by one foot, reminded Hank more of someone tossing a rag doll rather than a flesh and blood child. But the infant's screams made it all very real. The man swung the child in a circle and Hank watched as if the moment was frozen into devastating, slow motion. Then the man released the infant. The baby arched up into the sky and then came down, directly, onto the upheld bayonet of the second soldier, impaled. The act took place so fast, so casually, that it seemed they had done this before, and Chamberlain wondered if he could trust what he had seen. But already, he knew that he could. The woman's cries were more anguished even than the baby's, as the soldier pointed his bayonet rifle down and the baby's body slid off the blade and onto the dirt floor, still screaming. The woman dove for the baby, the soldier bayonetted her with the same bloody blade, one stab into the abdomen, and she was dying, but it would be slow agony, breath by dwindling breath.

Hank's truck was still idling in the traffic entering the town and he watched from his motionless perch as the Japanese guards regarded the slow death of mother and baby, some laughing. The baby's mother wrapping herself around his broken body. And then the baby went silent, into the mercy of unconsciousness and fell permanently still. The mother was not as fortunate, her body writhed from the pain and sorrow, and Hank watched in horror until the truck rolled back into motion.

Chamberlain exchanged a look with the medic seated next to him to see if he had witnessed the same thing. The man's haunted expression was his answer. But they didn't speak. The guards were at their side and would laugh if they saw a POW disturbed by what he saw. The image of that mother and baby, however, would play out in his mind over and over for the rest of his life.

They came to their final stop in front of a sprawling, grim, stone and concrete fortress, and the driver killed the engine. This was Bilibid, an infamous Filipino penitentiary that the Japanese were now employing to quarter civilians, internees, and POWs until they could be moved to more permanent sites. By the time Chamberlain arrived there were about six thousand prisoners onsite.

The guards rammed, shouted, shoved, and prodded the prisoners down, and many stumbled onto the street in front of the gate. Filipino merchants sat along the roadside, Japanese soldiers marched past. As he stepped down Chamberlain wavered on his feet, his headache dimmed his vision in the bright light. He fought the urge to release his bowels there on the street.

When they entered the prison gates the men were ordered to empty their musette packs and pockets and to remove any watches or other valuables. A guard approached Hank and snatched his bag, sliding his hand over the goods. He looked over Chamberlain's handkerchief with initials "HC" sewn into it, toiletries, and then the photos. When he saw them, he cried out in pleasure. Hank's red-headed mother posed in front of their home in Omaha. The other was Cathy, laughing as she leaned against the trunk of a pine tree in the Spokane park where he used to meet her. The guard gestured to those standing within range and the Japanese men circled the pictures, laughing and pointing.

The pictures went into the man's pocket. Guards proceeded to take what he wanted. Hank's comb, soap, underwear, mosquito netting, canteen, and cup came out of the bag and were handed around. Hank cared about none of them, only staring at the pocket where the pictures of his mother and girlfriend had gone.

He broke back to attention, however, as the guard turned the bag over and ran his hand over its seams. The one valuable he'd hidden well was that knife. The guard's hand passed over the seam, no reaction, and he then threw the bag back at Hank. The POW caught it with relief but seething with hate. The bag, his knife, and a few items rejected for unknown reasons were all he had left in the world.

When he was slapped he wasn't sure if something he had thought had inadvertently escaped through his mouth, "You thieving bastard!" Whether or not they understood the words, the disrespect was plain. With the slap, pain radiated across his face and then it happened, he returned the blow. His closed fist was out, striking, before he was even aware of what he was doing. Did he do that? His malarial confusion might have helped it happen. But the repercussions came to him bright and clear.

One guard grabbed each arm, the third stripped off his uniform—it was already a flimsy arrangement of rags. The beating then involved punches, kicks, while the other prisoners watched. They'd seen it before and could only hope, just as Hank hoped, that it would end before they killed him. At that moment he served as an example for his fellow American POWs of Japanese rage against their country, people, and culture. By the time it was finished, his eyes were swollen nearly shut, his ribs frozen, refusing to expand with the breath of air he desperately needed, and he waited to be dropped to the floor.

Instead another figure approached him, this one dressed as an officer, a cigar in his hands and his eyes boring into Hank's. The prisoner tried to yank loose, realizing what was happening. The cigar pressed into his arm, the pain so hot he thought he'd lose consciousness. He could smell his flesh burning. The cigar raised and dropped into his arm again, burning a new hole in his forearm, and the searing sound of burning flesh drowned out by his screams. Or had his breath been entirely taken from him? Did he even make a sound?

They weren't done yet. The man guided the cigar down between Hank's legs, and he thrashed like he never had before, but couldn't stop the burning that now dug into his scrotum. Finally, consciousness slipped away and the curtain fell on the indignity and agony.

It may have been only seconds before he was aware again, being coaxed, supported, and dragged up a set of stairs and into the cell with his fellow prisoners, other medics. He lay on the floor with his cheek pressed against the concrete, pain radiating from his groin, his arms, and head.

The concrete prison cell came with no door and an open window with shutters—no glass—that looked out over a busy Manila Street. There was no reason for bars on the windows. No one would survive a drop to the ground. And while the window was only waist level, Hank had no interest in looking out to orient himself. Once his friends rested him on the cement floor he lay there, motionless. There was a purpose to his method beyond pure exhaustion. Because there was so little food, and because he could feel the gravity of his injuries, he knew he needed to conserve energy. An infection could kill him, and that would be a miserable way to go.

It wasn't the first or last beating he would endure, but this one would leave both physical and emotional scars. The next few days passed in confusion. Food was brought in once a day. Time passing both slowly and fast somehow, morning and night. Some men leaving with guards and returning. They said they were being put to work in Manila: lifting or hauling, moving the spoils of war—metal, coal, fuel, any material that could be of use in Japan—toward the wharves.

As he became more aware of his surroundings again, Hank listened to the sounds of city life going on outside the window. He heard voices speaking Japanese and Tagalog. If he heard vehicular traffic it was military equipment motoring through the narrow dirt roads. More commonly came the sound of wagons and the hooves of livestock

There were women and children in the prison, who the POWs encountered occasionally in the communal yard. Filipina women were teaching classes to the cluster of children, all looking hungry and exhausted, but focused on each other, indifferent to the American prisoners moving around them. Eventually Hank saw familiar faces with the admittance of a new large group of POWs, Col. Schwartz—he recognized his voice and authoritative tone even before he saw the face. He saw others: Earl, Bill, Dr. Brown. They didn't have a chance for a reunion, merely waved to acknowledge that they were again among friends.

Although Manila had previously been an impoverished city in many areas, now it seemed much of it had been destroyed by bombing. An open sewer had previously run beside some roads, but now human waste—feces, urine, vomit—littered the road where others walked over it, and the smell in the heat drifted into the jail cell. It had become, Hank recalled, one of the dirtiest, filthiest places he had ever seen. And the people were suffering.

The Japanese could be heard shouting at the citizens: men, women, boys, girls. Gunfire occasionally rattled, and voices would fall silent. Once he could stand, looking out the window, and even venture into the city on work details, he saw how much the Filipino people were suffering from this war and occupation. Their faces drawn and starving, mirrored his own. Orphan children wandered through the streets holding hands, no parents to care for them, nowhere to go for shelter or food.

Within the concrete cell Hank began to take more notice of those around him and the help many needed. He was, after all, a medic first. A bucket in the room served all the men in the room for their bodily functions. By the end of the day it was filled to the top with diarrhea and urine.

As the sun dropped low and the cell's light dimmed, a POW with a handcart came to pick up the loaded bucket and leave an empty one.

Another delivered a similar bucket of food for the men to share, which was mostly balls of sticky rice. Hank found they were peppered with maggots, but also with grit and even broken glass.

After the food bucket delivery had passed and silence filled the room, one of the POWs started to moan. Occasionally a man would act out, and the other prisoners watched this one warily. The prisoners knew that attracting attention from the guards was always a mistake.

"I gotta get out of here," the man said once, twice, louder, and then louder still until his thin voice was laced with panic, and the sound rose in tenor. He had to be silenced because any attention that brought the guards into the room would be regretted by everyone there.

Hank shook his head at the wallowing. His head ached and the burns were so painful that a shimmering light hung in front of his eyes. "You damn asshole, knock it off," Hank called out and the others chimed in. When the man started thrashing around, attempting to stand, to run for the door, they jumped on him. Hank helped hold the man down until his protests dulled to a whimper and then stopped.

Guards posted out front sat smoking Philippine cigarettes, with their strange scent, talking between each other. Up the stairs through an open door, there was one or two, or three or four talking to each other. To the prisoners it sounded like "Gabble gabble gabble."

If they entered, they always came in a pair or more. Never alone. They carried rifles with fixed bayonets either at the ready, in front of them, or over one shoulder. This time they didn't come and Hank relaxed enough to close his hot, dry eyes.

About a week after Hank had arrived, and after the other medics and doctors had joined him, the prisoners were told they were going to have their pictures taken. Hank was immediately uneasy. They were told to comb their hair and look their best, maybe their families would see the pictures. Hank thought of his bruised face, his swollen lids that still obscured his eyes from the beating he'd endured.

The best option was to be completely unrecognizable. If the Japanese wanted the men to look good, then they were going to look bad. That was the war effort they could contribute.

"They're not going to get away with using us for propaganda," Bill and Hank agreed.

They ran their hands over the floor picking up dirt that they smeared over their faces. And until now they had found ways to keep shaving, sharing razors with those few men who still had them. They abruptly stopped shaving. "We just did everything we could to disguise our looks," Chamberlain recalled. The dirtier and nastier the better. And if they were going to show the Japanese world in their newspapers what the enemy looked like, the POWs weren't going to make that easy for them.

It wasn't much effort. Chamberlain knew what he looked like. It was reflected in the face of his fellow POWs with the collapsing cheeks around cheekbones and eyeholes filled with shadow. Collar bones pressing through the collars of their shirts. They were the dead version of their old selves.

In the meantime, he was fighting an infection in his groin and on his arms. Any break in the skin could turn to infection. His options were meager: keep it washed clean, scrub it with water, and if you have soap use it. Now he had only a cup full of water a day to drink, but he saved enough to splash over his wounds.

Around this time a disturbing incident again drew Hank and his comrades' attention: a crime against one of the American female prisoners. Hank recalled the story this way: the prisoner was taken to a private cell and raped by a single guard. After the assault ended and the guard left her there, she waited for the opportunity to tell the prison leadership what had happened. Hank and other POWs were summoned to see the results of this crime and accusation.

The commandant of the prison gathered an audience in the central yard between prison cells and ordered a lineup of Japanese guards. "Which man attacked you?" she was asked. The woman stood there staring at the row of men, wearing their uniforms, rifles at their sides, and needed almost no time to make her identification.

"This one," she said, pointing. The response was swift. She was told to stand back, and several curt orders were shouted and the other members of the lineup stood facing the culprit. They drew their rifles and peppered the man with bullets before he could even speak in his defense.

The woman let out a wail, a deep anguished cry that turned Hank's gut and that would haunt him for years. "Why did you do that? I didn't want that, how could you!" The lifeless body was thrown into the back of a truck the way Hank might have thrown a stick of firewood before the war. "Until those days in Manila I had no idea that any human beings could be so brutal to others," he said years later.

In the meantime, new prisoners were crowding into the penitentiary: men who had managed to miss the Death March. Hank and his fellow POWs knew these cells couldn't support their growing population. He avoided thinking about what might be on the other end of another journey.

11

MAY 30, 1942

TRANSPORT TO CABANATUAN

Before dawn, the sound of footsteps pounding up the stairs to the POWs' wide cell startled Hank awake. Words were exchanged with guards at the door, and two of them pushed their heads in. One hundred or more American POWs, leaning back to back on the concrete floor—most covered in hungry flies, too tired to swat them away—stared back at them. Hank already knew this kind of bluster of activity meant they were about to mobilize. One gesture and a shout and the men started climbing to their feet.

The first shipment of American POWs had departed from Bilibid three days before, and the flow had been taking place since then. They were heading for their more permanent home, the new Cabanatuan POW Camp, fifteen miles from Cabanatuan City.

They were each handed a sticky ball of rice before they marched out the gate. It wouldn't be Hank's last time inside Bilibid's cells, but he couldn't have imagined returning at the time; his thoughts were only on surviving that day.

Still aching from his beating, Hank was struggling to keep up. His face had swelled around his eyes, blurring his vision. His ribs stabbed with fresh pain at each breath. And while the bruises on his trunk were turning yellow and green as his body reabsorbed the blood, the burns on his arms and groin were inflamed and open. The burn on his scrotum viciously rubbed against his clothing with each step. And the illnesses he'd brought with him to the prison had not subsided. He was desperate to lie down, but he forged ahead, always aware of what happened to men who dropped to the back of the line or fell.

Some of his companions were worse off than he was. Dysentery bent them over like old men, shrunken over their aching bellies. In Bilibid the sickest spent most nights taking turns shuddering, moaning, and trembling over the bucket, relieving themselves of bloody diarrhea. For some the malaria was retreating, and fewer mosquitos at Bilibid meant the disease was no longer being pumped back into their bloodstreams. The coughing remained, and for Hank, each hack was agonizing against the bruises on his chest and abdomen.

Both Earl and Bill appeared in similarly dire conditions, and Hank protectively watched over them and those who were most likely to fall, lose their balance, or expend their energy when they couldn't afford to do so. The sun rose over this sickly group trudging to the Manila train station where they would board their latest mode of transportation.

Each metal freight boxcar that awaited them seemed to have transported livestock, either horses or cattle. The floor was littered with clumps of straw and carpeted in manure. The cars weren't designed to accommodate livestock, but it was being accomplished anyway with carabao, horses, or other beasts of burden breathing snatches of fresh air through an open hatch on the roof. The cars were better designed to accommodate temperature-sensitive produce with a cage on top where blocks of ice could be stored. Airflow over the moving car carried past the ice and into the car's hatch provided a marginal cooling effect. On this morning, a hunk of ice was melting in that cage, probably the remnant of a block used for horse transportation.

With dread Hank climbed in, near the front of the group and therefore pressed against the opposite wall. The Japanese used canes or rifles to push and prod in more and then more. When it seemed there was no more room—prisoners were stepping on each other's feet, pressed hot and slick against each other—yet more men were shoved inside. Altogether about ninety men were crammed into each car. By the time the door was rolled shut Hank was packed between the car wall and other humanity so tight that he couldn't raise his arms. Hank used the support of those around him and, to keep his wits about him, he turned his face up toward the air above their heads, breathing deep the barnyard smell as the air warmed. The train mercifully rolled into motion after about an hour of standing this way, but the car heated so fast that some fainted during the trip. Hank could feel someone go slack against him. A few men had been pushed to their limit and they died there on their feet, supported by those around them. The other men were oblivious of the man's condition, the corpse standing upright between them.[1] Hank knew, however, all too well when a man's life had ended. Another patient who couldn't be saved.

For the survivors though, the endurance test went on. Men who had been trained as warriors were crying or whimpering. There is a pain to sickness and hunger, Hank recalled. "It's certainly a different kind of pain. It's a horrible mental condition. One symptom plays on another." As the train lumbered and creaked around bends the men stumbled and protested. Sweating made everyone slick and urine and feces dripped onto the floor and made the straw lining slick as well. Despite the crowding, some still ended up falling. Those at the feet of the rest suffered being stomped or stood on. Each time the train turned or stopped or started with a jerk, men lost their balance, stumbling between each other, cursing, trying to steady their feet. And the train stopped often. The train ventured through the jungle where small villages marked the passage of the miles, but the POWs could see nothing of that. Carabao frequently wandered onto the track, grazing for meager edibles growing between the rails. They were oblivious to the turmoil underway in the human world. The Japanese, just like the Filipinos, didn't want to kill these working animals. So they stopped, and they waited, crept ahead, and then stopped again. The men lifted a few fortunate prisoners to the overhead hatch on the boxcar ceiling where they witnessed the causes for these delays and described them for the others.

Eventually Hank took a turn, climbing on the backs and shoulders of others to gasp a few breaths of the muggy breeze, cooled by ice. Never again, Chamberlain thought, would he take fresh air for granted. Those under the hatch licked at any droplets of water from the ice melting inside.

It was late afternoon when the train reached its destination. The doors rolled open, bright light streamed inside as the sick and exhausted group blinked against the sun to see the soldiers standing there. A shouted order, the word "go" in English, and they stumbled their way out of the car into Cabanatuan City. They had traveled 114 kilometers; it had taken them about six hours. Now they began their march. Once, in the middle of the journey, the Japanese ordered them to stop and then handed out water and fruit. Men were permitted to sit, if momentarily, as they devoured a piece of mango or papaya and gulped water from a canteen or ladle. Then they were back on their feet. Some were too slow to stand and were knocked back down, forced to try again, but this time frantically, fearfully, as the guards laughed. Even after his drink, Hank was obsessed with water, watching the environment around him—farm fields, rice patties, imagining drinking from muddy puddles beside the road.

Just as the heat peaked in the late afternoon, clouds filled the sky, and a deluge of large, hot drops of tropical rain mercifully soaked the men. Hank opened his mouth to the sky but was rushed on. Ahead he saw Filipinos, who had been walking on the road ahead with several carts, quickly disappearing into the fields, far out of range. When they saw the prison groups approaching, the locals usually made their way off the road, to avoid the wrath of the Japanese guards.

After hiking thirteen kilometers they reached a schoolyard, with bamboo hut-style structures and a playground. This play area was now a locked-down holding center for prisoners. And they weren't the first to have been there. The yard itself was stripped of any playground equipment. All metal structures—slides, swing sets, monkey bars—had been dismantled by the Japanese and loaded on ships to be used as scrap metal in their own country. That meant not only was that schoolyard empty, so too were homes and businesses—all metal objects scavenged.

Filipino prisoners had passed through shortly ahead of them and they too had been sick—maybe in worse shape than the Americans, judging from the sight and smell of the yard. Where once children had played hopscotch or baseball was earth hard-packed by hundreds of soldiers, coated in urine, feces, and vomit. Even mucus was smeared on the ground, fences, and bamboo brush.

Not long after they were secured inside the fenced-in yard, Japanese soldiers walked among them searching each man's pockets and bags for anything worth taking. All items of value—watches, pictures, food—had long since been confiscated and the search didn't yield much.

Chamberlain assessed this new holding area, searching for straddle trenches or pits for capturing sewage. There was nothing. Schwartz and Brown serving both as officers and doctors combed the yard and designated a corner to serve as a toilet for 150 men.

In the meantime, the Japanese drove a vehicle to the yard with an iron cauldron, water, and a bag of rice. The men started a small fire and boiled the rice and divided it among the group. Rice was washed down with ersatz tea that was ladled out of a bucket with a wooden spoon, splashing into each outstretched cup or canteen.

The rain came again, and the men looked around them—there was not as much as a single tree for shelter. By the time the rain had stopped the muck that had carpeted the yard was liquidized. Hank watched the men scraping the ground with their bare hands to clear a space for their heads. Hank, Bill, and Earl laid claim to a dirty patch of ground toward the front of the playground, and they too attempted to clean the area so they could lie down. Hank left his friends to search the yard, his eyes fixed on the periphery when he spotted an oily piece of cardboard stuck against the fence. He dove on this treasure and peeled it loose, marveling at his good luck. When he returned to Bill and Earl slumped against each other on their claimed space, he showed them his find. The three friends got to work clearing a space, using the cardboard to scrape the scum away and lay the cardboard flat for their heads to rest on. As long as the setting sun provided sufficient light, others were scavenging any material—stones, a fragment of a uniform—that could be used to render the ground clean enough that they could lie on it.

Flies swarmed everywhere, mean flies that were feasting on the filth underneath them. Cicadas rattled their call from the trees. Other biting insects included mosquitoes and ants. Gray lice, known as "graybacks," crawled through their hair and pubic areas sucking blood. Chamberlain, Earl, and Bill set about picking the parasites out of each other's hair, squishing them between their fingers while slapping angrily as the flies bit bare skin and swarmed around their eyes. The men thought nothing of helping relieve each other of these parasites, even in these most private areas: there was no modesty left.

Several men died in the yard that night and the next day, May 31, 1942, the Japanese instructed the POWs to carry them to the side of the yard and lay them out straight. They were immediately covered by flies.

The living then stood at attention as they listened to their captors' orders. They were to march fast and follow directions. There would be no stopping unless authorized. Those who stopped, those who sat down, or simply fell would be shot on the spot. Chamberlain didn't doubt this. He staggered forward as the group headed out, the sun beat on his head, the insects chattered around them. Although it was still early, the day was already hot, and the light brutally bright.

They made their way onto the highway and marched twenty-nine kilometers. At first Hank kept up, but at some point, when he could no longer recall the beginning of the march, or imagine the end, he stumbled. Every body has its limit, and his could no longer go on. He felt his legs collapse beneath him. Time slowed. He knew once he felt the hard ground against this body, he would be executed. He also knew he had no choice; all he could do was wait for the sweet relief of lying down and then the vicious retribution that would follow and end it all.

Fate had other plans though, and arms grabbed him under each shoulder before he could fall. "Come on Hank, get'yer footing," Bill encouraged him. Dr. Brown grabbed the other arm and he was ferreted along as his feet stumbled and skid against the ground.

The guard came at them in a rage but he carried a golf club; his rifle still over his shoulder. The blows came indiscriminately, and Bill and Dr. Brown were on the receiving end, along with Hank. They were all suffering for his survival. Hank clamored to feel the sole of his foot hit the ground and rose up on his weight. He would keep walking.

As they continued on Hank noticed an object on the side of the road, and then another—they were small bottles and cans, and when a POW saw his chance, he picked one up and lifted it, pouring its contents into his parched mouth where the Japanese couldn't see him. He turned then and smiled at the others: water. The bottle was passed to a few more men before it was empty. Hank watched closely for a similar opportunity. The Filipinos were leaving the water for them, risking their own lives to do so. More often though, the guards spotted the bottles before the group reached them, and they kicked them off the road with their boot. Hank could see the water spill out of them, wasted, into the ground.

Their group kept a steady pace but stopped occasionally to let six-wheel trucks or convoys pass. Several times they were allowed to sit when the guards needed a break. With thirsty eyes they watched the Japanese men drink water. "It was very disturbing to watch them drink," Hank remembered later.

That night the men came to a Cabanatuan camp, part of a sprawling compound the Philippine Army had managed, now controlled by the Japanese. There was no water. Chamberlain watched a man scrape at the ground with a stick, digging as deep as he could, reaching into his hole and shoving handfuls of dirt in his mouth, trying to suck any fluid out.

"Hey you stop that now," Hank called out and the man looked at him, dirt staining his mouth, chin, and neck. "Don't do that, it's going to make you sick, just wait, the rain will come." The man turned away and returned to his digging. His thirst had brought him beyond reason. But then he squeezed the mud between his hands and stared at it and let it fall between his fingers. He would wait for rain.

Eventually the afternoon sky turned dark, and a shower released over their heads. It was such a relief they turned their faces up in exaltation, mouths agape to drink from the heavens. Soon, water was pouring off the eaves of the bamboo structures and they took turns collecting it in their hands, pressing the precious fluid to their mouths.

The Japanese watched. This downpour relieved them of the task of bringing water to their prisoners. They did eventually hand out balls of rice the size of a baseball and dotted brown with weevils. It was the second such meal they'd had that day and some men stuffed them in their mouths whole.

Chamberlain looked at those dead insects and Dr. Brown noticed his medic's scrutiny, laughed, and patted him on the shoulder, "Better eat 'em, it's the only protein you're going to get." The ball went down in two then three bites. Once the rice was gone, his sore and angry stomach would try to leech any nutrients that could be transformed into energy before the rest ran out as bloody diarrhea. Bill took longer, picking the critters out with his fingernails. Again, Hank recognized behavior that would just hasten weakness illness, even death. "Stop picking at your damn food, Bill, eat up, you need it," Chamberlain scolded but Bill grinned at him and shook his head. "That ain't food."

The following morning the group was herded to the road and marched back the way they had come. They retraced five kilometers of the journey taken the day before, then turned in to another Philippine Army campsite, which was then known as Philippine Prison Camp 1. It was now June 1. The guards clearly expected them to settle in here, and they wouldn't be leaving soon. Hank's medical unit, what remained of the original Bataan General Hospital 2 group, would stay together, including Col.'s Schwartz and Gaskill, Capt. Brown, Earl, Bill, and Hank.

12

JUNE 2, 1942

CABANATUAN POW CAMP, PHILIPPINES

There were four camps to house prisoners: one in Cabanatuan itself—a city of fifty thousand. That camp closed fairly soon, leaving camps 1, 2, and 3. Camp 2 was dedicated to receiving new prisoners, who were then transferred to Cabanatuan Camp 1, a sprawling compound occupying the site of what had been a training camp for the Philippine military. Because Camp 2 had no ready access to water, it was soon closed and all its inhabitants relocated to Camp 1. All camps were assembled between rice patties and other agriculture fields as well as swampland where cogon grass grew wild, ten feet or higher.

Camp 1, which would be Hank's home for more than two years, quickly became the single largest Philippines POW camp during the war, with as many as ten thousand prisoners at its most crowded. It occupied about twenty-five acres of grassland and was surrounded by farms, near the Cabu River, and with a road cutting through its center. One area of the camp Hank would rarely see was the space dedicated to housing the Japanese guards. The rest of the camp consisted of the bamboo "nipa" barracks previously housing Filipino soldiers, now home to hundreds of prisoners. Eight-foot high barbed wire surrounded the camp.

This new abode for POWs was known as Camp Pangatian and left much to be desired. The ground was a wide expanse of packed mud and a few determined weeds. However it had dozens of permanent structures made of bamboo and cogon grass—barracks built by the Philippine Army. These long rudimentary structures could house dozens of men. They were windowless, but the doors were open to the air on each side. That feature could serve as a wind tunnel on stormy days.[1]

For water the men lined up at a single trickling tap to fill canteens, often waiting two to three hours in line to get a half canteen of water.

The day after Chamberlain's group arrived at the camp, the deaths began. The journey from Bilibid had taken its toll. Although the men had traveled a comparatively short distance, the maladies they brought—starvation, dehydration, over-heating, and exhaustion, along with numerous diseases—were killing them. Men who had been the very definition of youthful vitality months before were collapsing by the hour, their young hearts beating final feeble beats. Then they were gone, leaving the rest to continue.

From day one, doctors recognized the need to separate the sickest from the general population and give them the best care they could. Some camp survivors would claim later that the hospital offered little more benefit than providing a place to lie down where no one would step on you. The care would have to be provided without medicine or tools. But on those first days Chamberlain paid no attention to this effort. He was still suffering from the unhealed wounds of his beating and the parasites and bacteria occupying his body. He lay down on the hot soil listening to insects, smelling death, and fighting back his queasiness. Vomiting meant losing more precious bodily fluids. Yet ants crawled over him, flies landed on him, and he didn't care. A voice came from a distance, and with a start he realized it was directed at him.

"How are you feeling, Chamberlain?" He looked up at the face of Dr. Brown, the doctor had grown gaunt, bedraggled but still recognizably his old friend. Hank wondered if the doctor had been fetched by one of the medics. He couldn't recall anything that had happened in the past few hours. Even his arrival at the camp was a blur.

He took a breath. "I feel fine," he found the strength to lift his head from his arm.

"Can you drink?"

Hank was already pulling himself up to a seated position. "Yessir, I'm fine, sir."

"You can rest awhile if you want, Hank."

"No, sir." He was grateful for this interruption, for a reminder that he wasn't dead. He pulled himself into a seated position, waved impatiently at the flies on his face.

"We can use more hands at the hospital." Hank nodded, fought for his balance, and climbed to his feet. He knew one thing—getting up, moving his muscles, circulating his blood—was the only way he would stay alive. He accepted a drink of water from Brown and made his way to the barracks where the prone bodies of the sick and dying were being laid out to be admitted. Dr. Schwartz looked up as Hank approached. "Oh good, Chamberlain, let's record these men's names, then we need to arrange them inside according to symptoms. Remember, anyone with the runs goes on the bottom level."

Like the other barracks, the hospital was composed of two levels of platforms that made up the bunks, under a bamboo thatch roof. Hank accepted a scrap of paper and pencil and knelt next to the closest patient, "Name, private?"

In the meantime, Col. Schwartz went to camp leadership for official approval to dedicate one section of the camp as a hospital, with patients sequestered from the others, and tended to by doctors and medics. Hank marveled at the unending flow of patients coming to him who needed care he couldn't provide. Nourishing food, quinine, and antiseptics would alleviate the majority of their ailments as well as his own. He had none of these. His aspiration to help others as a medic seemed ridiculous now.

"What can we do for these guys? We've got nothing!" Earl echoed his thoughts and Hank could only shake his head, what could he say? "We've got our hands, and water," he answered.

"That's a hell of a way to treat a dying man," Earl answered.

By the next morning, the sunrise illuminated dozens of stiff bodies scattered in and among the other living patients. And still more needed those spaces so they were filled as soon as the corpse was carried away.

Within the first few days, the Japanese officially agreed to establish a hospital operated by the medical staff among the POWs and furnished them with a limited number of straw mattresses. Hank helped lay out the mattresses but soon they were discarded; saturated in waste and crawling with insects. There would be no mosquito nets so patients who brought their own netting fared best, but most lay exposed to these voracious bloodsuckers.

The buildings serving as a hospital were designed to hold forty men each. More commonly, as many as one hundred men lay inside each one, crammed on the sleeping platforms, usually with about a two-foot-wide space for himself. New patients reported or were delivered to the hospital most commonly in the mornings. Most had to be carried. One patient came in carried on a litter by his two friends. He was groaning and his friends tried half-heartedly to boost his spirits. "They'll take care of you here," one was saying to the man as Hank approached.

"They can't do shit for me here, no one comes back alive from this hell hole," he was muttering.

Hank frowned at the man, "Shut up with the belly achin' and maybe we can do something." He felt more frustrated than ever, the damn whiner was probably right. But Hank was determined to try what he could.

Routine was established for the POWs in the first few days. The camp was swelling into a city, and multiple kitchens sprang up, one dedicated to the hospital, medics, and doctors. A barrel-sized cauldron, over a wood fire, boiled a new bucket of rice twice daily. The guards delivered the rice peppered with long-snouted weevils and maggots and cooks steamed it all together. Occasionally the Japanese granted the prisoners some mongo beans or small fried fish as well, and that was thrown in with the rice.

Seated with Bill on the ground by the hospital kitchen Hank watched his friend picking at the rice and sighed. He couldn't convince him that insects could be food. Bill had been fortunate enough to eat reliably wholesome meals three times a day as a boy. It would have been a far cry from the hungry days and nights Hank had endured in Omaha. He recalled the odd soups he'd eaten during the leaner years of his life, watery brews of weeds on the lawn of the Nebraska Territory capitol building in Omaha, and protein from small animals—usually rabbit—that provided that vital energy for muscles, brain, and heart. That lesson wasn't lost on him now.

"Watch this," he grinned at his friend now as he scooped a spoonful of infested rice and shoved it into his mouth and swallowed. "Nothing to it." Since he'd arrived at Cabanatuan, with access to water and rest, his health had improved and he rarely vomited. He let out a laugh as Bill drew his eyebrows together in a frown. "I ain't eating that, I'll never get it down," and he used his grime-covered fingers to pinch out the curls of worms.

Hank, along with each POW, was assigned a bunk in a numbered barrack (Barracks 7, group 2) and a number that would be the identity for each of them for the rest of the war—his POW ID. Since Hank was among the first one thousand American POWs of the Japanese to be recorded he was assigned the number 999. His first task was to memorize this number in Japanese. He learned to shout it out multiple times a day during Bongo—the lineup and roll call that ensured they were there, living or dead. "Kuh ya ku—kujuku." He ran the number through his mind—if he forgot it there would be a penalty to pay. "Kuh ya ku—kujuku." The words settled into his memory and he would never forget it once, for the rest of his life.

Others were not as lucky. Hank watched his comrades as they struggled with the foreign language. When guards pointed at them during bongo, a few went blank, or the pronunciation caught in their throat, or they simply forgot. In some cases they tried to get away with calling out their number in English. The result was the same though, immediate punishment. Sometimes it was a slap across the face. If the prisoner continued to struggle he was knocked down. Everyone knew they had to stand quickly. If they stayed on the ground the beatings could be fatal, so the prisoner would leap to his feet as the guard fired out the demand again, "ID number!" Hank stared ahead in misery as a medic mispronounced his number, each time the beatings more savage, until they finally left the man to do better next time. With each blow the man endured, Hank imagined that he would soon do what he could to stop the bleeding, wash the wound, wrap it, if it was possible.

The Bilibid prison group from Hospital 2 hadn't been on site for more than a week when a parade of trucks pulled past a small duck pond in front of the camp, through the gates, then came to a stop inside with the squeal of brakes, one by one the engines falling silent. Hank and his fellow medics made their way toward the vehicles to see what was happening. The trucks were filled with men, bare from the waist up, staring at the camp around them, or down at their feet, with hollow, blank expressions. These were among the American soldiers who had fought to defend Bataan, survived the Death March, and had since been held at Camp O'Donnell.

He watched the pathetic disembarking of these survivors, a total of about six hundred, stepping, stumbling, falling out of the trucks. He saw their beaten faces, bruises on backs and chests. Their mostly bare feet were swollen, bleeding, and nearly every man seemed to suffer pain with each step. Earl and Bill stood at his side, Bill muttering "poor bastards."

Each truckload carried about forty men, but not all were alive. Those who had the strength helped lower the bodies of those who didn't survive the trip. There was some effort at lowering them gently to the ground, but some simply fell and rolled in a heap on the ground. The bodies were then stacked like cordwood beside the road. Later Hank and Bill would help fill the cemetery pit with these departed souls.

The Death March survivors who lined up to be counted stood in their ragged shorts, their ribs defining their deeply tanned, hollowed chests. Their eye sockets were ghoulishly deep and their stares were vacant or simply exhausted.

"Death march," Hank was thinking, and the three friends shook their heads in wonder.

A Japanese guard caught their expressions and strode over to the medics, singling out Earl for his attention, shouting in Japanese. Earl's blank look of confusion earned him a crack across the face. The guard then reached for a handful of Earl's auburn hair. Since his capture, Earl had attracted attention for his red hair, his helmet was long gone and when the sun shone down on him, he drew attention from the Japanese. Now he froze, his expression steely as the guard yanked a tuft of hair from his head. With a chuckle the guard wandered away, stuffing Earl's hair in his pocket.

More Camp O'Donnell prisoners streamed into the camp over the following days. A bucket of steamed rice was delivered in the front of each barracks. The cooks provided smaller and smaller portions of rice.

"What the hell are you doing with all the rice?" Hank asked a cook, "We'll all be dead in weeks on this diet." The cook shook his head, "Take it up with the Japs. We're doing the best we can. We have to share with everyone." The rice provisions had not increased with the additional prisoners.

Hank looked at the small scoop on the new wooden bowl he'd carved himself from a chunk of wood scavenged behind on the barracks. He glanced around him at his fellow prisoners, finishing the rice in several careful bites. If one grain was lost, the men would search the ground as if they'd dropped a precious gem. Col. Schwartz met with the camp leadership again to request more food to feed the additions to their ranks, but he was sent away with nothing. Hank could have resented these new skeletal campmates from O'Donnell—they looked as if they could eat the rations for the entire camp by themselves—but he was also a medic, and that meant he had to tend to their needs.

The Death March survivors required varying levels of medical care. Many went straight to the hospital. At each of the hospital wards a doctor was typically assigned to oversee the treatments, and he would meet these hapless patients upon their arrival and try to evaluate their symptoms. Almost all brought in diarrhea and vomiting, some too weak to swallow even a spoonful of rice or sip of water, despite the assistance of other POWs. Some were finding sources of food that were making their problems worse.

The camp had an expression: "Anything that'll make a turd." But the problem was that some of the food they selected—like grass or toothpaste—was doing nothing more than making them heave up the scant contents of their bellies or increasing the flow of diarrhea. The doctors suffered the same ailments the patients had. They were sick, skinny, existing on the same provisions, and had no medicine for themselves. Patients, doctors, and medics were all dying; their bodies piled under the ward for pick up by the burial detail.

The Death March survivors had more acute malaria and dysentery than Hank had seen before, however. And the ulcers on their feet needed immediate attention. Not only did they have infected blisters and sores from walking miles on bare feet or in badly fitted boots, but malnutrition also exacerbated the problem, causing painful swelling.

At first Hank went about treating the new patients while limiting interactions with guards and avoiding the camp leadership. Eventually though, he got his first look at the camp commandant: Lt. Col. Masao Mori. Before the invasion, Mori had operated a bicycle shop in Manila. Hank had frequented that shop, renting bikes he and his friends rode around the city. He hadn't noticed Mori at the time and barely registered that the store's proprietor was Japanese. There had been nothing during the prewar days to indicate the way the man would someday be treating those in his care—overseeing thousands of prisoners who were enemies of Japan. However some speculated that Mori was already serving the Japanese government from his small store, watching the arrival and training of army personnel like Hank. Mori was first charged with Cabanatuan's Camps 1 and 3. He lived first at Camp 3, then moved to Camp 1 in September 1942.

Chamberlain had heard stories of Mori's savagery before he finally encountered him. The prisoners referred to the middle-aged man alternatively as "Blood" and "Bamboo Mori," and knew him to dole out indiscriminate punishments for any possible transgression. The epithet Bamboo Mori referred to the stick he struck men with, always in the most vulnerable part of the body he could. The name Blood referred to what flowed freely from prisoners who had encounters with him, Hank explained later.

Typically Mori strode past the prisoners with an expression of disdain, the bamboo stick ready to strike for any provocation: a failure to bow, an unpleasant expression, or not understanding an order in Japanese. He was a smaller man than most of the POWs, about five feet five inches, carrying approximately 140 pounds. He wore a crisp Japanese Imperial Army uniform and stared at prisoners through thick round glasses. Each time he made his appearance in camp he was surrounded by guards, most commonly accompanied by an especially brutal guard named Kasayama Yoshikichi. Like Mori, Yoshikichi was shorter than most of the Americans, wearing a trim haircut and black mustache, but he compensated for his small stature with relentless aggression. The prisoners knew him by the name "Slime," and he proved to be the terror of the camp.

When Blood and Slime could be spotted approaching, Hank tensed in dread. Anxiety was now ingrained in him, since the first time he saw unjustified beatings and executions. Logic was a useless commodity here. It was impossible to predict where trouble was coming from. A guard could burst into the barracks at night and seize a man from his bunk. They could enter the hospital and shoot a patient, or a medic dead, or bolt at an unexpected victim with a fixed bayonet, driving a fatal hole in a man before he knew it was coming. He carried this anxiety with him to the latrines, through the day at the hospital, and into a fitful sleep each night. Still, when Hank spotted the camp commandant or his enforcer, the anxiety amplified.

In the barracks one early morning these tormentors came through the door swinging at the prisoners before the men were awake. Slime's golf club handle struck a blow across the soles of each man's feet sticking out of the end of the short bunks. The men bolted upright. Hank pulled his feet in fast enough to avoid the punishment and looked away as Blood scrutinized his face. They continued down the bunks until Slime seemed satisfied that he had identified a culprit. Just what the man had done, or whether they had the right identification was a mystery. Slime clamped a hand on the man's shoulder and dragged him out of the barracks.

The POW who'd been seized was a medic, and Hank figured they may see him in the hospital soon, as a patient. Or he might be strapped up in the sun in a display of torture meant to intimidate anyone who might commit a similar crime. Or maybe his body would turn up for burial. Hank never saw the man again.

To keep himself out of the hospital as a patient, Hank focused on his food and exercise. But cleanliness mattered too. He shaved his beard regularly with his grandfather's straight-edge razor, scrubbed himself with bamboo leaves under the water pouring off the eaves in the afternoon downpours. His toothbrush now long gone, he cut wooden toothpicks out of scrap wood that could be found in the kitchen or discarded in other parts of the camp.

Meanwhile, the transmission of dysentery, the mosquitoes, and the malnutrition meant the number of patients was growing. The camp's population made their way either on their own or carried by friends to the hospital's thirty-one wards. By early July about six thousand men were in the camp and half were patients in the hospital.[2]

Still without medicine, the medics had to consider what options they had for treatment. The wretched smell of diarrhea and vomit in the hospital and the filth the men had to lie in were compounding their misery and possibly accelerating deaths. After a meeting with doctors and medics, it was decided they needed a more aggressive effort at cleaning the men. Hank waded into the thickets of cogon grass growing as high as his chest near the fence and broke off pieces that he clumped together and tied onto sticks in an attempt to mop the floors. He was aware of Japanese guards watching him and tried to be slow and deliberate in his motions.

Once he had a mop built, he waited for the first heavy rain and used a puddle of rainwater to scrub the floor, then the bamboo shelving the men lay on, one space at a time. It wasn't the quality his mother would have approved of, but he had marginally reduced the odor and lessened the swarms of biting flies. Hank tied the softest ends of the grass together to make sponges that could be used to gently clean the bodies of the sick. He recruited a group of men to help weave new mats for the patients which raised them from the hard surface of the bunk but could be cleaned.

He and the other medics began bargaining with prisoners to help reduce the population of rats that were scurrying through the hospitals, no doubt spreading disease while often biting the patients and gnawing on corpses waiting for burial, under the ward. For each dead rat delivered to them, the medics would roll a Filipino cigarette for the men.

Killing the rats reduced the spread of disease and offered a little protein in the food rations as well. As Hank fetched water or made his latrine runs each day, he passed numerous figures hunched over narrow drainage ditches that crisscrossed the camp, a rock in one or both bony hands, their eyes trained on the grass for any sign of movement. Any dead rat was then delivered to the kitchen to be properly gutted and cooked.

Since the first week, the physicians attempted to separate the dysentery patients from the others. Their feces came out watery, uncontrollable, and most were too sick to walk to the designated toilets which were about one hundred yards from the hospital barracks.[3] If anyone was unlucky enough to lie in the lower tier beneath a dysentery patient they would be soaked in diarrhea as it dripped between strips of bamboo that supported the bunk.

Hank's days were filled with tending to the patients, interrupted by his visits to the latrine. After the afternoon rains, that journey required wading through mud. The hospital section itself dwelled on what had been a rice patty before the Philippine Army occupied it, and the low ground was quick to fill with water and mud.

Despite any cleaning, the filth and frequent rain meant every footstep landed in bacteria-filled scum. His bare feet were covered in sores and abrasions and the mud and diarrhea only agitated those sores. He snuck his grandfather's razor from his musette bag's hiding place and began carving himself a pair of wooden clogs similar to those worn by the Filipinos. With a flat wooden sole and a piece of string nailed to the top to insert between his big toe and the one beside it, they slowed his step and were awkward. But they kept the soles of his feet out of the mud. Soon other men were asking him to make something similar for them.

There were times when the medics and doctors could do something for a patient. But the procedure was sometimes nearly as bad as the suffering they would endure before an untimely death. So Schwartz, Gaskill, Brown, and other physicians started providing surgical support if it was desperately needed, although the typical anesthesia, antiseptics, scalpels, and oxygen were absent. Surgery would be a matter of boiled water, a knife sharpened on rocks, and marginally clean, reused strips of cloth for bandages—often made up from the clothing of patients who hadn't survived. They dedicated an area in the back of one hospital barrack, walled off in the hope of reducing the swarms of flies that otherwise harassed the patients.

As bizarre and unorthodox as some surgeries would be, Chamberlain drew from inner willpower rather than follow his instinct to leave the scene and retch. He wasn't the only one who was sickened by what he saw and what had to be done. He was one of the youngest of the medics, but he had seen enough in his childhood during hunting to tolerate more blood and gore than most. What he struggled with was the pain, and he suffered each agonizing loss when a patient crossed the fragile line between survival and death. He hated to see a man die.

One man came to the hospital with a badly infected eye, so swollen it was clamped shut, the red flesh of his lid engorged like a tomato. Brown took Hank aside to prepare a plan.

"This poor man's going to die if we don't operate. We're going to take the eye and I'll need your help."

Hank nodded, glancing at the patient seated on the table, his head in his hands. There was no antiseptic so they would boil some water for the scalpel that the doctor used. Rags that had previously been wrapped on other patients were washed and hung to dry. Those would swaddle the empty socket after the procedure. There was no sulfa or other antiseptic, so if the surgery introduced bacteria, it would be up to the man's immune system to knock it out. And with anesthesia long gone, he would feel the entire procedure.

The patient lay back onto the wooden table dedicated to surgery, hastily crossing himself with a shaking hand. Hank enlisted a team of medics to hold the patient down, one for each leg, each arm, and a fifth to hold his head still.

"I've got no way to relieve your pain soldier, so you'll just have to endure it," Brown said. The man nodded, stiff with fear, and the doctor patted his shoulder the way he might have comforted a child who was going to have a shot, before the war at Fort McKinley. "You're probably going to pass out Private, and that will be a kindness, but until you do, there's nothing I can do about it. I'll be quick as I can, OK? I know you're going to be tough." Dr. Brown looked into the young man's face and added "I'm sorry." Hank secured a scrap of wood between the patient's teeth to clamp down. The patient looked from Brown to Chamberlain with one good eye before nodding approval to start.

Several men got a grip around the man's jaw and the top of his head, others locked their hands around the arms and feet. When his eye was propped open and the blade sliced into the socket, the screaming and thrashing began. Chamberlain focused on his task of helping Brown complete the procedure. After the man went cold, they moved fast. Usually there were only about twenty minutes before the patient regained his consciousness and the fighting returned, no matter how involuntary it was.

As the man's consciousness returned, Hank washed around the wound, massaging his sore limbs and distracting him with stories from Omaha. Like most patients, the man was grateful for the care. "Thank you, Hank," he called out a day later as he walked out of the hospital, a bandage strapped over the empty eye socket. The medic nodded and waved back, "You take care of yourself now, keep it clean and keep away from the Japs. Don't do anything stupid."

In these early months at Cabanatuan, despite the afternoon deluges of rain, the camp had limited access to fresh, clean water. Although a water tower stood within the campgrounds, there was no way to distribute its contents since the machinery for pumping was gone. Once water could be accessed, each prisoner was allowed a single canteen of water per day.

But thirst and hunger were still driving the men to make mistakes. When Hank caught POWs with grass stains on their faces, he warned them, "That'll kill you, don't eat that shit." He knelt beside them and pulled at a clump of crabgrass. He put a blade in his mouth demonstrating, "Chew on it, suck out the nutrients, then spit it out. Grass is indigestible."

Each morning, medics carried out the patients who didn't survive the night and recorded their names. If they had been resourceful and fortunate enough to hold onto their dog tags, Hank or other medics made use of those for future identification purposes. It was an idea concocted by the physicians. They opened the body's mouth and pushed the dog tags inside, pressing the metal tag between the top front teeth when possible, then clamping the jaws shut. They hoped the bodies could be identified if this hell ever ended. Typically the bodies had already been stripped of their belongings, usually by the closest POW. The naked bodies were then piled under the raised hospital wards where they were spared from the direct scalding sun until they could be buried. But with or without shade, the hot conditions meant that bodies began rotting, bloating, and even split in the sun so that both the sight and smell became more disturbing by the hour. Medics and doctors were in agreement that something had to be done.

For burials early into the imprisonment the men took advantage of existing trenches that weren't in use for latrines and created mass graves. But as several dozen men died each day the bodies piled up. Even a modicum of respect and hygiene would be needed for the bodies of those poor souls, a contingency of doctors told commandant Mori. Schwartz and other officers persuaded the camp leadership to designate space for a cemetery. Mori agreed to use a relatively small area at the southern portion of the camp. The healthier men dug the graves with what tools they had; most typically sticks and their bare hands.

Tending to the dead was a task for a large fleet of the living prisoners, but all were operating with starving bodies, battered with diseases. They moved like old men with the strength of children. The flow of the dead to graves dug by men who might not live more than a few weeks themselves was a disheartening sight for Hank and the other prisoners, but still they refused to turn away. Instead the men took up the practice of standing at attention along the trail as the burial detail carried the bodies to their graves. As the parade of bodies approached each day, the highest-ranking man onsite would call out, "Be ready to salute, on the count of two." Then as the group lumbered toward them, he counted, "One. Two." Men's hands snapped up in unison, providing a last gesture of respect.

For the living, the thought that gave them hope was first of rescue, but as that grew more remote, they turned to personal survival strategies. Two balls of rice per day was a starvation diet, so those with the energy and will started seeking food from other sources. Filipino vendors had set up makeshift storefronts along the dirt road between the city of Cabanatuan and the camp, across the shallow river. They sold food and drinks, although they would often hurry away when the Japanese were near. Some of the healthier POWs started considering how to reach those vendors.

Hank, Earl, and Bill were among several staff in the medical wing who were thinking along these lines. It was clear now that the Cabanatuan Camp would be their home indefinitely and the Allied rescue they had been waiting for wasn't coming. Chamberlain wondered just how long any of them could survive. He believed the Japanese were crazy with hatred. They doled out slaps, kicks, hits, and verbal abuse not only to the prisoners at the slightest provocation but also among each other. Officers treated the enlisted men with little more respect than, in some cases, they offered the prisoners. It seemed to Hank that this untethered rage would cause the

Japanese to lose the war, but it could be the end of the prisoners too if they didn't find some way to help themselves.

So Hank and his friends considered their options. They noted that there were working ponies that were grazed in the area, rarely closely watched. All three medics were familiar with riding, and with their starved bodies, the pony would hardly notice a POW's weight. The three watched those ponies and spent the evenings imagining, planning, and fantasizing about their escape.

During the first month of captivity, however, a group of six men did make a break for it, to steal food. They got out of the camp without detection, reached a nearby barrio where they accessed food and water. Then they were caught on their way back in, with food stuffed in their shirts.

The Japanese guards personally beat the men severely for several hours, and then propped them against a fence in front of the Japanese headquarters. Here the torture device was a rope. They were tied in such a way that they could neither stand nor sit, but try to hold themselves up against gravity, bent at the knees and hips in a way that would cause the most pain.

They remained there for two days and two nights, without food or water and the other POWs were forbidden from approaching them or helping in any way. The sun beat down on their bare heads and scalded their unprotected skin. By the time they were untied, they were near death.

But the torture was not over. Four were taken to one side of the camp and executed. The two remaining were taken to the hospital side where Chamberlain first saw the men, and the agony they had already endured. They were ordered to dig a hole near the cemetery that would be their own grave. The Japanese gave them shovels for the task and ordered the Americans on the hospital side who could stand to be the audience for their execution.

As many as five hundred men were summoned to watch the spectacle. One hospital chaplain later recounted that the kitchen had recently received some flour, sugar, and oil, which was made into made donuts that the men consumed as the hapless prisoners prepared their graves. Chamberlain too had grown hardened to the death and suffering, but not enough that he could watch the loss of a fellow soldier without feeling. He stared ahead, miserable.

What happened next caught the Japanese guards by surprise. When one of the men climbed out of the hole he had dug, one of the POWs spoke to him across the barbed-wire fence that separated them. "You've got a shovel, take one of these Japs with you!"

The man didn't betray any sign he'd heard the comment. He stopped and looked into the face of the guard as he put the shovel over his shoulder. He broke into a grin, then summoned up the strength to swing that shovel over his shoulder and slice like a blade through the guard's abdomen. Chaos broke out, Chamberlain recalled. The remaining guards opened fire and shot down the two prisoners, firing multiple times before kicking the bodies into the fresh hole. "Dear God, I hope they find some peace," Chamberlain murmured to himself for those two men's souls.[4]

Later, in September three officers were among escapees who were caught. They would die for their audacity, which was no surprise, but how they would die and what would come first was still an agonizing mystery.

Their savage death was unforgettable for the thousands of prisoners as well as local civilians who witnessed it. The men were tied to posts in front of the gate and beaten. Filipinos passing the gate were forced to beat them across the face with a two by four board. If they didn't strike hard enough they were ordered to hit harder. The officers remained in this position in the blazing sun for two days without water. After the torture was over the colonel was beheaded and the other two men were shot.

Following the execution, the Japanese established ten-man death squads. "If one man escapes, we shoot ten," they announced. These "blood brothers" would be rounded up as soon as the man was found missing. As a result of this new rule, not only did no one escape again, they kept a close eye on their blood brothers, especially at night.

The American leadership took extra precautions by imposing its own additional rules to prevent even the perception of a POW trying to escape. For instance, while the Japanese dictated that men stay within ten feet of the fence, the American leaders made it thirty. A walking, unarmed patrol of POWs was formed to watch for anything suspicious. The patrol wore white armbands with MP printed on them.

To improve their authority over the men at night, the Japanese also went about rigging electricity so that they could shine lights on their prisoners. They installed moveable searchlights in the towers that guards could use to illuminate a section of camp when they heard anything suspicious.

For Hank and his friends, the thought of innocent members of their squads being lined up against the fence and shot down in front of the other prisoners brought their escape plans to a halt. Bill and Hank still talked through the plan, but knew it would never be more than a daydream. "What about the patients?" Bill asked.

Hank laughed, "No medicine, no casts, no bandages, what good are we? We've got nothing but water and our hands. I spend half my day just brushing flies off those poor bastards."

"That's something though." They sat on the dirt patch in front of their barracks watching their fellow POWs shuffling along paths that connected barracks, the "mess hall," and the latrines. Handmade signs, stuck on leaning poles of bamboo, declared familiar names from home, "Times Square" and "Main Street."

"You're one of the only surgical technicians they've got," Bill added and Hank nodded his agreement. As medics they had to be there. If water was all they had, they would have to make do with it.

In the meantime, Mori seemed indifferent to the rising number of deaths taking place at the camp. Most were dying from easily remedied ailments—starvation can be quickly alleviated with increased rations and starvation led to the majority of deaths, Chamberlain noticed. And medicines that could have saved hundreds of prisoners' lives like quinine, disinfectants, and sulfa tablets were never made available.

At times the guards seemed bored and found amusement in harassing the prisoners. One game was the binta or slapping contest. A guard came across Chamberlain and Bill seated together in front of the hospital barracks. The two had started one of the most common conversations in the camp, sharing excruciating details about the food they ate back at home.

Bill's mother made the best roast beef he had ever had, with steaming potatoes topped with a pat of butter and smothered in thick brown gravy. Talking about it, a dreamy smile lit up his face. Hank was ready to top that: "That sounds good, but it would have to be finished with my mother's apple pie. We had apple trees across from our house that had the sweetest you ever tasted. Eating a slice of that pie was better than se . . ." The guard stopped in front of them, yanking at Hank's arm and gesturing for both to stand. The man then swung back and placed a slap across Bill's face, then Hank's. Hank let out a deep sigh, exhausted, waiting for whatever cruelty may be next.

The guard laughed at Hank's expression, then the frown on the two medics' faces, then pointed to Bill, "You hit," he pointed to Hank.

Bill hesitated only for a few seconds. "Go ahead, let me have it," Hank muttered. Bill gave his friend a soft slap and received another blow from the guard, enough to knock him off his feet. "Do it like you mean it, Bill," Hank said. Bill hit him again, his palm open, the slap cracking out loud enough that a few POWs wandered over to see what was happening. Hank staggered back on his feet. The guard pointed at him now, then back to Bill. His turn. Bill wasn't looking very strong lately, Hank hated himself, then hit his friend with as much weight as he could manage.

"God damn you son of a bitch," Bill said, "What the hell," under more pressure, he hit Hank again and they took turns abusing each other until the guard lost interest in the bizarre contest and wandered away.

Bill stuck out his hand. "You've got a pretty good swing for a scarecrow, pal," and the two laughed, patching up any sore feelings. The swelling on their faces wore down over time.

One of the primary purposes of the Cabanatuan Camp was labor. The commanders made it clear they expected Americans to work on the neighboring farms, on a runway expansion near the camp for Japanese planes, as well as various other jobs. The prisoners would be paid too, although the payments were paltry, officers got more than enlisted men, and Hank later insisted he never saw a dime.

The weakened condition of the men didn't discourage camp leadership from enlisting the men for manual labor. They would need harvesting, then planting for sugar fields, sweet potatoes, beans, corn, and rice on five hundred acres of fields where food was grown for feeding the prisoners and Japanese. Runway work involved repair and expands on a takeoff and landing strip at Cabanatuan airport to accommodate Japanese planes. Still more men were used to care for the carabao they kept in the camp.

Each morning work parties of one hundred men each were assembled and marched out for their day's efforts. When there were not enough healthy men in the main camp, guards went to the hospital section and asked Colonels Schwartz or Gaskill to provide a list of healthy medics or recovering patients who could accomplish the farm or construction work. Despite the physicians' protests, the Japanese demanded that a percentage of hospital patients and medics march into the fields.

Eventually the morning came when Schwartz came to Hank and said he'd been put on the work detail list for farming that day. "Your turn, Chamberlain, I wish I didn't have to send you." Hank nodded. He'd seen other medics leave with the rag-tag unit of farmworkers, carrying rudimentary tools taken from Filipino farmers. Now he was among them. It was miserable work for twelve hours in the sun, punctuated by beatings.

Each one-hundred-man team was overseen by ten armed guards including one supervisor who carried a short club or golf stick at the ready to dole out beatings.

Hank had done his share of farmwork as a boy in Omaha, however he'd had some machinery, healthy farm animals, and plows. He'd had a team of two horses that stayed together, one wouldn't work without the other.

While those horses went about the work, Hank walked alongside, picked up harvested corn, hit the bang board pulled behind the team, and the corn dropped in.

It was different now, starting with a complete lack of tools. They would be working with their hands, digging holes for planting, and using sticks they scrounged around the fields to care for the seedlings.

Hank was surprised when he and another soldier were instructed to collect and carry a bucket of feces dipped from the latrine. It was heavy, sloshed against their legs, but the sight and smell went largely unnoticed. They carried their load to a field where yam seedlings were emerging from the soil. The guard's pantomimed their instructions: scoop a small spoonful of feces for each plant and press it around the stalk with a twig, delivering the fertilizing nutrients straight to the roots.

Later they would harvest fully ripened yams, ready to eat. Handling these swollen yellow vegetables, smelling their sun-warmed flesh was agonizing. Hank's mouth watered as he palmed each yam then reluctantly dropped it into the assigned pail. He had seen one prisoner nibble the meaty tip of a yam when all attention was turned the other way. But the guards examined the teeth of each man as the group returned from the fields and spotted flecks of orange. He was beaten with one blow that knocked him to the ground, then strikes on the back, head, and neck with the butt of a rifle until he lay still. Hank waited, then reached for one of the man's arms, someone came around to the other side, and they helped him back up the hot trail to the camp, his legs shuffling to hold his weight.

Hank learned though, that if he was fast, he could eat the yam leaves, but only if he swallowed them whole. Any chewing would stain their teeth green and often the guard's inspected their teeth. His dry throat balked at the wad he forced down, but it gave him just enough relief to get through the day.

Before each work detail, the Japanese kept track of the men through their roll call which began with shouting into the barracks or hospital "bongo" and the men hurried to their feet, out the door and into a semblance of a military lineup. From the first day though, the prisoners recognized one advantage: the guards had trouble telling them apart. It was a mutual confusion brought on by a lack of exposure to each other's culture and race. The Japanese all looked the same to the Americans and vice versa for the guards.

As a result, the ID numbers were crucial to keep track of accurate counts. The men became so good at milling around in a confusing fashion that getting a simple headcount was almost impossible. Eventually the Japanese drove two poles in the ground and ordered the men to walk between then, single file to be counted. Even then, the Americans sometimes circled through several times, upsetting the count.

On some mornings, each man was ordered to call out his number in Japanese, other occasions the guards read off a list. When Hank heard 999 he shouted out "hai!" Japanese for "yes," and was checked off the list. Those who didn't respond were typically dead.

On one of the early days in the camp two guards entered the barracks door. One shouted "Bongo!" at the top of his lungs while the other walked past the POWs, striking the feet of those who didn't stand fast enough. Hank and the other medics collected the numbers from those who had been admitted to the hospital, or who had died, and shouted them out, one by one, to the guards. This time the guards had a tall American POW at their side. The man was unfamiliar to Hank. He was clearly a trusted assistant to the guards though, and in some limited Japanese, he translated some of the identities of the patients to the guards.

When they left, the Japanese men took the tall American POW with them. Hank watched the three walk away. "There goes Dumb and Dumber, and whoever the hell that American is," Hank commented. Bill laughed, "That's Tom Snead. He's cooking for them. They let him sleep in their barracks."

"Traitorous bastard," another medic commented, "look how fat he is."

The two guards weren't back for several days, but when they did they put the men through the same process. "Ok Dumb and Dumber," the medics laughed when Hank spoke up, assured they didn't understand. Their American companion frowned at Hank and the others laughing at his expense.

"Hey, Asshole, why don't you share some of that free food you're getting over there," someone commented, and Snead walked away. He stopped the two guards and spoke with them for several seconds, they turned angry faces toward the POWs who were now preparing to return to the barracks.

"Stop!" the order was shrieked from Dumb, and the man raised his bayonet over his head and brought the side down hard on the first man within range. The beatings went on for some time before the two guards grew tired.

The prisoners bit their tongues as their tormentors and their American companion walked away. The men kept the monikers, but no one spoke it to their faces again.

In the meantime, news was coming in from the outside from a group of prisoners who had built themselves a radio, possibly inside a water canteen. They could wrap the radio in wax paper and bury it when there was any risk of being caught. Hank heard reports regularly about the American war progress, but he found the news was often wrong. The man said he had access to a station out of San Francisco, but Hank suspected what he was learning was not exactly the cold, hard facts of what had come across the airwaves. The man relaying the news seemed to always indicate the Americans were closing in on the Japanese, and that rescue was coming any time now. Too many times disappointed, Hank didn't take any news seriously.

13

JULY 1942

CABANATUAN, PHILIPPINES

One warm summer night Hank was awakened by the roar of wind battering the compound, followed by a sudden deluge of water. As the typhoon passed through Cabanatuan and thousands of men incarcerated there, barracks swung and swayed in the heavy wind and rain. The prisoners clung to their bunks. Because the barracks were open on both sides, the wind whipped a tunnel of chilling water through some buildings, soaking the bunks. However, the medics' barracks included shutter doors that could be closed when the winds were high. At times like these, the Japanese guards took cover at their side of the camp, and the POWs' greatest threat was no longer their captors, but Mother Nature.

Hank, Earl, Bill, and the others could do nothing more than wait out the weather as the wind rattled the structure over their heads.

In the morning, after the storm had passed, the guards were back, in pairs or groups up to four, counting living and dead to identify every prisoner, while assessing any structural damage. The storm had punched several holes in the hospital roofs, and prisoners hacked down the tall cogon grass to patch up the holes.

The hospital patients had not fared as well. In the days following, the typhoon deaths continued at an accelerated rate. Their crowded conditions helped transmit disease between the patients. Those who died lay where they were until someone could retrieve them for burial, and that gave other prisoners the opportunity to pick through any possessions the man left behind that would be of use.

Summer heat was exacerbating the misery of the prisoners. Oppressive, maddening temperatures that were inescapable. Even shade was nowhere to be found. Many days were also punctuated with a soaking tropical downpour that left a steamy, sodden mess for those trying to run the hospital. Deaths were compounding, in the dozens each day, and the graves were filling.

To reduce overcrowding and disease transmission, Hank helped arrange the patients so that they lay beside each other head to foot and men's faces were never in direct range of someone else's coughs or vomiting. Eventually a head physician, Col. Gillespie, supported by a team of doctors, requested a barracks dedicated to those in the direst condition.

In July the Zero Ward was in operation. The building stood at the lower end of the camp and it was the most miserable of all the barracks. It came with no raised beds or other furnishings. Patients were typically laid on the bare floor, often without any clothing, with only their blanket for comfort if it hadn't been pilfered by their guards or other prisoners. Most of the patients suffered from advanced dysentery, and as a result they typically had no choice but to lie in their filth.

Hank had a sinking feeling the first time he looked upon this gloomy place with its half-dead patients. Sometimes he could see death in the eyes of those who had given up hope. But Hank was reluctant to give up on any of them, even after the doctors had. He and the other medics did their best to keep the men and building clean because that was one of the only treatments they had left. Their greatest resource consisted of a cold water tap in front of the building which provided a reasonable stream of water when they cranked it on.

Each morning the medics carried patients out of the building, laid them on the grass near the structure, and hosed them down to clean off the bodily fluids that they had been lying in. In the meantime, the floor inside the ward was scrubbed as often as it could be. But the smell could never be tamped down for long.

When Schwartz assigned Hank to death detail again, with a dozen other prisoners, he was leaving his work at the Zero Ward to care for the bodies of those he had cared for as living patients the day before. There could be as many as forty deaths a day, and with those numbers, the graves—large holes dug out by hand—filled fast. After the heavy afternoon rains they might be filled with a foot of standing water or more. And if the grave wasn't covered over with heaps of dirt at the end of the day, these bodies that had been unceremoniously piled together were exposed to wildlife.

On that July day, Hank worked in a party of four to carry a single body on a homemade litter to its grave. Hank helped tug the bodies out from under the building, then rolled them one by one onto the litter—nothing more than blankets strapped between two poles. The four men hefted the poles onto their shoulders and trudged as far as they could, stopped to rest, then continued until they reached the burial pit. Disposing of the bodies was the worst part of the operation for Hank. He had often been the last to speak to the man when he was living, and now he would be the last to see him to his grave. He had been physician, minister, and undertaker, and he couldn't bring himself to throw the body in.

So, as they rolled the body off the litter and the men bent down to begin the "heave ho," Hank put up his hand, "Hold on, not yet." He looked at the body, just bones and skin, his eyes pulled shut, but his face already frozen by rigor mortis. In the absence of a preacher, loved ones, or family, these young men had only Hank and the other burial duty prisoners to send off their souls.

"Lord, please look after this man's soul, may he rest in peace," he muttered the words, loud enough that several others chimed "amen," and they steeled themselves to the task. Pulling the body to the edge of the hole they gave it a roll and it landed on a pile of others.

They covered the bodies the best they could, with handful after handful of dirt, and Hank recalled the words of Col. Schwartz, "Cover as deep as you can." The greatest concern was Bataan's wild dingo-like dogs that frequented the area, slinking through camp and competing with the men for small animals to eat. Hank saw the tall gray, round-eared canines around the camp, rummaging around the kitchen, and the POWs generally threw rocks at them, although rarely hitting their mark.

When Hank returned to the hospital the image of the wretched graves stayed with him. "I guess I won't know any better, but I still would hate to end up in that damn hole," he told his friends.

That night he was woken by unnatural sounds in the distance he had heard before: grunting, barking, howling. It was the wild dogs. "Oh God, don't let those dogs be in the graves," he thought to himself. The next day, however, the grave detail found the damage. Fresh dirt everywhere, the pit had been partially dug up, bodies or parts of bodies pulled out and thrown like rubbish around the area, half-chewed or eaten by the dogs.

Hank came to despise the canines and night after night he heard them howling and desecrating the bodies of his comrades. He imagined bludgeoning these dogs to death. One morning he saw one slink into camp and he came at it with a club, swinging hard, catching it behind one ear. It yelped but continued out of the camp. Hank watching it go with loathing. Eventually someone spotted the silhouette of a dog with its familiar lope slinking along the perimeter of the fence and he hurled a rock. The rock caught the dog in the head and it fell.

"You got that son of a bitch!" Hank congratulated his friend, and the men dragged it by the tail to the hospital kitchen, filled with smoke from the pit fire, cooks stoking the flames. A caldron six feet across was suspended over the fire, where the entire hospital's sustenance for the day was cooking.

The kitchen crew laughed when they saw it. They would have some meat to work with, no matter that it would amount to scrawny muscle divided among hundreds. Hank walked away before the butchering, chopping, and cooking took place. Later he stood in the mess line as usual, about thirty minutes for his turn at the caldron. He held out the bowl he had carved, for the ladle. "Make sure I get some of that dog in there," he joked, although when he ate his watery rice soup the usual and familiar taste of rice and dirt was all he could detect. Later, men would catch the dogs in traps that ensnared them alive. Several times Soochow was caught in these snares and quickly released to the care of the Marines. The wild dogs were not as fortunate. Several veterinarians among the POWs' ranks were enlisted to kill the canines humanely, and the animals' tough meat was cooked into the rations. No one commented on the unholy circle sustained by dogs eating human flesh, men eating dog flesh.

What they ate was not always nourishing to their starving systems, and in some cases it introduced parasites. During a surgery in which he helped Dr. Brown open up a patient's abdominal cavity, Hank saw worms writhing around the man's intestines. Several were as long as eight inches. "Everybody's got'em," Brown said. "But they sure aren't helping this poor bastard. Pull out what you can." Hank reached in pulling them out with fingers, then tweezers until he could find no more. When he sewed the unconscious man back up, he was unsure just how much they had helped him. Over time Hank would see such worms in nearly every patient on the operating table, some small, some larger. He had the same revulsion each time, knowing that what was in that man was probably in himself as well. At times he was doubled over with abdominal cramps so strong he could drop to the ground. And he wondered, was it the worms?

Hunger and deprivation brought out both the best and worst in the prisoners. Hank saw fights break out over food rations, the butt of a shared cigarette, or even the unintended splatter of diarrhea. Few had the will to break up these battles, and most often they fizzled out on their own. "Most of us took it as entertainment and didn't try to break it up," Chamberlain said. Once fists were being thrown it wasn't long before they ran out of breath. Chamberlain came to blows with another prisoner in one instance in which, in his rage, he might have smashed the man's face in, under healthier conditions. He could see his adversary felt the same way. They lunged at each other, swinging bony arms, kicking with bare swollen feet, and throwing fists as furiously as they could, but they couldn't cause as much as a bruise. Minutes later they were so exhausted they both collapsed in the mud, panting and staring at each other in rage. The two saw the absurdity of their situation, in the same instant, and laughed.

"Oh what the hell are we doing?" Hank asked, and his former foe shrugged. Then they shook hands and helped each other to their feet.

At other times, even more pathetically, a fight broke out between patients in the hospital, and then Hank stepped in. "Knock it off, neither one of you can afford to do this. You're losing energy," he would say, pulling the two apart from each other.

Many of the patients suffered both injuries and illnesses. If the skin broke, an infection often followed. Here parasites also found themselves a host. The soap had been exhausted so at times Hank then got to work cleaning a man's wound by reaching into the open sore, pinching each squirming maggot between his finger and thumb, pulling it out, and depositing it in a can, one after another.

While Hank was undertaking this process on a man's hip wound, Dr. Brown approached and leaned over the pus-filled sore. He then stood straight and rubbed his chin, "That's a hell of an infection, better off just letting the maggots stay where they are. Let's give them a chance to eat up some of that pus."

Hank let out a sigh. "Yessir Doc." The patient looked up at the medic and doctor who were strategizing his care.

"You're going to leave the maggots there?" The man's eyes were in a panic and Hank felt a pang of sympathy for him. He patted the patient's skeletal shoulder. "I'll keep a close eye on it, don't worry. Maybe they can do some good before we get them out."

Later the patient called out to Hank as he walked past, "Medic? I feel them crawling on me."

Hank bent down to examine the wound. It looked cleaner. The swelling had reduced. He grinned at the man, "Good news, it looks better, let's give them a little longer." He made a mental note to return in the evening. By the time he did pick the fattened maggots out, one by one, they had significantly cleaned the wound, and he was pretty sure this patient was going to make it.

Hank had been hungry many times in his life—occasionally for days at a time—but he saw now the stark line drawn between hunger and starvation. Food deficiency can have cruel and painful effects on the bodies of previously healthy men. Some grew breasts, filled entirely with pus. The condition was so painful the doctors opted to give a few of them mastectomies. In some cases this was done without anesthetic, and Hank helped stitch up after the drainage was done, while others clamped the patient down.

Scurvy caused hemorrhages which blood vessels broke in the skin, muscles, bones, and organs. Teeth loosened and gums bled. It also contributed to blindness many men began to suffer from, as well as hypersensitivity to light.

Hypoproteinemia withered the muscles. Pellagra hardened their skin and caused mental confusion. The disease, resulting from a lack of vitamin B, gave rise to burning eyes, cracked lips, sores on the face, and ulcers on the legs. Men began cutting the metal rim away from their army-issued cups to help prevent burning their sensitive lips while they drank tea.

Eventually POWs also developed dengue, a disease inducing severe body- and headaches. A condition known as limber neck featured drooping eyelids and weak neck muscles that led to a distinctive feature in which prisoners dropped their chins helplessly on their chest. In some cases they couldn't fix their vision on an object and might be found drooling, unable to eat with weakness in all their extremities. This condition was worsened by physical activity. Doctors later diagnosed the problem as mild chronic botulism.

Beriberi also stemmed from vitamin B deficiency. This was a disease that few of the doctors had encountered in the United States and the symptoms were horrific. Those with dry beriberi lost muscle function. Early on it caused the prisoners a distinctive toe-dragging gait. Worse still, wet beriberi was characterized by swollen legs and arms, often bloating two to three times their normal size. "What we had guys do is elevate their legs when they were sleeping," Hank recalled, and some formed a harness with blankets or rags that kept their legs raised. Then their testicles might blow up like softballs. Their trunks or faces bloated painfully. Hank began feeling an ache in his legs during the day and they began swelling, Looking down toward his feet he saw the ankles were gone. He combed the vegetation around the camp seeking the most likely plants to carry the vitamin B that his body needed.

Malaria and dysentery were the most common and ultimately the deadliest diseases in camp since they took the lives of men by the hundreds, and eventually by the thousands. A cleaner environment and quinine would have saved nearly every life, he noted. His friends too were sick. One medic collapsed in exhaustion between two patients, and Hank lugged him up onto a bunk with the help of several more men. The medic was now a patient himself. The man's frustration was painful to see. He cried, tears collecting in the corners of his eyes.

"Now stop that Mack, stop your crying you need your body fluids," Chamberlain warned him. The man simply let out a wail and cried harder. "It's over Hank, we're not going to survive this, we're going to die here." Hank took a breath and slapped the man across the face. The crying stopped. "You stop talking like that, and stop crying. You're only making it worse for yourself."

That night Hank lay down to the sound of that man's anguished crying still echoing in his ears. Before sleep he clasped his hands together as he had taken to doing, every night, a moment alone with God. And he had the same prayer, an entreaty that brought him just a glimmer of solace: "Please God, end this suffering. Please bring an end to this war."

The next day though, Hank found the medic ready to be propped up. Once Hank had the man upright, the patient opened his mouth like a young robin when he was offered a spoon of rice. "Thank you, Hank, I was feeling pretty low yesterday, but I'm better now." Hank later learned that that man survived the war.

Others did not do as well. Several times patients attempted to take their own lives, finding a sharp implement to slash their wrists or throats. One night Hank heard a patient calling from his ward and hurried to the voice that was bleating like an injured animal. He found a heavy flow of blood soaking the man in question as well as the bedding and even the patient beside him. "I don't want to die, you got to help me, I made a mistake," he cried out. Already Hank had found the source of the bleeding, the patient's two narrow wrists, and grabbed the closest fragment of cloth, used as a rag, to wrap tightly around each arm. Whether or not the patient survived the war he didn't know, but the action did spare the man another day of life, he knew that much.

While Hank was engrossed in the challenges of the hospital and the Zero Ward, more men continued to fill the camp, bringing yet more patients. In late October though, circumstances changed nearly overnight with the arrival of the North China Fourth Marines. These Americans, who had served in Corregidor, were older than most of the prisoners— some were middle-aged and exhibited little sign of starvation. These Marines were elite forces who had come from Shanghai, then fought the Japanese from Corregidor, before being captured. They had missed the brutality

of Bataan combat, the weeks of starvation in the jungle, as well as the Death
March. They had missed the deprivations of Camp O'Donnell. They had
been housed at Camp 3 before arriving in this crowded, disease-stricken
sister compound—Camp 1. When they came upon their new home, they
appeared to be appalled at the conditions the men were living in.

One of these Marines—Lt. Col. Curtis Beecher—spoke fluent Japanese which he had learned in China. These Marines had been stationed in
North China for years, some closely connected to a Japanese community
there.[1] The forty-five-year-old officer offered something the POWs had
lacked until then, a source of direct communication between the guards
and the prisoners. He could read the Japanese instructions and notes that
the other prisoners had referred to as "chicken scratch."

Beecher also brought with him a leadership that had been lacking at
the camp. So upon the Marines' arrival, Beecher strode through the camp,
shaking his head at the squalid conditions, the naked patients in the Zero
Ward, the dead bodies awaiting burial in mass graves. The men dragged
around weakly, fought amongst each other, and resembled walking skel-
etons, he would later recall. Overflowing graves emitted the stench of
human decay, while feces and vomit seemed to coat everything and every
place. He noted with distaste the need for a battalion of eighty men enlisted
each day to bury up to forty bodies in the mass graves.

Beecher was a unique personality and historical accounts have credited
him with bringing order to the camp. Hank saw it the same way. Along
with the other Marines and with the support of the officers, doctors, and
prisoners at large, Beecher got to work planning just how the camp could
be made cleaner and healthier, thereby reducing the overwhelming flow
of patients through the hospitals and—all too often—in the mass graves.

Hank and the other medics noticed the Marines whenever they passed
and appreciated having them in their midst. He was startled the first time
he saw a small animal scurrying at the Marines' feet as they made their way
to their local "mess hall" where rice was cooked and served from a stained
caldron. Hank and his friends had come to regard all animals as edible and
fair game for hungry prisoners, but something was different here. The
Marines were watching over this critter like a child and as soon as the little
dog wandered in another direction, one man scooped him up and carried
him under his arm.

When they collected their food rations, Hank watched as the Marines
each saved a spoonful of rice for their pet. The dog was known as Soochow, named for the town in which they had rescued him in China. The
small, square-nose terrier was not only a POW but a war veteran himself.

He had stowed away to Corregidor with his human companions when they left their Chinese post and had dived into foxholes along with the rest of the men when they were fired upon by the Japanese. Now, as the Marines were serving their time as Japanese prisoners, so too was Soochow. The Marines had trained their pal to stay silent, but the dog still caught the guards' attention. At times Soochow, who had taken an intense dislike to the Japanese, would bark and snarl at the heels of guards, challenging them as they counted roll call. Occasionally a guard would lunge at the dog with his bayonet, but only half-heartedly.[2]

For multiple reasons the China Marines either kept the dog close, carried him, or tied him up to protect him not only from the Japanese guards, but from the starving prisoners. Hank would have eaten the little dog himself if he'd had the opportunity.

In the meantime, Beecher organized the installation of a network of wooden walkways that would keep men's feet out of the mud and sewage. The Japanese willingly provided the wood needed, once Beecher requested it. Under Beecher's instructions, prisoners took shovels provided to dig out drainage ditches, rerouting runoff and sewage that inundated the camp after heavy rains.

Chamberlain helped with this effort as well as the next one—building covers for the latrines. To date, men relieved themselves by squatting over trenches. The Japanese guards had a similar accommodation, although their latrine was segregated from the prisoners. Universally the latrines not only reeked, but they also bred the fat black flies that carried diseases from the latrine waste directly to the hundreds of men already fighting malnutrition. By the fall of 1942 there was a constant drone of the flies from sunup to sunset in the camp.

And while maggots might help eat away an infection, the thousands and thousands of maggots and flies caused untold disease transmission around the hospital and camp. Hank swatted flies away from his eyes and struck at them in his sleep. The hum of winged-creatures was a relentless concert at Cabanatuan and if someone or something died, the flies would descend upon that body like a black cloud.

Beecher directed that some of the wood delivered by the Japanese be used to build covers to the latrine trench. Holes were then cut into planks so that men, for the first time, sat as they relieved themselves and had better control of where the waste went. That didn't stop the flies much: they continued to swarm, breed, and thrive under those planks so that any man emptying his bowels was sitting over thousands of flies, many of which bit. Beecher then assigned the men to eradicate flies. Chamberlain was among those who cut cogon grass and tied it in clumps, then lit the end at the kitchen stove fire. The men lifted one latrine seat cover at a time and shoved the torch down into the crevasse of flies and human waste, killing as many of them as possible.

That didn't address the larvae though. Looking into the latrines revealed thousands upon thousands of the fly larva writhing in the waste. If the men could kill the maggots before they were flies, it would benefit the entire camp. On the suggestion of Beecher, Hank joined work parties pouring scalding water over the latrine waste, effectively burning, and drowning them before they took up wings. The Japanese seemed to appreciate the results. They soon took up the same practice at their latrines.

On December 15, 1942, the camp had its first day without a death. The cleanliness efforts were paying off. Better latrines led to a reduction in patients. Chamberlain noticed a gradual reduction in the flow of sick men coming into the hospital and to the Zero Ward, and more of the cases were related to hunger than to disease.

There were other ways to boost the health of men in the compound too, and Hank served as a relentless advocate of bathing. By this time, many prisoners were so covered in grime their skin was festered with sores. Hank knew all too vividly what became of the sores when left untreated. One practice that had helped the men keep the sun from burning them was to coat themselves in mud and that mud rarely was completely washed off. Now they made a practice of standing under the barracks eaves not just to drink water but to bathe in the runoff. They even scrubbed each others' backs.

Kitchen staff began washing their hands and avoided wiping their hands on their faces, eyes, or noses. As time went on Hank found more purposes for the straight-edge razor that he had hidden in the seam of his musette bag. He used it not only to shave, to cut his hair, to make tools, and to carve wood, but also in some cases to help his friends. He offered men a haircut and in some cases a head shave.

When cutting his friend Earl's red hair he commented on the angry, swollen patches in his scalp where at least one guard had continued to yank tufts of hair from his head, and Earl said, "Do me favor and cut it as short as you can, so they can't get a handful."

"I can do better than that. Let's shave it off," Hank responded.

Earl laughed at the idea. "That's just what I want, shave it all off." Hank sharpened the blade on a rock and then slid it over Earl's scalp. Within ten minutes his friend had a smooth bald head, and he ran his hand over it appreciatively. It offered multiple benefits—it was cooler, reduced the risk of lice, and made it harder for guards to differentiate between Earl and other prisoners.

Both POWs and guards noticed Earl's new clean-shaven look. Bill was the first to ask for a shave. "Take it all off, I want to feel that fresh jungle air on my scalp," he joked, patting his head. Another prisoner soon followed and offered a trade—a cigarette consisting of a fragment of a *Reader's Digest* page wrapped around Filipino tobacco. Hank found he was in business. Soon the same guard who had snatched a clump of Earl's hair so many times, approached his victim and demanded to know where his hair had gone. "Who shave?" he asked.

Earl stared ahead resolute, refusing to turn in his friend. When the guard caught Hank in the act of shaving a POW, however, the secret was out. Hank's heart plunged as the guard strode toward him shouting in Japanese. The guard stood looking at Hank, the straight-edge razor in his hand, a prisoner seated on the ground in front of him with a half-shaven head.

"You shave my head?" the guard asked.

Hank stared at him, confused. Wasn't the man going to confiscate his razor and commence the beating? "Shave your head?" he asked the guard, his voice uncertain.

"You shave my head," the guard repeated, with more conviction. Hank glanced at the POW seated in front of him before responding.

"You have rice? Food? Tobacco?"

The guard laughed then nodded, "Okay I give you food, you shave." Hank hurriedly finished shaving his friend's head, working carefully around mosquito bites and sores, willing his hands to stop shaking. Then he started on the guard's head, leaving shorn hair piled with that of the POW at his feet. When the guard rejoined his comrades, they gave his bald head an appreciative look. At least for a few weeks his head would be cooler and head lice would have no hair follicles to cling to.

"He couldn't find a Jap to shave his head?" Earl asked Hank later, sharing the extra rice his friend had earned.

"No straight-edge razors, I guess," Hank shrugged.

"I can't believe you asked for food."

"I figured he'd either take off my head or feed me," Hank responded and they sat in silence, considering that the decision may not have yet been made. He marveled at his luck when the guard returned the next day with a piece of rehydrated fish. He savored each salty bite that night, sharing pieces with his closest friends. The Japanese guards were a mystery.

As 1942 proceeded American soldiers were being sent to places like Normandy, France, to fight Hitler's troops, and the attention of the

American public was largely focused on Europe. Frank Hewlett, a US war correspondent in the Philippines summarized the situation for the American soldiers' plight in the Pacific with his poem "Battling Bastards of Bataan":

> We're the Battling Bastards of Bataan.
> No mama, no papa, no Uncle Sam.
> No aunts, no uncles, no cousins, no nieces,
> No pills, no planes, no artillery pieces
> And nobody gives a damn.

In Cabanatuan the hospital situation seemed to only grow more wretched. The sturdier POWs stood out from the others simply by surviving. Sick or not, eventually they were taking part in jobs. One of the more coveted duties was caring for the camp's small herd of carabao.

About twenty of the beasts were corralled near the camp, confiscated from Filipino farmers. Most carabaos bore a steel ring in their noses, indicating they had served as a working animal, most likely pulling a plow. Now they would provide food for the camp, although the Japanese officials and guards seemed to be the only recipients of the meat.

Regularly, the Americans—a group of about fifteen men referred to as "cowboys"—who cared for the animals were instructed to butcher one. Hank recognized the racket when a carabao was butchered. Often the Japanese would come to watch. Hank too saw every piece of meat was carefully portioned, wrapped, and delivered to the Japanese who stashed the meat away. The starving prisoners would see none of it. After the slaughtering was over though, some desperate men crawled in the yard where the butchering took place, sucking blood from handfuls of dirt they squeezed over their open mouths.

Hank shuddered at the sight. "Starvation is a terrible thing," he recalled later. "You throw caution to the wind. We would try almost anything."

When the underfed carabao were nosing through their straw one day, the POWs assigned to care for them came up with an idea. They could never kill one of the animals for their purposes, but maybe they could get some meat without actually taking the carabao's life. When the opportunity arose, one of the cowboys stashed a sharp knife in his pocket. Another pilfered a hot coal from the kitchen fire.

They had to move fast. Several men reached around the animal's neck and held its rope to restrain it and before it could react, the man with the knife sliced off its tail in one quick action. The tail was quickly hidden away while they got to work on the bleeding and angry animal.

That's where they used the hot coal—to stop the bleeding, cauterize the wound, and ensure the animal survived the ordeal. Within weeks all the carabao had just stumps for tails, and although the guards seemed aware it was happening, they chose not to dole out punishments or even prevent them from eating the tails.

These small meaty appendages were like gold for the hungry POWs. There's quite of bit of meat on a cow tail, Chamberlain remembered, "More than you'd think." The cooks shaved the meat off the bone, chopped it, and flavored the soup with this protein, shared by the prisoners. A piece of the bone went to Soochow. When Chamberlain saw where the bone was going, he approached the cooks to talk about the patients. There were protein and calcium in bone, and hundreds of men would benefit from that too. He insisted on having a vertebra for the hospital.

Once he had secured that small bone, he held it in his palms, gazing at it like a man of great wealth. But it was going to require processing. He put the bone out behind the hospital where it could sit on a plank in the tropical sun and dry out, the POWs agreed to leave it there, and it was never moved from its spot as the heat baked out any fluids. Once the bone was dry enough, Hank used a rock to pulverize it into a powder. It was a slow process requiring shifts of workers. Each one took a turn grinding, hammering, pausing to catch a breath, feeling the occasional breeze cool their chapped skin, resting their sore muscles. Then they went back to work, pounding and grinding.

Once Hank collected enough powder, he carefully wrapped it like gold nuggets in a scrap of an old shirt. He ate a pinch of granules every day, shared it with his co-workers, as well as spooning some between the dry lips of some of the sickest patients who still showed a glimmer of spirit.

The hunt for protein went far beyond rats and carabao tails, however. Any animal that found its way onto the compound risked its life. Birds were pelted with rocks, snakes strangled. The occasional cat made the mistake of prowling into the camp as well. Chamberlain found a POW squatting behind the kitchen with a fist full of cooked meat once, seeming engrossed in an unusually large meal. "What do you have there, Smitty?" he asked. "What are you eating?"

"I's eatin—rabbit," the man grinned at him. Chamberlain looked at him suspiciously. Rabbit? In Bataan? He shrugged and left shaking his head. Later he saw a cat dart around the corner behind the kitchen and Chamberlain guessed this was probably a relative of the "rabbit" the GI had been consuming. That last feline was soon gone as well.

He also noticed some men gnawing the soft tips off the end of feathers, fresh plucked from an unlucky bird. Chamberlain approved. It provided them a little calcium, he suspected.

The conditions were still taking a toll on those who weren't almost obsessively seeking out nutrients. Hank worried about his friend Bill who didn't care for rice and wouldn't touch the critters found cooked in it. At chow time Hank and Earl ate what they had without reservation while Bill paused to pick out anything undesirable. Bill hadn't endured childhood hunger the way Hank did in Omaha and now Bill's more privileged background was no asset.

While the camp housed thousands of American POWs, it was also home to hundreds of guards, some of whom Hank became familiar with as much by their reputation or behavior as by their appearance. First Lieutenant Oiagi was the camp quartermaster. He was tall and had played on the Japanese Davis Cup team in America. Unlike most of the prison guards, Oiagi was relatively fair and pleasant and he spoke a little English. The ability to communicate was a rare commodity that most guards didn't have, and as a result, he may not have been as frustrated, or feel the need for gestures, threats, and beatings to make his point.

But Hank hated and dreaded most of the guards. The prisoners didn't know the names of their tormentors, so they gave them nicknames to differentiate one from another: Big Stoop was named after a comic strip character. He reminded Chamberlain of a sumo wrestler, stout and heavy set. He wasn't fast, he recalled, but he was mean. Big Speedo and Little Speedo were dubbed for the English word they used most frequently: "Speedo!" they ordered when men weren't moving fast enough. Little Speedo was the meaner one, who was quick to take advantage of a chance to cause some abuse.

Laughing Boy was known for mocking the prisoners' suffering, and Hank despised him for the beatings, which he followed with an exaggerated belly laugh. Donald Duck was named for the Disney character because of his distinctive voice. With the limited English he had learned at the camp, he asked prisoners who this Donald Duck was. "A famous American movie star," the prisoners responded with serious expressions. He walked away with a smile and stood a little straighter with pride when the prisoners called him by his new nickname.

Hank made a habit of keeping a safely wide space between himself and the guards when he could, and he focused on his patients. His days were defined by bringing as much comfort as he could to those who needed it and left the recovery to their bodies. He could encourage this healing process by bathing, comforting, and distracting the patients. He hated the sound of the men's crying or screaming—from pain, sickness, or frustration at their miserable condition. He tolerated it but never got used to it. At times he simply laid a hand on a man's shoulder and gave them a no-nonsense order: "Stop your damn screaming, it's not helping."

Often patients could be soothed though, with something as simple as a wet sponge gently scrubbing the grime off their limbs, torso, or face. While he administered these sponge baths, Hank would talk to them about his youth in Omaha, ask them about their own homes, families, girls waiting for them. When they were frightened, many of the prisoners shared their secrets as if it was their last chance to unburden themselves. "Medic, I have to tell you something," he heard from the beds. If he could have summoned a priest or minister, he would have, but sometimes there was no time for that.

"They made private confessions, very private," he recalled later, and many will never be spoken.

The most common admission was stealing from others in the camp. One prisoner admitted in a wavering voice that he had snatched the belt off a patient lying beside him the week before, knowing the man would die within hours, a day at the latest. He was now haunted by what he had done.

"The inner workings of a starving, tortured POW is mindless and unfulfilling," Hank remembered. "The thoughts that we were having were frightening and boisterous." Sometimes these thoughts and worries were too devastating to bear. "I believe it would be difficult for the average American reading these words to understand."

Sometimes when a man knew his time was ending, he would ask for a last favor from Hank. "Do you have a slip of paper?" one patient in the Zero Ward called out. He was a man Hank had believed to be near death hours ago, yet here he was, propped up on his elbow, holding his hand our frantically as if the paper was just out of reach. "I have to write a note to my mother." The man was so distressed Hank searched the hospital, the barracks, and even the library—a makeshift pile of shared books and magazines the prisoners had somehow brought past the guards. Hank tore a tiny scrap of paper off the bottom of a magazine page and brought it with a pen borrowed from the doctors. When he returned to the Zero Ward his heart plunged at the sight of this patient, his head on the floor staring up at the ceiling. When he approached, he found shallow breaths still moving the man's ribs.

"I have some paper for you, Private," he said.

"Just write down that I love her," the man said. It was the same message nearly every man wanted to convey to those at home. Hank wrote it down, put the paper in his pocket, and stashed it with the others in his musette bag, with addresses in places like New York or Texas or Minnesota. None of them made it through the war.

In October 1942 Lt. Col. Mori, the camp commander, nicknamed Blood, vanished from the camp and was replaced by Major Iwanaka, a man in his sixties standing only about five feet tall. He wore glasses and spoke with a high pitch through yellowed teeth.[3] He engaged rarely with the prisoners and Hank saw him less frequently than his predecessor. The operations of the camp remained the same, however, and the change of command went largely unnoticed by medics.

One morning the guards came to the hospital demanding one hundred farmworkers to harvest corn. Schwartz's eyes flashed with anger when he understood what they wanted. There were too many POWs in the hospital, the guards told Schwartz. These men were not sick, they suffered from laziness. They gave him a few minutes to select their farm labor team.

Schwartz moved with resigned determination, first looking for medics, and then the least frail patients. He patted Hank on the back. "I can't hardly afford to lose you every day Chamberlain, but if you can take today, I don't think we have any surgeries planned. There's nothing I can do about it, so go on. We'll manage alright." Chamberlain joined this hospital team of the sick and dying, trudging down the gravel path to the fields.

Earl, Hank, and several other medics sang under their breaths in rhythm with their step, songs they had composed to occupy their time in their barracks. "No balls at all, no balls at all," they picked up enthusiasm as others joined in, and the guards waved their bayonets at them to move faster. "She married a man who had no balls at all."

It was a hotter day than most, and Hank felt sweat dripping down his chest, depriving him of body fluid he was unlikely to replace until the next rain. When one man didn't come out of the thick growth of corn the man-count number was off by one, and guards, in a rage, ordered the men back into the fields to find him. Heart hammering, Hank hurried back into the corn stalks not knowing what punishment awaited if the man had escaped. Instead, he turned down one row after another until he heard someone call out to him, "Medic!" The POWs gathered around a dark shape slumped on the ground. The object of their search was unconscious but alive, overcome by heat and dehydration, Hank helped carry the man back out of the field.

As he picked up his shovel, Hank swung it up over his shoulder and felt it hit an obstacle behind him with a soft "thump." He spun in horror to see one of the guards fall to the ground. Hank had clobbered the man, in the head, with his shovel. Adrenalin pumped fire into his veins as his eyes met first Earl's gaze, then flashed over the other prisoners. All their faces were wet with sweat, grimy with dust, and mud, they seemed momentarily stunned. In an instant, Earl got into action and the others followed: the group began milling around Hank, creating a confusing crowd of prisoners. As the guards ran to their comrade's side, guns drawn, they helped the man to his feet and then turned to the Americans for retribution. What they saw was a huddle of men each seeming to be otherwise occupied, with no tools in sight that could have done the damage. One guard shouted a string of Japanese words at the prisoners then pointed at them to start marching, "Speedo."

Later that week the same guard was seen heading for a day's work on the farm, this time wearing a homemade piece of head protection—a crude tin helmet. The helmet not only amused the prisoners, the guards laughed openly and teased the man about it as well. That guard earned his nickname from the POWs that day, "Tin Hat."

Sunday service was one of the few opportunities for distraction and most men attended sermons led by POW chaplains. Prisoners not only enjoyed a passionate sermon, they sang hymns with enthusiasm they never had in church as children. After a few of these Sunday services, prisoners agreed that some of the men had good voices, and several volunteered that they played decently with instruments too.

When Christmas approached the climate on Luzon was cooler than the summer months, but still temperate. The trees and grasses grew thick, insects chirped loudly from trees, and POWs wandered the camp on bare scarecrow legs with little more than a scrap of clothing to cover their privates. It was hard to believe that somewhere it was snowing and people were warming themselves by fires, celebrating.

One of the chaplains secured permission for a religious service, and a large choral group started practicing carols and hymns. The music was strikingly beautiful in this place of suffering. Men stopped what they were doing to listen, goosebumps rising in the hot humid air. Soon doctors requested the choir at the hospital to boost patient morale. It eased the suffering of the patients, but also of the medics and doctors, if only for a half-hour. It wasn't just the Americans who appreciated the music either. On Sunday mornings the guards would come to church services to hear the melodic sounds of these despised prisoners, and for those few minutes seemed to forget the conditions and their rage. It was as if, for those fleeting moments, the war entirely stopped.

The effect was not lost on the musicians or their organizers. They informed the guards that many had formal music training and could handle wind and string instruments. Over the next few weeks, the guards began scavenging instruments from Cabanatuan City and delivered them to the POWs. They were granted time to practice, and they began playing in the relative quiet of the carabao corral, where only the large grazing beasts could hear their efforts. Other men began creating some skits, and on Christmas Day, everyone who was able gathered on the muddy center grounds of the compound to hear sermons and Christmas carols, hundreds of men singing along to *Silent Night* and *Jingle Bells*. Again, the guards gathered silently to listen.

In December the camp also received its first delivery of Red Cross packages.[4] Hank nearly wept with pleasure when he was handed two packages, one from the Red Cross (which he was required to share with four other men) and one from his mother. Both had been pilfered. Still he sat in front of his barracks, lost in the joyful effort of prying the tape (already broken) off the top of his mother's box.

Inside he found a Christmas card and letter. Another letter from Cathy was packed beside it. Most of what was written in the letters was blacked out so that he could understand little that was written to him.

He was able to make out one sentence clearly: "I hope you enjoy the candy and cookies." He tore out the packing paper, turned the box over, pried back the flaps, but couldn't find as much as a crumb. Any goodies had already been consumed by someone else. He went to bed that night imagining the sweet smell of her oatmeal cookies as she cooled them on top of the oven.

Hank got two letters throughout the war from his mother that were cut up—both received in the Philippines. Chamberlain would learn later that around this time the Japanese had selected names from the POW list and sent a notice to the Red Cross that those individuals had died.

It was around this time that a disturbing letter from the Red Cross arrived in Alvina's mailbox. The American agency had received a list of those who died at the crowded Philippine camp and Hank's name was on the list. Dr. Brown's name was on that list as well. Chamberlain never knew just why the Japanese had informed the Red Cross that he was dead. They kept meticulous records based on the daily roll calls, so there was little doubt that he was still living, as was Dr. Brown. Chamberlain believed that the inaccurate information was about damaging American morale at home. Dr. Brown's young wife too got a message from the Red Cross that her husband was gone.

Hank's mother received a similar notice about her captured son. He never knew how she took the news, but he knew that she placed a gold star in the window of her house, declaring that she was a family member of a soldier killed in the war. The star honored sacrifice on the part of the family, bravery in a fight for freedom on the part of the soldier. She had no idea that thousands of miles away her son was in captivity and gradually starving as he cared for the sick and injured. She also placed a phone call to Hank's father and to Hank's girlfriend Cathy in Spokane to give her the bad news. They wouldn't learn the truth until the end of the war.

It seems that the Japanese picked names of POWs and told the Red Cross they were dead. The Red Cross then notified parents that the Japanese said their son had died.

Whether on the farm or with patients, one of Hank's most diligent efforts—like most POWs—was to avoid the notice of guards. The less they singled you out the better you were. Prisoners kept their heads low and stayed with the group as much as possible. But there were times when luck was not on his side. One afternoon lining up for the trek to the farm fields, Hank found himself in the wrong place at the wrong time.

He would never know what led to the beating. The guards were in an extraordinarily bad mood that morning, and everything the prisoners did was annoying them—too slow, standing in the wrong place, holding the wrong tool, sometimes just the wrong expression on a man's face was irritating them. But Hank was still caught by surprise when a guard rammed him in the gut with the back of his rifle and he was helpless to stop his fall. Once on the ground, the guard was kicking him where he lay. Hank had witnessed over and over how a man on the ground could be beaten to death, stomped, and kicked until his life escaped him and he was just another corpse for the burial pit. Frantically he tried to get his palms flat on the ground to push himself to his feet, and the guard brought his boot down with all his weight and fury on Hank's left hand. He sprung to his feet as pain exploded. The guards laughed as Hank held his hand up to look for the damage—it felt as if it had been mangled. And in fact, he could see that it was broken, his index finger and thumb immobile and misshapen. He hurried to catch up with the others. He marched to the fields, and he put in ten hours of work, wielding his shovel in his good hand. He held the injured one against his chest as it throbbed and swelled.

By the time he returned to the camp that night his hand was round and bloated like a sausage. He held it out for Dr. Brown who took a brief look and shook his head. His index finger and thumb were broken in several places. Brown went about devising a splint out of sticks and rags and strapped the hand against Hank's body.

For weeks, the hand was useless, since the splint inhibited his movement. Eventually Hank removed it and began wiggling his fingers to force movement. The pain eased over time, but he was unable to properly grip anything with that hand for the rest of the war.

The injury had inflicted damage to Chamberlain's mental as his physical health. He had seen enough beatings and executions to expect almost anything. But this seemingly unprovoked beating was one bridge too far for him. He had to get away from the Japanese. He was sure if he didn't he would lose his temper again, like he had in Bilibid, and that would be the end.

Henry Chamberlain grew up
with his single mother in Omaha,
Nebraska. Courtesy of the
Chamberlain Family.

Henry Chamberlain lived in
multiple homes before and
during the Great Depression, in
Omaha, Nebraska. Courtesy of
the Chamberlain Family.

Henry as a boy in Omaha, Nebraska, circa 1920s. Courtesy of the Chamberlain Family.

Henry Chamberlain. Courtesy of the Chamberlain Family.

	Last	First	Middle	Rank	Org	Serial No
1	Dempwolf	Charles	Martin	Capt	14th Eng(R)	O-326435
2	Harrison	Mel	Leon	1st Lt	43rd Inf(PS)	O-890372
3	Adams	Eulice	Noble	T/Sgt	91st BombSq	6244934
4	Armijo	Manuel	Anastacio	1st Sgt	200th CA	20843120
5	Barela	Pat	Frank	Sgt	Med Dept	20842378
6	Burkett	Jasper	Housten	Cpl	19th Bimb	18021441
7	Commander	Eugene	Carl	M/Sgt	4th Mar X	170402
8	Deal	Volney	Clyell	Cpl	60th CA	19006117
9	Fenton	Benjamin	Arthur	Sgt	Med Dept	6274307
10	Folio	Etalo	Edward	S/Sgt	54th Pur	6937859
11	Gammon	Eugene	Arthur	QM 1/c	USN	3719134
12	Garrison	Altie	Theodore	Cpl	4th Mar	280875
13	Hamm	William	Edward	1st/Sgt	59th CA	R-128528
14	Howton	John	Issac	BM2c	USS Quail	375-80-96
15	Karr	Austin	Carroll	Cpl	59th CA	18050416
16	Krysak	John	—	Sgt	24th Pur	6999983
17	Light	William	Lloyd	Cpl	Med Dept	6281898
18	Marcum	Sidney	Louis	Sgt	60th CA	19051246
19	Miller	Rufos	Jewel	Cpl	Med Dept	14026084
20	Orosco	Arnold	A	S/Sgt	200th CA / Med Dept	20842394
21	Sullivan	James	Victory	S/Sgt	31st CA	6138478
22	Petrochilli	Chester	Edward	Cpl	Ord Dept	13032279
23	Polk	Almus	—	Cpl	Med Dept	69245539
24	Ryan	Robert	James	Cpl	Med Dept	36006232
25	Scooby	Marion	LeRoy	S/Sgt	Med Dept	6277052
26	Terrell	Bishop	Wade	Cpl	Med Dept	18050101
27	Van Buskirk	Francis	Hall	Sgt	200th CA	20843168
28	Weoxsler	Ben	Robert	Sgt	91st Maint	6592495
29	Wright	William	Jesse	BM1c	USN	3211832
30	Adams	Robert	Marion	Pvt 1cl	Med Dept	19017504
31	Baer	William	Joseph	Pvt 1cl	Air Warn	15065877
32	Barnes	Richard	Henry	Pvt 1cl	Med Dept	6288889
33	Beal	John	Leonard	F1c	USN	Unknown
34	Berlin	Louis	Edward	Pvt 1cl	Med Dept	19000244
35	Bond	Stanford	Arthur	Pvt	Med Dept	18015124
36	Borruano	Angelo	—	Pvt 1cl	59th CA	17014491
37	Brown	Paul	Christian	Pvt 1cl	31st Inf	19021000
38	Bundy	John	Arthur	Pvt 1cl	4th Mar	Unknown
39	Burns	Robert	Thomas	Pvt 1cl	Med Dept	38002614
40	Butler	Edwin	James	Pvt	Det Med Dept	692-8088
41	Chamberlain	Henry	Tilden	Pvt	Med Dept	17011542
42	Crupper	Charles	Glenn	Pvt	Med Dept	19010415
43	Decker	Paul	Eugene	Pvt	Med Dept	19013600
44	DeLude	Leon	Wilfred	Pvt 1cl	27th BombGp	11009233
45	Diaz	Pablo	Aguilar	Pvt 1cl	200th CA	20842501

Roster for Building 7 of Hospital 2 listed Henry Chamberlain among hundreds of medical staff members. Courtesy of Philippine Archives Collection.

Japanese officers question General Edward P. King, American commander at Bataan, at the surrender, April 1942. Naval History and Heritage Command.

American prisoners after the fall of Bataan. Naval History and Heritage Command.

RG407 - Adjutant General Philippine Archives Collection
Entry 1054 - Invasion + Surrender Bataan + Corregidor

Bataan Field Hospital #2

Private Harry R. Browning,
Gen. Del., Tupelo, Arkansas
Private Eugene Castle,
Route #1, Saltillo, Texas
Private Wallace Casto,
Rt. #1, North Little Rock, Ark.
Private Henry T. Chamberlain,
203 S. 25th St., Omaha, Nebraska
Private Ernest D. Collingsworth,
San Clemente, California
Private Doyle F. Collins,
Route 9, Box 662, Houston, Texas
Private Charles G. Crupper,
Clyro, Kansas
Private Raymond N. DeCloss
10774 Bluffside Drive, Hollywood Cal.
Private John Edward Dempsey,
326 N. Austin Blvd. Chicago, Ill.
Private John G. Denver,
21 Monterey St. Salinas, Cal.
Private Samuel H. Dorr,
117 North West St., Anaheim, Cal.
Private Henery H. Dyer,
Gen. Del. Oceano, California
Private Albert W. Everett,
425 University Ave., San Diego, Cal.
Private Austin Everett,
Rt. #1, Mendenhall, Miss.
Private Eugene H. Evers,
725 E. Dewitt St., Dyersville, Iowa
Private Malcome C. Fitch,
2521 State St., Milwaukee, Wis.
Private Donald L. Fitzgerald,
220 Castro St., Mountain View, Cal.
Private Richard W. Freeman,
3625 Vine St, Cincinnati, Ohio
Private Alvin L. Fry,
Rt. #3, Box 248A, Hood River, Oregon
Private Robert E. Galbraith,
1455 Gaty Ave., East St. Louis, Ill.
Private Douglas H. Graham,
Rt. #1, Emmet, Idaho
Private Woodrow H. Haines,
14 S. Richill St., Waynesburg, Pa.
Private Loyd E. Harvill,
Rt. #1, Huntington, Texas
Private Gardy J. Havlichek,
Branch, Wisconson.
Private Burchard A. Hays,
Motley, Minnesota
Private Reinold M. Hoem,
1624 E. 27th St., Tacoma, Washington
Private William L. Hubrecht,
285 Shipley St., San Francisco, Cal.
Private Bernard F. Humphreys,
RFD #1, Imperial, Nebraska
Private Phillip J. Hurley,
1021, 7th Ave., Oakland, California.
Private Frederick P. Jenkins,
Conway Springs, Kansas.

Private Joseph R. Janson, Jr.,
45 West 2nd North St., Logan, Utah.
Private Robert G. Jones,
RFD #1, Ringgold, Va.
Private Alfred Jolley,
2943 Sacremento St., San Francisco, Cal
Private Leonard P. Kacsorowski,
4515 Richmond St., Chicago, Ill.
Private Arthur H. Kelder,
Rt. #2, Virgina St. Crystal Lake, McHen
Private Richard C. Kellogg,
51 Mule St., Apt. #1, Salinas, Cal.
Private George J. Kusek,
605 N.W. 10th St., Oklahoma City, Oklah
Private Zachary Kush,
Elburt W. Va.
Private Junior Ladd,
Rt #1, Balling, Arkansas
Private Walter A. Laffoon,
Rt. #1, Warner, Oklahoma.
Private James E. Martin,
1132 C-7th St., Santa Monica, Californi
Private George H. Morris,
285 6th St., Oakland, California
Private Ernest O. Norquist
RFD #34, Dayton's Bluff, St. Paul, Minn
Private Robert C. O'Donnell,
256 W. 60th St., Chicago Ill.
Private Ernest Ouellette,
RFD #6, Concord, New Hampshire
Private James A. Patterson
8432 Magnolia Ave., Riverside, Californ
Private ames L. Peyton
726 Parade St., Erie, Pa.
Private Robert E. Ross
1217 West 1st St., Coffeyville, Kansas.
Private Clyde E. Samson
RR #6, North Vernon, Indiana
Private Everett H. Schneeweis,
181 Albert Place, Costa Mesa, Califor
Private Merrell Schultz
244 Glenwood Ave., Ludlow, Kentucky
Private James W. Simmons,
1507 S. Jennings St., Ft. Worth, Texas
Private Jay R. Snell,
86 Adams St., Rochester New York.
Private William G. Strong,
Huntington, Utah
Private Darrell W. Summers,
Gen. Del. Fort Towson, Oklahoma
Private Elbert L. Templeton
Gen. Del. , Troup, Texas
Private Robert W. T. Trafford,
Glidden, Iowa
Private Clifford G. Vose,
Main Street, Wilton, N. H.
Private Robert E. Ward
Gen. Del. Norton, Kansas
Private Lowell L. Washburn,
8th St., Colby, Kansas
Private Joseph W. Wolf,
Star Route, St. Mary, Mo.

4

One page from the official listing of men seized after the fall of Bataan. Courtesy of Philippine Archives Collection.

Showing the strains of the long, desperate battle for Bataan, American prisoners Private Samuel Stenzler, Private First Class Frank Spear, and Captain James Gallagher await the horrors of the Death March. None would survive the war: Gallagher died within a few days, Stenzler within six weeks, Spear in July 1945. National Archives and Records Administration.

POWs under guard during the death march. National Archives and Records Administration.

Prisoners are forced to sort equipment for the Japanese, April 1942. National Archives and Records Administration.

POWs at the beginning of the Bataan death march. National Archives and Records Administration.

Prisoners on Bataan. Naval History and Heritage Command.

Casualties of the Death March. National Archives and Records Administration.

Soochow served alongside the 4th Marines as they defended Corregidor and then as a POW in Cabanatuan Camp, The Philippines. Pictured with Sergeant Paul Wells, circa 1946. United States Marine Corps.

Henry Chamberlain, weighing less than one hundred pounds, was routed to a Japanese hospital after liberation from his work at the mine at Sendai Camp 3. He is pictured here, seated on steps in front of the hospital. His recuperation took more than a year. Courtesy of the Chamberlain Family

Henry Chamberlain reenlisted in the US Army shortly after recovering from his POW experience, around 1946. Courtesy of the Chamberlain Family.

Henry Chamberlain, who had a lifelong love for dogs, is pictured here with his dog, Petey, in 1945. Courtesy of the Chamberlain Family.

Henry and Dorothy Chamberlain at their wedding in 1946. Courtesy of the Chamberlain Family.

Henry and Dorothy Chamberlain lived in Okinawa where he served as Staff Sergeant, supervising medical services before transferring back to the Philippines. Courtesy of the Chamberlain Family.

Henry Chamberlain with his mother, Alvina Louise Soper, shortly after he re-enlisted in the US Army. Courtesy of the Chamberlain Family.

After the war, Henry Chamberlain shipped out to Greenland with the US Army. Courtesy of the Chamberlain Family.

Henry used his sharp shooting skills for hunting before and after the war. Pictured here in 1949. Courtesy of the Chamberlain Family.

Master Sergeant Henry Chamberlain, 1959. Courtesy of the Chamberlain Family.

Henry and Dorothy were married more than sixty years before Dorothy's death in 2007. They are pictured here in 1996. Courtesy of the Chamberlain Family.

Following the war, many Philippine Scouts immigrated to the United States, and Hank maintained a friendship with many of them that lasted decades. He is pictured in the center, front row. Courtesy of the Chamberlain Family.

Visiting the site of the Sendai Camp 3 mine, as the last survivor, in 2017, was both painful and a source of relief for former POW Henry Chamberlain. Courtesy of the Chamberlain Family.

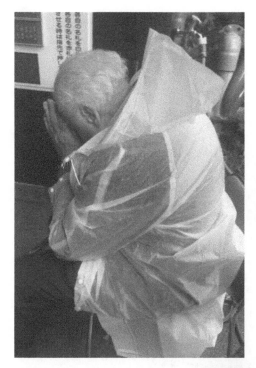

In 2017 Henry Chamberlain said two prayers: one for peace and one for forgiveness for all those who had been part of the War mining operation. Courtesy of the Chamberlain Family.

As a guest of the Japanese Ministry of Foreign Affairs, Henry Chamberlain returned in 2017 to the mine where he labored as a POW more than seventy years before. Courtesy of the Chamberlain Family.

Henry Chamberlain visiting the Flying Heritage and Combat Armor Museum in Paine Field, Washington, poses in front of an ambulance similar to the one he drove as a medic and paramedic during and after World War II. Courtesy of the Chamberlain Family.

14

JANUARY 1943

CABANATUAN, PHILIPPINES

With Christmas behind them, Hank and his fellow American prisoners began staring into another year of captivity. After hundreds of deaths in the past few months, the most determined—those graced with strength, perseverance, and good luck—were hanging on, making the most out of what they could scavenge, finding ways to stay alive. For others the battle was getting harder. Food deficiency can have cruel and agonizing effects on the bodies of previously healthy men.

Hank noticed his friend Bill looked worse daily, but weren't they all? Bill was so thin and so sick, sometimes Hank worried that his friend had given up any hope. Despair was the enemy to medics and patients alike. After an especially long day at the hospital, one medic collapsed into tears, and Hank had to help him onto a bunk—medic was now a patient. "We can't treat patients like this, they just come here to die and we're just here to watch them do it," the man said. "Where's MacArthur, where's the army? No one gives a damn that we're here." Hank had little solace to offer.

"All we can do is the best we can," he offered and looked from the medic to the row of patients, some lying still and spent, others groaning and twisting where they lay, still others talking to someone nearby, to themselves, or to God. The noise in the hospital was constant. "We have to keep trying," Hank added. The medic heard him but he was beyond responding, his face gaunt. He fell into a fitful sleep. Hank knew he wasn't going to make it. A person dying had an unmistakable odor, he learned. It was not the rot that hovered over the dead, for Hank it was more disturbing and made his stomach churn when he caught the waft of it.

When the medic died, Hank grew alarmed about Bill, who seemed like he could easily fall into the same pattern. He tried to draw his friend with talking about their favorite subjects: women and food. Since the Red Cross packages had come, men carried love letters from their girlfriends or wives next to their hearts and both Hank and Bill were no different. The letters, blacked out with maddening mysteries in the missing phrases and words, were neatly folded and tucked in their shirts. "It felt so good to have that letter there, next to your heart, I can't express how that felt," he recalled.

Now Hank asked about Bill's girl, the one who wrote him the letter that he had folded so carefully in his shirt on Christmas, "Where are you going to take her when you have your first night out?" he asked, but got no response. Bill closed his eyes, "I'd like to rest now."

There were ways that the POWs were boosting their morales. Long after Christmas was over, the POW band known as the Cabanatuan Cats continued to perform popular music: swing, jazz, and dance numbers for the camp and would visit the hospital to raise the moods of those who could not walk to the main compound.

In some cases the men acted out plays and periodically brought their performances to the sickest. Hank helped support, or carry, the men out of the hospital wards to see a gathering of actors performing comedies, musicals—dressed as both men and women—wearing handcrafted costumes: cogon grass skirts strapped around their waists, or grass wigs tied under their chins. Slapstick comedies entertained POWs and their captors alike. And stand-up comedians poked fun at Cabanatuan camp life, while they were careful not to insult the Japanese who listened closely.

In April 1943, the aircraft of the Japanese Navy marshal admiral and commander-in-chief of the Japanese Combined Fleet, Isoroku Yamamoto, was shot down by American fighter planes. Major Iwanaka, still the commander of Cabanatuan's camp, assembled the Americans and decreed that all men were forbidden from singing or smiling for two days. A record-high number of prisoners were also sent to the farms to work at this time.

Shortly after this Major Iwanaka called out American senior officers and announced to them that he should be congratulated, for improving the conditions in the camp and took credit for the reduction in death rate. He regretted the beatings, he said, however they were the result of POW laziness, lack of cooperation, and language barriers. He then announced that "when the war is over, you will rejoin your families in good health."[1]

By this time Hank had returned to using his broken hand freely, although the aching was almost excruciating at night. The next time he was lined up for work on the farm, a guard—he never knew if it was the same one who had stomped on his hand—knocked him down with a blow to his lower back with the flat side of a shovel. Pulling himself to his feet with his one good hand he wondered how many more of these days he could endure before his temper flared, or he couldn't get back to his feet.

There was one escape for him, already established as part of the camp's medical system—the "Dip Ward." Here the men suffering from the dreaded disease diphtheria clung to life and often lost their grip all too quickly. The compound had become a breeding ground for the bacterial disease; the first cases were detected within months after the camp was established. Sores erupted in mucous membranes—noses, throats, tongues, eyes—and that wasn't all, it also affected men's penises, urethras, and rectums. Once skin lesions took root doctors knew the entire body was under attack.

This was the ugliest and potentially most contagious and fatal disease in the camp, and doctors realized just how grave that situation could be for a population that was already weakened by malnourishment. Under normal conditions for otherwise healthy individuals, diphtheria has a mortality rate of no more than 10 percent. In this case it was proving to be much higher. Once a man was brought into the Dip Ward, he was more than likely to survive only another day or two.

Early on, men admitted to the hospital had been separated once they were diagnosed with diphtheria. Jack Schwartz and Col. William "Rhiney" Craig (who had led Hank's transit from Manila to Bataan in 1942 and who would die on a hell ship in 1945) appealed to the camp leadership, Mori, for a separate ward and an antitoxin to treat the disease. "This disease could be as deadly for the Japanese," they pointed out to the head of the camp, "as it is for the rest of us."

Eventually Mori agreed and the Dip Ward was established. The Japanese constructed barbed wire around it and instructed their men to stay away at all times. Like the other wards, it was soon overwhelmed with filth. In the past, Hank had not regarded it as anything more than another house of misery for the prisoners. The barbed wire itself was so thick with black flies, it seemed as if it was moving, even on still days.

After his recent beating though, Hank looked at the Dip Ward anew, wondering if the place might offer him a solution. If the Japanese didn't dare enter the ward, that was the place for him. He found Col. Schwartz reviewing the kitchen chow, assessing a pile of charcoaled black rice that had been scraped from the side of the cauldron. It could help reduce diarrhea; he urged the cook to save the darkest part for the hospital.

"What can I do for you, Chamberlain?" Schwartz said as they stepped away from the kitchen, swatting flies away as they went.

"Colonel, I really need to get away from the Japs, they seem to be after me lately. Even for a few days, I was thinking, do you need help in the Dip Ward?" he asked.

Schwartz glanced in the direction of the small barrack surrounded by packed dirt and barbed wire. "We always do, but I really can't risk any surgical assistants getting sick, Chamberlain."

"Oh that's alright, Colonel, I had diphtheria when I was a little tyke."

Schwartz gave the medic a glance, "Are you certain about that?"

Hank thought back to his time in the hospital around the age of eight. In the 1920s an epidemic of diphtheria swept through Omaha, and he picked up the disease at school or church or around the neighborhood. There was no way to be sure. What he did know was that his cough and fever made him so sick he was sent to the hospital where he recuperated alone in the children's ward. He remembered the daily shots, the hacking, vomiting, headache, the loneliness since even his mother was forbidden to come near him.

"Yes, Colonel, I'm sure of it, I was sick quite a while."

That summoned a smile and Schwartz patted him on the shoulder. "That's good news, Chamberlain. They need a helping hand in there. Alright you go report to the Capt. Schultz and let him know I said you could transfer, see if he needs you."

Those who have survived diphtheria are not fully immune from a second infection. After several weeks in the ward one of the doctors secured enough vaccine through the black market—smuggled in by local Filipinos—that he could inoculate Hank further.

Hank was only peripherally aware of an active black-market underway between select Filipino visitors who came as clergy, messengers, or workers for the Japanese, and a few exceptionally discreet POWs. Col. Schwartz was one of those black-market participants, receiving food and medications for the hospital from Filipino civilians, including a Catholic nun, until the group was apprehended. After the war Schwartz revealed that he made contact with civilians through a few POWs in working parties to procure drugs, money, and food. They never spoke of their activity to other prisoners. Schwartz did not reveal his name to the Filipino civilians, who referred to him by his codename "Avocado." In May 1944, the Japanese caught twenty-three POW participants in this clandestine group and all were either beaten, placed in solitary, or executed. Only a few survived this experience, including Schwartz.[2]

Charles Brown, a warrant officer and POW at the camp, also received goods through another church connection. The Sacred Heart of Jesus parish where Brown and his wife had been married in Manila was his source. Through the parish priest, Fr. Theodore (Padre Doro) Buttenbrunch, Brown received and distributed money, tobacco, and medicine. Buttenbruch was captured, tortured, and executed after he refused to reveal the names of his fellow smugglers. Occasionally Hank saw packages passed between civilians and the physicians and turned the other way. The less he knew the better.

Once settled into the Dip Ward, Hank had some opportunity to consider treatment options. He had already aided with the diagnosis process in the main hospital wards and many of the patients at the Dip Ward already had been through that diagnosis with him. The most immediate way to identify diphtheria was to look in the patient's throat. To spot the characteristic white ulcers the men needed light, something that was in short supply inside the dim windowless hospital wards. So the process took place outside, where he used a broken fragment of a mirror to reflect sunlight into the patient's throat for a clear view. There were plenty of symptoms beyond the ulcer though. For one thing, the sound emitted from the Dip Ward was unlike any of the other wards. Here the patients didn't cough so much as they barked out loose, rattling hacks to loosen phlegm. The sound of that cough and the resulting struggle for air, Chamberlain said, remained with him long after the war: deep, long, ragged gasps. When the cough was productive, nickel-sized gobs of mucus, sometimes bloody, would fly from the victim. Blood was a bad sign. Many of the men already had some lung irritation from smoking. The American cigarettes that came in Red Cross packages never reached the prisoners, but they had taken up the habit of smoking wild tobacco leaves found growing around the camp. Among the distinct odors that hung over the camp was the earthy fragrance from burning wild tobacco leaves.

Treatment of those with diphtheria, like the other patients, required taking some individual time with each man. Hank could often be found spoon-serving the men water and rice mash. Before the war he had been one of the more muscular medics, and he still had more strength in him than most, but he was unable to prop a prone patient into a seated position. So with the help of another medic or two, he would wrestle the man upright until his torso was vertical. He pounded on the man's back, encouraged him to move his arms and legs, look out the door, show an interest in the world, even for a fleeting moment. Then he lowered the patient back onto the bare wood shelf or ground.

Occasionally a Japanese guard displayed the early symptoms of diphtheria. American doctors and Japanese leadership were in agreement that he needed to be removed from the population and put into the Dip Ward's enforced quarantine. Several times Hank walked into the ward to find one of his hated guards lying prone, feverish, and coughing on the plain bamboo shelves with the rest of the prisoners. Hank would feed the man, coax him to drink, wrestle him upright and pound on his back, just as he did the Americans. And just like the Americans, Hank encouraged the Japanese patients to force water down their throats, and he provided the help needed in keeping clean.

More than one medic muttered, "I could kill that son of a bitch," but the treatment was always the same as it was for any other patient. And if the man was lucky, he walked out of the ward to live another day, even to pick up his cane, club, or rifle, and resume his brutal ways. The bodies of Japanese guards who died, however, were quickly removed by fellow guards to be cremated, far from the American cemetery. American medics and doctors were forbidden to touch a Japanese body after death.

Seeing so much death, while watching his friend deteriorate, was taking a maddening toll on Hank's health. In addition to the dozens of illnesses circulating through the camp, there was one more condition, known by the doctors and medics as "give-up-itis," and it could be the deadliest of the afflictions. Sometimes he spotted it in others, and he would help them sit up, or stand on their feet if possible. If they could walk two or three steps that would be enough to keep the muscles going. "In doing that we helped them but we also helped ourselves. That helped us stay strong."

Anecdotally, the survival rate of medics skewed higher than that of the other POWs and that could have been the result of the purpose they shared. Hank felt a responsibility to stay alive for the patients. "If we didn't take care of ourselves, we couldn't take care of the patients." It was a responsibility that weighed on every medic and doctor, but also kept them going. Hank focused on his patients as not only his mission but his distraction, a way to have meaning in a meaningless place. The Marines took some comfort in caring for Soochow. It seemed as if having someone to care for helped a lot of men stay a step ahead of despair. Just like the medics, though, some doctors didn't survive. They contracted the same diseases the others suffered. "If a doctor died he got dumped in the hole with all the others."

On June 6, 1943, Hank registered a personal milestone. Most men were older than him and some were well beyond forty. There was a disproportionate number of officers in the camp and that skewed the ages higher than that of the enlisted men. So for Hank, June 6 meant he joined the majority of the prisoners as a legal adult. It was another day of lining up to be counted, and a Japanese officer arrived with a clipboard and paper, indicating an interrogation was going to begin. These interrogations often took place individually—with prisoners taken away to be privately questioned, and sometimes beaten, based on their responses. Other times the Americans were asked a battery of odd and sometimes highly personal questions in front of the other men. Hank and his fellow POWs lied whenever possible, even when there was no benefit to lying. They gained fleeting satisfaction from watching the officer busily writing their false information on a sheet of paper.

This time, however, Hank couldn't resist a positive response when asked the day of his birth. "Today!" Hank responded, a grin on his face, "I was born twenty-one years ago today, June 6. It's my birthday." His interrogator gave him a doubtful look, his pen hovering over his clipboard, and Hank added, with some sarcasm in his voice, "Now I'm old enough to vote!"

He heard chuckles from the other men travel down the line, and the guard watched them, his face growing steely. Laughter was never something the Japanese liked to hear. He pulled his hand back and struck Hank across the face, then shouted at him in Japanese. The interpreter, standing at the man's shoulder leaned into Hank, close enough that the American could feel his breath on his face.

"Explain what you mean that you can vote?"

"When we're twenty-one we can vote in elections," Hank answered, now looking around him, wondering if his joke had been a good idea. "You know, for president."

Another crack of the man's hand exploded across his face and he righted himself, his feet planted firmly in his wooden shoes. He stood straighter and stared over the officer's head, fixing his eyes on the cogon grass growing beyond the camp fence. The man moved on and several POWs later pounded him on the back, "Happy birthday, Hank."

As he later sat whittling at the soles of his shoes, shaving down a section that was tearing at the skin under his toes, he gazed out at the matted soil where weeds were growing. He noticed the yellow flowers of the dandelions that reminded him of home. When Earl sat beside him, Hank motioned at the weeds and commented, "Those dandelions look just like the ones back in Omaha." Earl nodded, "Yep, those damn weeds grow all over the world."

Hank stood and walked closer to get a better look, he knelt to touch one of the blossoms. "They're edible, you know."

"Is that right? Well, let's have it then." Earl stood as if prepared to pluck it right out of the ground, but Hank put a hand up to stop him. He remembered his hungriest days in Omaha and the dandelions he had seen growing in the yard where he had slept for a stretch during the Depression. He remembered the dandelion soup, which had tasted pretty good to a hungry kid.

"If we just pick it, that will be the end of it. The flowers turn to seed, you've seen that. Let's do some farming."

"Farming dandelions?"

"They grow fast, we could have a whole dandelion garden if we do this right." By this time another medic had joined them. "Go ahead and pick the leaves, but leave the flower, that's where the seeds come from."

Earl plucked the leaves off the plant and stuffed one in his mouth, handed one leaf each to Hank and the other medic.

"Like a salad," Earl said.

Hank picked the rest of the leaves and doled them out, a dozen or so, to the most malnourished of his patients, one limp green leaf provided vitamins C and D. He didn't know it at the time, but the leaves have also been known to reduce swelling and potentially fight infections.

In September 1943 a Japanese general visited the camp, escorted on his inspection by Col. Beecher. The general noted the listless nature of the starving men, the unhealthy demeanor of those not in the hospital, and the sheer number of men in the hospital itself.

"We have many sick men in this camp," Beecher said when asked about the prisoners' appearance.

"Why?" the general asked.

Beecher pointed out the meal of rice and a thin broth that the men were making one of their two meals for the day. "This is why," he said.

The general was unconvinced. "The prisoners are sick because they need more exercise," he said. The farm detail expanded soon after.[3]

As more of the sick entered the ward, the patients were squeezed tighter, sometimes as many as a few hundred men in a barrack—about eighty feet by sixty feet in size—intended for about fifty.

Bill didn't work with Hank in the Dip Ward, but Hank still kept an eye on his friend who was no longer tending to patients with the other medics. He was ever slower to pull himself to his feet, and his face had lost all color. It was a bad trend. Hank set aside a space for the soft-spoken medic who had been at his side for nearly three years. He left Bill there for the night, resting as comfortably as was possible, but in the morning Hank found him barely responsive. His heart plunged. As gently as he could, Hank raised Bill's head to dribble a spoonful of water into his mouth. This suffering was so unnecessary, if the man could only have some real nourishment, Hank thought, infuriated. Starvation is not a natural death, Chamberlain recalled. It is slow, painful, and ugly. And throughout it all his friend still refused to eat the maggots in the rice, then eventually couldn't take the rice at all. "I know I should, I just can't," he said. Hank was desperately frustrated. Bill may not have had as much hardship in his early life as Hank did, it was impossible to know why one man was starving and the other was holding on. "I just kept trying to get him to eat."

Bill had been an average-sized man, muscular, and radiant with good health when they met in training. Now he was a bag of bones, his cheeks caving in, his eyes vacant. They had spent most of their time together since that first meeting and Hank stayed by his side all day, personally delivering him to the Zero Ward when there was no more choice. By that time, Bill didn't have the strength to sit up, let alone walk.

Hank massaged his arms and legs, talked to him about the time when the war would end, and what they might do together. "Maybe I'll meet that girl of yours finally," he said. Bill was silent.

When he did speak, at last, it was with an effort. "When I die make sure my body stays right here in the Philippines, even after the war. Let the people know what we did here, that we didn't die for nothing." Hank nodded, held his friend's bony hand, and wrapped his other arm around his shoulders.

"Hank?" his friend had one more thing to say. "Thank you for being my friend." Bill's voice was soft and weak, and within minutes his life slipped away. Hank saw to it that a minister came to his friend's side, but he may not have been the right denomination. If there was no Catholic priest, a protestant minister would give last rites, and the same courtesy was provided in reverse.

Hank brushed the flies away from Bill's closed eyes and sat, the droning of insects all around him. He spoke his prayer softly. "Thank you God for giving him relief." He and Earl made a marker out of wood with his friend's name—there were no dog tags—and pressed it into his mouth.

Last, Hank, Earl, and several other medics—Bill's best friends—carried his remains to the burial site, along with a parade of a dozen other bodies. They couldn't rest Bill in his grave gently, no one had the strength to make that possible. They simply lay the body by the communal hole and rolled him in. Hank spoke a prayer for the group, then his own, he recalled later. "I remember I said 'rest well my friend' and sent him over the side."[4]

He stayed to help cover the bodies securely, providing as much dignity as he could. They worked together—the men of burial duty—scooping, tossing soil. The guard watching was growing impatient. It was a hot day and there was no shade from the sun.

"Ok fast," the guard shouted, waving his rifle, and Hank scooped faster. "Push! Push!" By the time they finished at least four feet of dirt covered Bill and their other comrades.

He went to bed in the barracks that night with Bill no longer there. Some day he would mourn his friend, but for now he felt numb to it. "So many men dying, you just couldn't think about it," he recalled. For a long time Hank kept a scrap of Bill's clothing as a remembrance, something he could give to the man's family after this was all over. Eventually he lost that too.

15

1943

CABANATUAN, THE PHILIPPINES

As the second year of the Cabanatuan camp ticked by, the Japanese guards were adjusting to life there, just as the misery had become something of a routine for the prisoners. Occasionally the Japanese spent time with the prisoners and learned some English to better interact. Since the prisoners often addressed each other as "Hey, asshole" the Japanese took up the same habit with each other, in a friendly greeting, sometimes with a bow and salute. Hank smiled when he heard the Japanese call each other "Turd-bird," another expression they'd collected from the Americans they were guarding.

Many of the medics still wore a semblance of a red cross on the left arm, although it had yet to benefit them. What it did do, however, was draw attention to others who needed help. Sometimes that meant the Japanese. On one summer afternoon an American truck rattled along the road to the Cabanatuan camp, driven by a Japanese or American driver, and a rut in the road caused a Japanese guard to be jolted out of the back. His arm took the weight of his fall. The result was a bloody compound fracture.

A fellow guard noticed Hank, wearing his red cross, as he made his way back from the main compound on an errand for one of his patients. "You!" the guard shouted. Hank paused, hoping someone else was being summoned but he turned to see the guard making his way toward him, his eyes planted on his face, one hand over his rifle, the bayonet fixed. The guard punched one finger at Hank's red cross patch, then pointed behind him. Hank followed the man to a cluster of guards standing over the victim, arm bloody, the jagged edge of broken bone jutting through his sleeve.

"You fix," the guard pointed at Hank's patch and the patient again. Hank nodded, the Japanese didn't often seek medical help from the Americans, but this injury looked like an emergency that wouldn't wait for a Japanese doctor.

"Ok let's go to the hospital," Hank pointed across the compound, then helped the man to his feet, with what feeble strength his starved limbs could provide.

They hobbled together in a small group to the ward where Dr. Brown worked and was Hank's most trusted physician and who he was certain could manage this medical situation, diplomatically. Once the patient was seated on the makeshift table dedicated for surgery, Dr. Brown took a close look. They wrapped a tourniquet around the bicep and gave the patient a piece of wood that he clenched between his teeth. Hank helped yanked the arm straight as the guards held him still. He was stoically silent.

Once Dr. Brown had the arm strapped tight to his chest, the bone realigned and the bleeding slowed, he motioned toward the compound gate. "You need to take him to a doctor to get plastered up," Hank raised his hand and pantomimed the instructions by walking two fingers toward the gate. "Doctor."

The guards nodded. It was the last he would see of that individual. Although there were so many guards, Hank wouldn't know if he returned to duty. There may have been some Japanese doctors in the camp as well, although Hank never saw any. He did, however, hear from prisoners in a burial party claiming to have seen a disturbing sight: bodies cut up in strange manners, as if they have been subject to experimentation or autopsy. He never saw signs of such things.

One of the best parts of any day was when the rain came, and Hank and the other medics took an afternoon shower in the rivulets of cool water streaming off the hospital ward roof and onto their sore backs. They scrubbed each other's backs to wash away the mud, and to clean the infections and ulcers wherever they had breaks in their skin.

Nearly everyone suffered some array of sores on their backs from beatings, insect bites, sunburns, or disease. Like many of the lighter-skinned prisoners, Hank, with light brown hair and blue eyes, suffered from occasional sunburns, and so he coated his skin with mud whenever he was going to be out in the fields or otherwise working in the sun.

One of the men to be admitted to the diphtheria ward, coughing long, racking coughs, was a chaplain in his late twenties, still wearing a soiled white collar around his neck. At first, he seemed destined for the Zero Ward, but Hank continued to dribble water in the man's mouth, wash off his face and arms, and wipe the blood from his lips. Eventually the morning came when Hank walked through the open door of the ward to find the chaplain sitting up.

"Why, pastor, you look better today!" He sat next to the man who was seated with his arms crossed, smiling.

The chaplain patted Hank's hand. "I thank God for the support you and the other medics have given me, Chamberlain," he says. "It was His Will that I stay in this camp longer," he smiled. "So maybe I can help here in the ward, now that I have immunity."

Hank called over Dr. Schwartz, who agreed. "Yes, that's fine, we can use your help, and your background."

The chaplain took to working alongside the other medics, conducting any task that needed to be done, whether carrying bodies, washing floors, or caring for the patients. He would patiently scrub the men clean with a sponge, using heated or boiled water when that was possible. There was no soap. Hank showed him how to make bandages out of whatever material he could recover. The chaplain hand-fed the patients too. Hank would find the man working at the side of a patient, mashing a spoonful of rice with a few drops of water so that it could be swallowed.

Like Hank, he was not one to give up on a patient who had reached the end. "If there was a life in that person, no matter how bad it was, maybe you could see them breathe, their eyes blink." That meant there was hope. Later the cold hard stare meant it was too late. A shallowness in their breath, a sickly gray coloration to their face, and the chaplain became the best man possible to offer him some comforting words, a prayer to ease him out of his painful life.

The chaplain could also help with the heavy lifting tasks such as turning patients over to prevent bedsores. Many of the men's skinny hips, buttocks, heels, and shoulders grew ulcerated simply from the pressure of lying on the ground, especially when the ground was fouled with liquid feces.

Other ministers were called upon at times to take confessions or to administer last rites. Unlike the chaplain who volunteered at the Dip Ward, these other clergymen didn't have immunity and were loath to catch this dreaded disease. Often they would report to the ward, Bible in hand, but remained outside. Because the ward's two doors were always flung wide open, the man of the cloth could safely stand in the doorway and provide the liturgical support that was needed without getting infected.

For those needing to confess their sins that meant shouting across the ward, and the medics, patients, and doctors all witnessed the unburdening of sins along with the minister. "It didn't matter much," Hank recalled.

"They all had the same sins." Most often the crime of stealing a morsel of food from a fellow prisoner.

Even while the POWs fought to survive in the sprawling compound of Cabanatuan, the suffering of the Filipino people was orders of magnitude worse. Families were killed, their possessions stolen, and homes burned to the ground. While Hank had seen suffering in Manila while at Bilibid, it was just one glimpse into the anguish of many civilians around the entire country—in small villages and large cities alike. Additionally, another Cabanatuan camp—a satellite location south of Hank's Camp 1—held thousands of Filipino soldiers, as well as civilians who had been deemed a threat or an enemy to Japan. All were being held in squalid conditions.

Most Japanese propaganda efforts to unite with the Filipinos against a common enemy—the United States—had been largely unsuccessful, in part because of the harsh treatment they doled out upon those living there. And although Japan occupied the country, fighting was still ongoing. The Philippine Scouts and guerilla forces had been trained as an elite force by the US military, and they had not given up the fight to recapture their homeland. One night, they brought their fight to Cabanatuan. Hank heard about the incident through another prisoner and saw the gruesome results.

Japanese guards watched over the camp from guard towers constructed out of bamboo, making it a relatively rickety climb into the tower. They shook as men climbed up and down. On this particular night Philippine guerilas penetrated the fence and approached one of those bamboo guard towers under the protection of a moonless black sky. Only those who climbed into that tower knew exactly how they accomplished the deed without shaking the tower, but they appeared to have caught the guard by surprise. They managed to kill him silently—no other guards were roused, and they then hacked off his head. They also removed his penis and testicles, leaving the rest of his broken body in the tower.

The head turned up in the morning mounted on a stake standing in a wide shallow spot in the river, near the bridge that many crossed on their way to and from their farm labor. The man's privates had been stuffed in his mouth.

Those prisoners who were marching to work across the river caught a clear view of the spectacle, at the same time that the Japanese guards did. There was much agitation on the part of the guards, Chamberlain learned. The men were hurried back to the camp and word was sent out among the camp leadership what had occurred. "I remember all of a sudden there was a tremendous amount of excitement among the Japanese," he said. Hank had seen so much death, so much violence, the beheading simply struck him as a solid point scored for the side of the Filipinos against the Japanese "When we heard about it we laughed," he recalled.[1]

In the meantime, Hank was serving as a surgical assistant when required. Increasingly, operations consisted of amputations. Nearly every POW ran a risk of amputation, based on infected sores they developed. If hospital personnel caught the infection early it could be scraped and washed clean, using water that was boiled or at least heated with a knife that had been scalded in the kitchen fire. In some cases though it was just too late. When the patient reached surgery, his arm or leg was gangrenous and had to be removed. Amputations were the most reliable way to halt an infection before it could take a man's life. By this time Hank had taken part in dozens of these operations. If the patient was lucky the surgeon had access to novocain, but mostly there was nothing between the patient and his pain. They would slice through the limb's muscle, tendons, and bone as fast as the equipment allowed and then tie off the stump and hoped the man survive.

Every patient fought the process, even when he swore he wouldn't. The four of the strongest medics holding him still, the man's instincts would still take over when the cutting began. At least once Hank was punched in the face as he helped Dr. Brown amputate a hand.

"Hold him still, assholes!" Hank shouted.

"Get it done, get it done!" the other medics called out as they held the thrashing arm and legs. The patient's screams were disturbing, but when the man lost consciousness and went silent, the medical team was left with the even more troubling sound of cutting bone, and the dreaded snap as it split, if gravity took control (that was the sound Hank heard late at night when sleep wouldn't come). The separated limb dropped into a bucket or onto the ground, and all effort was focused on wrapping up what was left of the man and nursing him back to health.

These amputations helped persuade Hank to diligently manage the sores on his own body, cleaning them as soon as the skin grew red, fluid oozed out, or insects clustered over the spot.

Without the companionship of Bill, Hank talked to Earl and the other medics when they were alert and in the mood. Often Hank would find paper pulled off a can or other rescued items and write letters to his mother and girlfriend, never knowing that they were both mourning his death. If a letter had gotten through, Hank's family would have been shocked to hear from the dead.

16

1944

CABANATUAN SATELLITE CAMP, PHILIPPINES

By mid-1943 the Japanese were urging the hospital's American doctors to begin discharging their patients. The camp leadership wanted to see the number of patients drop, by whatever means necessary. At times doctors received directives to release a certain number of patients a day under the diagnosis of "cured." The result was that many patients who could not care for themselves were sent back to the main camp, into the farm fields, or to the airport to fend for themselves.

In the meantime as the hospital population shrank, it eventually was moved to the center of camp where it required less space. By Christmas 1943 Red Cross packages were delivered that included food and medical supplies. Hank searched for letters, gifts, or care packages from Cathy and his mother among the parcels, but there was nothing. He had no idea why they would have failed to send him something, but assumed the package may have been stolen. Many others around him had been without packages or mail, including Dr. Brown who often spoke fondly of his young wife. She had sent nothing.

This year the POWs had appointed recreation officers who set up activities like boxing, baseball, and volleyball. The hardiest of the group still summoned the strength to participate. The Protestant ministers and Catholic priests also began working on improving the spiritual conditions of the men. One of those ministers, Chaplain Oliver, had suffered a broken neck in a beating by a guard but continued to visit the hospital wearing plaster of Paris around his injured neck. With Christmas coming efforts were begun to build a church. There were about eighty Jewish prisoners in the camp by December 1943 and they had their own house of worship with Hebrew songs and prayers that inspired some courage in the prisoners as well.[1]

The Japanese surprised the men, as well, with some American entertainment. The camp leadership had acquired several reels of American movies and a projector, and the prisoners sat dutifully during the scheduled time, accompanied by their guards, and both nationalities were mesmerized by the Hollywood movies and Disney characters that were so familiar to the Americans. Some of the guards had enough English-language skills to follow the stories and they chuckled along with the prisoners. However one conflict the POWs hadn't anticipated arose when Donald Duck appeared in a Disney cartoon. The guard whom they had dubbed Donald Duck for the past year watched his namesake waddle onto the screen. Reference to the name Donald Duck was unmistakable and the guard's face screwed up in anger while other Japanese guards laughed at his expense. From that day forward he was never referred to as Donald Duck and "we prisoners caught hell," Hank recalled.

In early 1944 Dr. Harry Brown was assigned to a new project in a part of Cabanatuan that had been off-limits to the men. In this satellite camp, linked by about twenty kilometers of narrow dirt road running through cornfields, about one thousand Filipino POWs were being held with no official hospital or medical care.

A sprawling POW camp dedicated to Philippine soldiers—Capas— had been vacated by January 1943, with men sent home in what the Japanese called a show of goodwill. They were granted their freedom under the agreement that they would not join the resistance. Most of them, however, did.[2] But some Philippine prisoners had not been as fortunate. A third satellite camp of Cabanatuan held Philippine soldiers along with some civilians, most from the Visayas Islands. These individuals had no transportation home, or neighboring relatives to go to, did not speak the local languages and were therefore kept at the site, under Japanese rule, with almost no food. (The prisoners depended in large part on food donated by local Filipinos.)[3]

The death rate was higher than Camp 1 and disease was running rampant. The Japanese leadership instructed Brown to bring one medic with him, and the doctor asked for Hank, his old friend, with the bonus of surgical skills, to join him.

For the first time in more than a year, Chamberlain was going to be leaving the camp. He didn't need to pack much. He shoved his few belongings into his musette bag: his blanket, cup with the rim cut off to prevent burns, and the board he had fashioned into a bowl. He ran his finger on the seam to ensure his razor was still there, the same way he had hundred of times before. He left his fellow medics with a wave, hoping they'd meet again. No one knew when he'd be back, and who would still be there when he did return. The uncertainty of their future meant there were no goodbyes.

He stepped into the back of a truck with Brown and they bumped along the road, the hard seat slapping their skinny butts, but the breeze blowing refreshingly through their hair.

The satellite Cabanatuan camp was another sprawling compound overflowing with the starving and the dying, but it was significantly worse than the suffering Chamberlain and Brown experienced at the hospital. They walked through the barracks and Hank felt a sickening dread at trying to address the suffering around him. Brown and Chamberlain toured the camp, shaking their heads as they went. Hank had numbed to human suffering, but this was unlike anything he'd seen before. The prisoners looked up at him, some beyond awareness of the world around them, others with a small wave and greeting.

"Hi Joe," they'd call out and Hank flashed back a wave for each of them. Those were the ones who would survive.

Diarrhea flowed everywhere in this camp though, as their latrines were little more than overflowing trenches spilling the waste back into the camp. Prisoners suffering from dysentery and other digestive infections had no control over their bowels, and where it landed, it stayed. The lack of latrine covers meant the fly was king here, swarming over everything and everybody.

The stench of feces was as overwhelming to the senses as the cloud of insects that hovered over the dead and harassed the living.

They walked through the kitchens and found they too were covered in human waste. It leeched into their water and even their rice, as cooks clamped their soiled hands around the large spoon. No one had bathed for months or even years, and their ragged remnants of uniforms hung off them, filthy and inadequate.

The camp's malaise wasn't just about the inadequate living conditions either, Hank learned—it was about communication. The prisoners spoke dozens of dialects specific to the region where each soldier had been raised, and that meant that many of the prisoners couldn't understand each other. Chamberlain and Brown knew little Tagalog, and the prisoners rarely spoke English.

There were women in the camp as well, Filipina civilians, who seemed as sick or sicker than the others. They lived in a separate covered area, and at times, they required medical help too. Chamberlain soon learned that they were being raped frequently at an institutional level by their Japanese captors.

One early morning Hank spotted a cluster of women working their way toward the makeshift clinic he and Brown had established in a thatched hut in the center of the compound. They made slow progress, stopping and then resuming their approach and Hank walked out to meet them. The group of a half dozen women was carrying another woman, middle-aged, slight, and unconscious to the world. Hank saw the remnants of a nun's garb, a habit around her neck and shoulders, but her head bare. He took the nun by the shoulders and helped deliver her to the clinic. The women told her story. She had been raped by guards and was not responsive. Their request was simple: save her. With sips of water at her lips, the nun opened her eyes and smiled appreciation. She appeared to be suffering from malnourishment like those around her. She responded to their English.

"I can clean you up," Brown said, holding the woman's hand in his, "You're going to be okay." She answered, "Thank you," in a calm voice. Hank stepped out of the clinic to snatch a moment of reprieve from what he saw. He inhaled the thick, humid air, wiped tears from his eyes, and returned to her bedside. They kept the woman at the clinic for several days, feeding her the same rations the other prisoners had, and at times listened to her praying in soft Tagalog, which seemed to sustain her. When she left the clinic she was able to walk and she clasped her hands together as she glanced back at the doctor and medic as if to say she would be praying for them.

Brown and Chamberlain sent teams of POWs to screen out the sickest prisoners lying in huts, or outside under narrow shafts of shade, against the sides of buildings; anywhere they could escape the heat. Those who were so severely ill they couldn't stand were separated from the less ill. They discovered that many of the sickest were dangerously dehydrated. Many of the prisoners suffered angry streaks of lacerated skin across their backs, arms, legs, and buttocks, caused by whippings from guards using a vine growing in the neighboring trees. Sometimes the streaks of bloody, infected skin crossed over a man's face.

Brown set up a system to ensure that water was being boiled before being doled out to the prisoners for drinking. Chamberlain got to work designing a bamboo rake similar to the ones they made in Camp 1 when they had arrived there. He provided his handiwork to a handful of prisoners, demonstrating its use, and they went about making more of them, using the wild bamboo and cogon grass growing around the camp. They then raked the floor of the kitchen, as well as other parts of the camp daily.

As it rained nearly every afternoon, Brown instructed all who were able to take a sponge bath in the rainwater. Men stripped down as the first drops fell, knowing the Philippine climate so well they could predict the downpour, then stand under the cool stream, cupping their hands to collect freshwater that was safe to drink. They used grass to scrub each other's backs, breaking through pus to clean festering sores. The prisoners used scraps of wood to build wooden covers for the latrines that opened and shut with hinges made out of cloth or bits of string.

After several weeks in the camp Hank saw a prisoner approach, his eyes focused on him as he strode in his direction. He was carrying his large frame with what seemed to be reasonably good health.

"Hey Joe," he said, his eyes had a spark of the cheerful confidence of the Philippine Scouts, and he stuck out his hand for a shake.

Hank greeted him with a grin, "How are you holding up?"

The Scout shrugged and then introduced himself as Ernesto. "We're happy to have your help over here," he said, taking a turn at shaking each of their hands with a strong grip.

"Great to meet you, Ernesto. Are you a Scout?" The man smiled and nodded. Although they had guessed as much, the Japanese had not, and Ernesto and the other dozens of Scouts living among the other prisoners kept their identity quiet. The Japanese had a special loathing for the Scouts.

Once communication was established, Brown and Chamberlain spent evenings or free time talking to Ernesto and the other Scouts. The men spoke English well, they knew American culture, and Brown and Hank felt they had good friends in their midst. The Scouts described their fighting in Bataan, how they had been captured, and the tortuous Death March. Hank was impressed with the group—they indicated they were still fighting for their country in any way they could. Each morning they still summoned the energy for calisthenics and they talked often about killing the enemy.

Brown noticed, however, that the Japanese had taken a liking to some of these prisoners as well and were campaigning to bring these men over to the Japanese cause. Ernesto told the American that if the Japanese were convinced of a Filipino's allegiance, they would release him.

"What if you started cooperating with the Japanese and get on their good side?" Brown asked one day. "They might free you, send you home."

Ernesto shook his head, no. They were reluctant to leave their fellow fighters to suffer in their place.

"By all means, Ernesto, you should go on out of here, get out of this Godforsaken place," Brown said, gesturing around at the wretched campgrounds and the skeletal figures seated or lying around them.

"I'm not so sure about that," he said, taking a drag from cigarette rolled from jungle tobacco. "Maybe we can do more for the war effort here."

Hank and Brown both shook their heads at this.

"You know what the war efforts needs? Guerilla units, fighting from the outside," Hank said, and then told him the story of the decapitated guard in Camp 1, killed by a stealthy group of Filipino fighters.

Ernesto was quiet but nodded. Brown continued, "You get out of this place, all of you Scouts, you can destroy anything that's Japanese. That's what your country needs."

They were pleased to watch the progress these Scouts had in ingratiating themselves with the Japanese. Within weeks, most of the Scouts, including Ernesto, had been released. In their absence, however, Brown and Hank had lost companions, and they missed their company. Those hundreds of souls in the camp who remained lacked the language skills or the training to secure their release, and Hank was struck by the brutal treatment they were enduring, beyond what the Americans were exposed to.

One afternoon Hank and Brown were abruptly summoned from their work by the guards to serve as an audience for an execution. It was the thing Hank hated most. "You watch," they were told. The spectacle was organized in the center of the camp and the POWs were positioned in a circle around a group of about twenty Filipino prisoners, weak and tired, resigned to their fate. There was no indication of what crime these men had committed. After nearly two years in captivity, Hank knew there was just no reason for what they were witnessing. Although there were several Japanese guards hitting the men and shouting insults at them, only one raised his rifle at the head of the first victim and squeezed the trigger. The prisoner, dressed in rags, no more than a boy who had put down his plow to help protect his country, dropped to the ground dead.

Hank watched with his eyes but kept his mind elsewhere. All he could do was pray, something that helped him through these horrors. He prayed for the boy's soul, he prayed for them all, he prayed for it to end, and then the rifle cracked and the next man fell. The exercise went on for ten minutes until twenty bodies lay before them. Hank frowned the worst grimace he could summon, and he turned that face of loathing on the executioners. That was the only power he had left.

Then the men dispersed, silent and despondent. Hank and Harry Brown returned to the patients who were too sick to attend the forced spectacle, and Hank took deep breaths trying to refocus on the living.

One of the Filipino women who came in for some medical attention caught Brown's interest due to her strange appearance. The woman was young, likely a teenager, with a delicate, pretty face, and, like other others, an undernourished body. But reddish-brown sores freckled her face and neck, her hair was so thin it exposed her scalp. Dr. Brown urged her to sit down to talk.

"What is wrong? Where do you have pain?" he asked. She listened to his question with sharp attention and nodded, seeming to understand.

"I am sick," she said, neither complaining nor embarrassed. He asked about the sores. Where else did she have them? She pointed between her legs. Brown ran a hand over her neck and glanced at Hank. "Swollen glands."

Hank nodded. He figured he knew what Dr. Brown was going to say, even as the man spoke.

"Young lady, you might have a venereal disease, have you been raped by the guards here?" She nodded. "How often?"

"Last night, night before, night before." Brown sighed and sat back. "If this is syphilis, and I think it is, it's only going to get worse. I don't have any medicine but I know ways I might be able to get something." Hank had heard Dr. Brown and the other doctors speak this way before when faced with a unique problem.

The young girl was shaking her head no. "No medicine."

"No medicine? You could get a lot sicker if you don't treat this."

"Those men, they get sick too, from me?"

"Yes of course you're spreading this disease."

She smiled then, something Hank had seen little of among the prisoners, especially here among all this suffering. "Okay," she seemed satisfied and ready to walk away.

"Are you sure you don't want treatment?" Brown tried one last time as she stood to leave.

"This is my gun," she said, "This is how I fight war."

Brown and Hank could only look at each other as she left, amazed at what they had heard. "That's one hell of a strong-willed girl," Brown said.

"I guess there's a lot of different ways to be a war hero," Hank said and they both shook their heads. Not for the first time, Hank felt admiration, while also being deeply disturbed.

III

HELL SHIPS

17

FALL 1944

BILIBID PRISON, MANILA

By the time Hank and Dr. Brown returned to Camp 1, in the summer of 1944, there were signs that the war dynamics were finally shifting. News accounts from prisoners who had access to radios were upbeat, Americans were on the move through the Pacific, and Japan was on the defensive.

Chamberlain watched as men were summoned by the Japanese, name by name, they were lined up and marched out of the camp, to the trains, and on to who-knows-where. The American population at Cabanatuan had already been reduced from approximately ten thousand in 1942 to four thousand by the end of 1943, in part due to deaths, and partially by the systematic removal of men destined for labor sites.[1]

So while the news was promising, the fate of the prisoners looked to be more menacing. Chamberlain couldn't know whether the news reports were true, whether they were exaggerated, and what any of it meant for POWs. He had given up hoping for a fast end to the war or sudden rescue. He solely focused on daily survival—his own and the lives of those he was caring for. Mending the tired, broken body of one more prisoner and seeking nutrients for them and him, those were his only pursuits. His dandelion farm was going well, other men were planting more seeds in other areas, and the availability of fresh greens was providing some badly needed vitamins.

Hank also found more room in the hospital wards, as the men were removed, and he paid little attention to rumors that the men were being taken as hostages for use by the Japanese. Or that maybe they were being taken to Japan.

By September 1944, the first US air raids were striking in the Philippines. Hank heard of these raids from those who could access the news, but there was no sign of Americans where they were. The removal of prisoners accelerated after that, and within about a week, Chamberlain's number was called. The number 999 was shouted out during lineup, and he stepped aside. They were shipping out. He had no regrets about leaving this miserable place. The unknown was better than the day-to-day monotony where he had seen so many men die, where so many men were suffering under his care. But he soon learned Earl would not be with him, nor would Dr. Brown or Dr. Schwartz.

In total 1,905 men were removed from the camp in September, including several hundred American doctors and medics.

One last time, Hank was able to visit his dandelion farm where yellow blooms brightened the worn earth behind the barracks. He gave some instructions to the medics who were staying although he had no idea what would become of the camp and its hospital now. He shoved handfuls of the seeds in his pockets. His pants were shredded to rags, the legs were torn to shorts, strands of string holding them together. They hadn't been subject to a decent washing for two and a half years. But the pocket was intact, and that's where his dandelion seeds would remain, as valuable as anything else he owned.

Many medics had been called up—among the several hundred men preparing to leave—and those medics stuck together with Hank, as they lined up at the gates, preparing for transportation. Among those comprising his bedraggled and anxious group was Boucher, a lanky infantryman in his forties—a career soldier—his musette bag slung over his shoulder. Hank knew him well as a man who had survived on his quick wit, but he was not someone who could be trusted. Dr. Gaskill was the highest-ranking among the group, and one of the few physicians. A big man, he stood with some authority among them, fielding questions from other prisoners, although he too had little insight into what was ahead. As they were marched out through the gate Hank turned back to see Earl wave to him, and the heavy loneliness of prison life weighed down on him harder than ever. He was again forging ahead without his closest friends.

The men were pressed into trucks, shoulder to shoulder. Unlike his journey out of Hospital 2, this time Hank had no patients to tend to. These were the survivors due to a combination of physical strength, smart choices, and good luck. The convoy of trucks growled into motion and launched the prisoners into the next episode in their ordeal. Once the trucks transporting them pulled into Manila and came to a stop, Hank gazed at the familiar, imposing walls of Bilibid prison. The gate swung open to receive them and his heart sunk. Then he followed the shouted orders to step down and line up.

The men were in low spirits as the gates swung shut with a clang behind them. They trudged up the stairs into the dreaded prison most had left two years before. Back into the cells they went, and Hank now knew what to expect: Predictably meager meals: lugao—a watery soup—for breakfast; a cup of steamed rice and barley later in the day; a bucket of water and ladle to fill canteens or cups. They had access to common areas for a half-hour a day. Here men peered at each other curiously, looking for someone to recognize. Hank saw some familiar faces and all had the characteristic, despondent shuffle of the malnourished. And some limped with rudimentary, hand-crafted crutches, accommodating amputations. He marveled at how much damage two years in captivity had caused.

By the next early morning at roll call, on September 21, 1944, the guard surveyed the lineup of prisoners in the common yard of the old penitentiary, walking down the row, stabbing a finger at a few. "You!" And then another. "You!"

Hank was among several dozen men selected who were marched out the front gates under armed guard, about two miles down Quezon Boulevard, a busy commercial street lined by huts, lean-to storefronts, and sidewalk vendors. It led to the port where the sun was rising over the piers as gulls swept noisily overhead. Hank took deep breaths of the marine's salty breeze. The port itself was populated with hulking, aging vessels, as well as a few non-seaworthy ships listing in their moorings. His task was to load Japanese cargo ships that would be carrying goods from the Philippines to Japan.

Back and forth he carried crates from the storage area onto the ship decks or down into their holds. The men carried a fraction of the weight they could have supported when they were healthy. These prisoners had little strength left in their bony arms and legs. Hank dropped one crate hard onto the deck of an aging ship when another prisoner muttered a question, "You come from Bilibid?" Hank nodded, glancing around for guards watching or listening, a habit that had saved him many times in the past two years.

"There's a lot of you then," the prisoner continued. "Looks like the Nips are getting ready to mobilize. Usually there's just a few of us working here, moving shit back and forth." Hank had a bad feeling about that. Every rumor he heard involved prisoners shipping out of the Philippines, and he didn't relish the idea of being one of them, ending up in Japan. So far every move produced conditions even worse than the place he had left.

As he walked down the gangplank for the next load, he heard the hum of an engine approaching. All eyes rose skyward and he spotted several planes traveling along the coast above them, probably Japanese, Hank thought, and the others around him seemed to come to the same conclusion. They all started returning to their work when Hank looked up again. He couldn't tell much from the appearance of these planes; they were high up and the markings weren't visible. Their silhouette against the sky was no help.

Suddenly their path veered into the Manila Bay toward the port where the men watched from the ground. The leading carrier aircraft, plunged into a dive, headed straight for the ships they were loading.

Japanese shouts filled the port around them, and guards were shoving the POWs, frantic, pushing them in every direction. Then abandoning the effort, the guards were gone, and Hank dropped flat to the ground, his face down, his hands protecting the back of his head. This, like nearly every action taken since the invasion, he learned through experience. "We did everything the best we could. There's so much about war that you just can't train for," Hank recalled.

Bombs exploded around him. Then he turned his head enough to peer up as the planes shot nose up toward the sky, directly over his head and he spotted white stars on the wings. Hank had never known American aircraft to have plain white stars for markings. All the same, there was no doubt in his mind—these were American aircraft.

It was the first time his eyes had set on an American plane since his capture. "They're back, they're back!" He leaped to his feet and waved wildly. The Americans around him joined in, all realizing at once, what they had seen. They shouted in sheer joy, even as the battle raged around them. Some of the POWs had wounds, but generally minor ones, pierced by sharp fragments or scalded by the flying debris. Japanese antiaircraft guns fired skyward, but they had been taken entirely by surprise.

The chaos following the attack brought an end to the celebration. Black smoke burst out of ships, several were already listing heavily and began sinking into the Manila Bay.[2] Sirens moaned their familiar air-raid alarm. The guards re-emerged from whatever cover they had taken, rounded up the men, counting and then shoving the prisoners into a line to mobilize back to Bilibid. Their day's work was over. Hank took a hard blow to the shoulder, but he didn't even feel the usual flash of pain. He was elated. For the first time in years, he had hope.

Back at Bilibid that night the men were giddy, talking excitedly about only one subject. "We're back!" "Lookout Japs, now it's our turn!" The air raids continued for several more days. The next day, however, the loading of ships went on despite the attacks. One afternoon as Hank carried his latest load, he noticed a strip of old rope coiled in a ship's corner. He knew something valuable when he saw it, he glanced around him before snatching it up and wrapping it around his waist.

On Sunday, October 1 in the midafternoon, Hank sat in on the concrete floor of his Bilibid cell, wiping sweat off his face with the fragment of a rag scavenged from Cabanatuan. He started, then felt dread set in, when he heard the orders he had been fearing. "Bongo!" Go line up out front. They were shipping out.

As Hank had feared, the Japanese were moving the POWs to their homeland to provide slave labor where they were running short of able-bodied workers. These POWs would be providing mining and railway work across Japan. They had been selected for their reasonably good health.

By residing in Japan, the prisoners would provide a second benefit to the Japanese Imperial Army war effort—as hostages in the event of an allied invasion. That, Hank thought, "Might be our only real value," at the time, "They've mostly used us up as slave labor." Looking back seventy-five years later he said, "We had been stripped of all our possessions, our freedom, our health, our dignity and as far as possible, dehumanized." But he wasn't broken yet. He had his musette bag, he had a letter from his mother and one from Cathy. He had his grandfather's razor and the board he had carved into a bowl that had fed him now for years.

About 1100 men were assembled in the prison yard and with more aggression than usual, the guards shoved, smacked, and beat the men, counting again and again, then marching them on the route Hank had become accustomed to: Bilibid Viejo Street, then along Quezon Boulevard to Pier 7.

The marching of thousands of POWs was a noisy affair with loud footfalls, Japanese shouts, and occasional gunfire. And it attracted attention in the city. Filipino civilians began to gather, some walking alongside, more and more flanking the street the Americans were marching down. In his bedraggled condition Hank still looked warily around him, as a matter of habit, but he saw the warm faces of the people of Manila, smiling in his direction and shouting out encouragements. They waved cheerfully, some held up the "V" for victory sign. He distinctly heard the tune of the *Star-Spangled Banner* being whistled from somewhere in this growing crowd. The Japanese hurried them along, shouting at them to move faster. But for

Hank, the encouragement from the Filipinos boosted his morale and he stepped more lightly than he had in a long time. He felt his back straighten, his strength improved. These civilians had helped him restore his dignity, even if only for minutes.

At the pier, guards divided the men into large groups and Hank found himself in the company of 1100 men assembled alongside a rusty ship with a Red Cross painted on the stack. Hank noted that it was riding high in the water indicating that no cargo had been loaded. It was the Hokusen Maru, also known as the Haro Maru or Benjo Maru. They would be embarking on one of the longest prisoner voyages of the war, on what would be commonly known as a "hell ship."

18

OCTOBER 1944

HOKUSEN MARU, NORTH PACIFIC

The *Hokusen Maru* had its origins in New Jersey where it was built to serve the US Navy, transporting horses during World War I. The ship was seized by the Japanese during the Second World War and the Imperial Army was employing it in part for its original purpose: transporting horses in one of its two holds, while coal was carried in the other. Before the October POW transport, the horses had now been removed, along with most of the coal, but remnants of both remained in the cavernous holds.

The Japanese counted the men once, then twice, and shoved them up the gangplank to the deck. The prisoners were directed to one of two hatches opening into these holds. Each employed a narrow steel ladder that prisoners climbed down about forty feet below deck, into a dark space measuring about forty by fifty feet. The rear hold was carpeted with chunks of coal—dirty, dusty, and sharp. Once the ship unloaded in Japan the coal could be used for heating, but it also served as ballast for the ship that would be carrying the marginal weight provided by human cargo. The front had no coal but was filthy with horse manure. The Japanese herded 550 men into the front and another 550 in the rear.

Hank was ordered into the back hold along with many of the medics and a few doctors who had come with him from Cabanatuan, as well as personnel from all military branches. Reluctantly, he ducked through the hatch and down the ladder, one step after another plunged him into darkness and stagnant, suffocating heat. A single American officer in charge and one medical officer along with cooks were permitted on deck, the rest suffered together in the hold.

Almost immediately the ship steamed out to the harbor's breakwater and dropped anchor. Then it sat motionlessly. The prisoners didn't have enough room to lie down, so they sat back to back and rested, dozing as the air grew hotter and more stifling. Night fell.

On the first night at anchor in Manila Bay, the tropical sea breeze still gently wafted into the hold and lifted away some of the oppressive heat. Hank turned his face up to feel it cooling his hot skin. That didn't last. The men looked up at banging sounds above the hatch and watched the evening light vanish. They were immersed in darkness and the air seemed to grow hotter and more oppressive in an instant. The Japanese crew had placed large planks over the hold and secured them down with steel cable. There would be no one trying to leave the hold. The next two nights and days were agonizing, the air rancid and stale. One of the doctors used a clinical thermometer he'd stashed in his bag to measure the air—it had reached its maximum temperature at 108 degrees. The men made estimates of 110 or 112 degrees.

Even seventy-five years later, Chamberlain had no idea why the Japanese chose to cover that hatch. Although the single, metal ladder might have allowed prisoners to climb out, they could only have done so one at a time, and with the POWs' weakened condition a guard could have quickly put a halt to that. "Oh well, you know, there's no explaining what the Japanese were thinking," he said.

During the night the Japanese crew painted over the red cross on the stack and replaced it with the number eight for reasons Hank and the other prisoners would never understand. Yet another mystery. As the wait crept from one day to three, sitting in the harbor, in the cargo holds, the men began to overheat, dehydrate, and panic. Men who had survived three years of starvation, beatings, and disease had now reached their limits. Some began screaming in anxiety or terror, demanding to be released. Others simply sobbed and begged for God to rescue them.

When the Japanese heard the clamor coming from the hold, they burst open the hatch and trained weapons down on the men cowering below. "Stop the noise!" they ordered. The Japanese suspected it could attract the attention of American submarines prowling near the Manila harbor. Through an interpreter the captors laid out the stakes—if the men couldn't be quiet, the Japanese would kill every one of them. It was as simple as firing into the hold until they were all dead.

Shortly after the hatch had been closed again, the cables winched tight to hold it shut, the dark hold fell silent. Then a few groans resumed, several men had lost all reason and started screaming, clawing at the walls of the ship as if there was a way out. Some tried to reach the ladder. Some men preyed on the others, from minor squabbles ("Get your damn feet off my balls!") to the organized horror of a group of POWs who strangled those who made noise, or bludgeoned them with a canteen until they fell silent. One prisoner was said to have killed another to drink his blood.

The confusion meant that Hank only understood some of what he was hearing. But the fighting eventually led to silence. If the men in the hold had any leadership, it came from Lieutenant Colonel Robert Gaskill who served as the ranking American physician and was well known by Hank. When the hatch was opened to admit an empty bucket for a toilet and filled bucket of rice, Gaskill asked to speak with the ship's captain. Once he climbed onto the deck Hank strained to listen and heard the shouts and unmistakable sound of blows on flesh. Gaskill was a tall man—over six feet—and was not well liked by the leadership of the Hokusen Maru. When Gaskill eased his bruised and bleeding body back down the ladder into the hold, Hank knew they had lost one more point of leverage with the Japanese.

At the dawn of the fourth day in the harbor, the *Hokusen Maru* joined a convoy of hell ships setting sail from Manila. Hank felt relief that something, anything, was happening. As they sat in the sharp, dirty coal many stripped off all their ragged clothing attempting to cool down but there was no relief. Not a breath of air stirred. Many men lost consciousness from heat prostration and no one could help. Yet still the prisoners attempted to bring some humanity to this hellish confinement. Those who had the energy and willpower amused the others with stories and tall tales. They talked about food. They recalled meals like roast chicken, pork chops, fried steak, and the food that offered the greatest allure in the hot belly of the hell ship—watermelon. They imagined the sugary liquid ripping down their arms, pouring down their dry throats.

"Oh would you shut your fuckin' trap!" eventually someone called out. Others played nonsensical games in the dark, in silence, tapping their fingers against each other one at a time, faster and faster until they missed. A pause, some coughing and groaning, then they started again.

Each day the Japanese pulled up two toilet buckets and replaced them with two more buckets with food and water that would be emptied and employed as the new toilets. The buckets couldn't accommodate the waste of 550 men, especially one at a time. The result was that many men soiled themselves and those around them. In the meantime the water bucket emptied fast, and dividing the water evenly among every man was almost impossible.

As the convoy of ships skirted the Philippine shoreline, stopped in Cabcaben, then steamed into the open water of the South China Sea it was forging into a deadly journey. The prisoners could not know that their lives were not only in the hands of their Japanese captors but also the American military prowling the waters for Japanese vessels.

As he sat there in the coal, his back pressed against another man's back (he had no idea who it was), Hank dreamed of a summer day in Omaha when the sun shone brightly on his mother's garden and the breeze was cool. He recalled his grandfather suspending a hammock between two trees and young Hank climbing in with him. The two rocked in the hammock and watched the clouds gently roll across the sky.

The memory gave him an idea. He still had most of his GI blanket intact and the piece of rope that he had salvaged at the port—about twelve feet long. He stood and strained to see in the dark. He took a step over the man beside him.

"What are you up to?" a voice called as Hank began knotting the rope around the edge of his blanket.

Hank recognized the man's voice, Boucher, the prisoner who had traveled with him since Cabanatuan.

"I'm making a hammock," he said.

"A hammock? What the . . . where will you hang it?"

"On the stanchions of course," Hank responded. He could imagine the man's face perk up in the darkness.

"Hey want to share a bit of rope with me? I think I know what you mean, and I can help you." Hank was reluctant. He didn't trust Boucher and he didn't want to share the rope, but he also knew tying the hammock in place by himself would be nearly impossible.

So Hank used his razor to cut the rope into quarters and tied two to each of their blankets. Hank took off his wooden shoes, he'd need bare feet for climbing. Boucher then boosted him up against the side of the ship, and Hank's toes found the holes cut in the steel stanchions to support his climb about ten feet up the side, just far enough be well clear of the heads of the men while not too close to the top of the hold. Hank tied the rope in knots around the stanchions, effectively suspending his blanket like a hammock. He then helped Boucher do the same, several feet forward of his own. Boucher helped push and shove Hank from below until he was able to swing himself in and then tie his belongings in a sack at his head. Hank stretched out in his hammock and sighed with some relief. He could recline here, comfortably, and also gave a little more room to the fellows on the coal. Soon Boucher was suspended in a similar style along the ship's side. In the following hours those who had similar equipment were doing the same and half a dozen more hammocks slung on the walls of the ship.

Chamberlain soon found there was a second advantage to his location. His thirst was maddening, but as he touched the side of the ship he felt the wet condensation from the sweat and breaths of the men below. He reached for the small rag he carried with him and wiped down the side of the ship, then wrung out the moisture directly between his cracked lips. This provided him with enough hydration to keep his wits.

The ship pitched and rolled as it churned into the South China Sea. As it progressed over the waves the Japanese periodically raised the two waste buckets which swung back and forth, striking the ladder or the side of the ship and spilling the contents on the men below. This probably accelerated the rise in diarrhea and dysentery. The nature of their diseases created an urgency that meant most men never made it to the bucket, especially when a line waited in front of it. So most were forced to sit in their own and each other's excrement. The toilet buckets were often rinsed out with saltwater and filled with freshwater for drinking. The Japanese laughed as the prisoners complained about this practice, so the men drank it anyway.

When the hatch was open Hank would look up at the square of light, blinking painfully at that little bit of sunshine. The air in the hold itself was gray from the coal dust stirred up by the restless men.

One of the doctors onboard eventually succumbed to the heat and efforts at reviving him failed. He died on October 4 and when the prisoners alerted the Japanese, the men were assigned to hoist his body up to the deck. The doctor had been kind to many of the POWs and medics alike, and Hank and the others were sorry that he had to die in such a way. He deserved a proper burial with a minister they agreed, but funeral services were forbidden. No chaplain was allowed on deck, so the men appointed as burial detail carried the man's body to the rear of the ship and as gently as they could, dropped him overboard. Afterward the chaplains in the hold stood and they all prayed.

The heat began claiming men's lives now on average one a day. Once per day the Japanese opened the hatch and lowered enough rice to provide one cup per prisoner. Hank knew the equation. This was a starvation diet. Every unnecessary movement burned calories, and their bodies couldn't afford to waste a single one. That isn't easy even when immobile on land, Hank said. "When you're on a ship on the high seas you're constantly moving," and to maintain balance, the body was constantly relaxing and flexing—wasting body energy hour by hour.

On October 6 another doctor took his last breath. The men waited hours until the hatch was opened and they shouted up for help. Another body needed burial at sea. Again they asked for a chaplain on deck with the body for a short funeral service, but the guards shouted their refusal. Instead they had two men—one of them a physical therapist named Joe who Hank had known since General Hospital 2—pull the doctor's body up to the deck and to the ship's rear. They then rolled their old friend over the side and into the water. The body was bloated with gas and wouldn't sink. A Japanese destroyer was following close behind their little ship and Joe described later to Hank how he had to watch the ship turn deliberately toward the body and hit it. The body slid alongside the destroyer and then into the screws. Joe bowed his head in silent prayer. The guard hit him on the side of the head and sent him back into the hold. The sight would haunt Joe for the rest of his life. From that time on chaplains held a short service in the hold before any more remains were hauled out of the hole. Then day by day, more men died of dysentery, heat prostration pneumonia, and starvation. Desperation was settling in over the group. The lack of protein and vegetables, and almost complete immobility, were aggravating the beriberi. Their bare legs and feet swelled up and the sharp charcoal compounded the pain. Although they sat back to back for support, they hardly had the strength to support each other.

Tempers flared at the slightest provocation. As tightly packed as the men were, the Japanese decided to shift some of the POWs from the front hold to the back. Those men told Hank that the front hold had been coated in horse manure. The prisoners had been forced to sit and lie in that manure, heavily infested with lice, fleas, and horseflies. In this foul condition, the men kept busy killing the flies, but there was little they could do about the fleas, and the bites became infected. They also had the same problems Chamberlain's group suffered: dehydration, beriberi, dysentery, bronchitis, and a new scourge related to the bad air of the ship—pneumonia.

One of the doctors instructed men to take deep breaths while another slapped him on the back with the flat of his hand. This seemed to loosen the mucus that was then expectorated into a small hole dug into the coal. Hank watched from his perch, no longer serving as a medic for this sorry lot. The violence and desperation taking place below him were too much to fathom. It was clear that the hammock was not only sparing him suffering but possibly saving his life, and he was the envy of many of those below. Some of the men, including medics who had become friends called to him. "Hey Hank, you gotta give me a turn in that hammock."

"You want to trade?"

"Anything, name your price."

"One spoon of rice for a half-hour," he offered.

"Deal."

He shared several times a day, keeping track of the time by counting off in his head, enduring the cramped, stinking coal and other bodies until he counted up to thirty minutes. He always insisted on the rice first.

After several days one of the POWs refused to relinquish the hammock though.

"Get out of there, it's been thirty minutes."

"It ain't been even twenty, I need more time."

Looking up at the shadowy bulge where his hammock and its occupant hung, Hank was ready for a fight. He leaped up the stanchions, while his adversary lay still, refusing to budge. Bracing himself against the wall, Hank yanked the hammock, swinging it with all the force he had until it spun enough to dump the occupant. It wasn't a short fall, but under healthy conditions a man could have jumped down and landed on his feet. That didn't happen in this case, like dead weight the man dropped ten feet to whatever lay below. Hank didn't look down or call out below, he climbed back into his hammock, muttering to himself, "God-damn asshole thinks he can take over." He didn't know if the man was injured or even killed in the fall. It was an action his former self would have avoided, but he had put saving others behind him once he got into the hell ship hold.

A day later the handful of POWs who were taking their short turn on the deck were rushed below. One of these prisoners, a Navy man, told the group what he had seen from the deck. A US submarine, he said, had fired on a large merchant ship and a tanker in their convoy, and the ships were now listing and sinking fast. It wasn't over yet. Hank heard several blasts and the hold fell silent as hundreds of men strained to hear. Chamberlain could pick up the ping-ping sound of the sonar against the hull over the breathing and occasional stifled coughs of his companions there. They could hear an explosion as the torpedo hit another target. They were under attack by their nation.

One of the chaplains led the man in whispered prayer and then all concentrated on their quiet thoughts and conversations with their God. They lurched back and forth, some rolling onto others as the captain zigzagged to make a less reliable target. In the meantime, they could hear depth charges exploding around them. Chamberlain knew his hammock hung flush with the waterline, where a missile could most easily strike. He said his quiet prayer, "If a torpedo hits us, dear God, let it be a good hit."

He knew a swift death would be better than any of the other options. Being wounded and drowning would be a tortuous way to go.

A ship in the convoy began rolling more depth charges over the side, and every time one went off, the ship would seize and bounce, shaking the men across the floor of the hold. Hank held onto the hammock as it slammed against the side. "I will always think the only reason we weren't sunk is because they didn't think our ship was worth a torpedo," Hank said. Following the attack, the remaining members of the convoy changed course and headed for Hong Kong.

The ship was under constant risk of attack from both above and below as Americans terrorized the convoy. There was machine-gunning from fighter bombers. That was both terrifying and delightful, Hank recalled. He remained sure, long after the war, that if these Americans had known their countrymen were being transported onboard, they wouldn't have fired on any of the convoy's thirty-nine ships.

But even if pilots had been able to see the men on the deck, there would have been little they could make of who they were, or why they were there. Any Americans on deck were discolored from lying on coal dust so long they were not recognizable.

More men died and their bodies were carried ashore by Chinese forced labor for disposal. Chronic coughs plagued every man onboard from breathing the coal dust and foul air that included feces and dried urine.

When it was finally Chamberlain's turn to go on deck he was shocked by the weakness of his arms and legs. By the time he was standing on the topside, he was racked in coughs and exhausted from the ladder climb. Beside him was another fellow medic from Hospital 2—Lou Vargas. He saw his old friend was in miserable condition, not only coughing, but nearly unable to stand, his legs were so engorged they could have been on an elephant. Infected ulcers from the sharp coal dotted the back of his legs and his buttocks. Hank felt a pang of compassion. The Japanese upturned a hose of saltwater and Lou and Hank were ordered to stand under it to bathe. "Hang on, Lou, I've got something for your legs," Hank tugged his rag out of his pocket and bent to rub his friend's sores, to clear away some of the pus. He heard the word, "You, stop!" shouted and the water abruptly switched off.

Two guards shouted directly at them, their wrath directed at Lou for unknown reasons. Lou looked at Hank, confused, and then he was pulled to the hatch and the beating commenced. The guards began kicking the man's swollen legs then sent him below, laughing at the slow painful steps Lou took, one after another. Hank knew that climbing the steel ladder with those bruised legs and feet must have been agony. He thought then he could have killed one of those guards if he had a chance.

The *Hokusen Maru* arrived in Hong Kong on October 11. The men in the hold had no idea where they were when they felt the ship's engines quiet, the anchor creak over the side. Only after men were brought onto the deck in small groups for their baths, those POWs who served in the Navy recognized their surroundings. They had been there before.

The ship's captain had sidled the vessel up against a large rock island, sprinkled with bird guano. The rock provided some protection from American bombs and strafing. On their first day there, Hank got his first chance to climb the ladder out of the hold and into the bright light of Hong Kong Bay.

The *Hokusen Maru* was living up to its nickname—Benjo Maru. Each day the ship became more of a stinking toilet. To reduce the buildup of waste in the ship hold, the vessel guards instructed the men to hold their bowels and bladders and relieve themselves over the ship's side during their scheduled five minutes on deck. By afternoon, following the anchoring of the ship, Hank was permitted on the deck, and with relief, he gulped fresh air. His first task was to relieve himself at the saltwater latrine—that was the Hong Kong Bay. Guards ordered him to climb over the deck rails, down onto a bamboo framework attached to the ship's flank, where he had to squat and defecate between the poles. This was no small accomplishment for most of the men who were suffering from the bloating of beriberi that shot electric pain up their legs with each step. Hank took his turn, feeling the urgency of the guards shouting "Speedo!" as the other POWs waited. Next he was directed to take another shower under the saltwater hose. Never fast enough, he was shoved from one position to the next, before he put his head under the downpour from deck hose that several guards held, shooting bay water skyward. "We had no soap and could not wash off the coal stain, but it sure felt good." The salt burned when it hit his raw skin, but the relief of cold water and the effect of some cleaning was overwhelming, and he basked in the hose's spray.

Hank was stepping away from the shower, making room for the next prisoner, when he heard a roaring sound approaching the ship and harbor. As he stepped further from the hose it became unmistakable: planes. Then American bombers—B-24s and B-25s—escorted by P-40 and P-51 fighter planes came into view. The bombers pummeled the seas and ships around the Benjo Maru while several of the fighter planes swept low overhead, and Hank dove for the deck. Strafing found its target in the Japanese ship next to the *Hokusen Maru*. This neighboring, anchored ship was loaded with fifty-gallon drums of fuel on its top deck and the fuel drums exploded.

The concussions from the explosion rocked the *Hokusen Maru* violently and Hank held on, covering his head, praying for survival. As more strafing whizzed overhead, four or five rounds hit the deck. Hank and a dozen POWs as well as Japanese ship crew, all pressed down, flat, in terror.

The flames, then smoke, shot up out of the cargo ship one hundred feet away as the planes droned away from the harbor, and the guards ordered Hank and the prisoners with him down into the hold. He would not see daylight again for days. He knew another attack could come at any time, and the thought haunted him on his way down into the dark hold where they would be helpless to save themselves. "I was thankful we were riding high in the water and not worthy of being bombed," Chamberlain recalled, "with so many other rich targets available" in the port.

The bombs claimed a freighter as well as merchant vessels and numerous small craft dock areas, drydocks, wharves, cranes, and shipping equipment. The attack would be considered one of the largest and most successful operations of the US 14th Air Force in the Pacific War. Japanese antiaircraft fire did little damage to the aircraft, while 85 to 90 percent of the bombs landed on their targets. General Claire Chennault, who had led the attack, indicated that it had signaled a major change in Japan's fate in the war.

For Hank and his one-thousand-plus fellow prisoners though, the battle was hardly over. Only war can deliver the kind of conflicting emotions Hank wrestled with as he climbed up to his hammock. He was accustomed to fear, but the bombings raised the stakes. If they were struck here in the harbor, their bodies would be trapped in this sinking toilet of a ship. But the sight of American bombers was exhilarating. It was the best welcome to Hong Kong the prisoners could have asked for and they talked about it excitedly, filling the hold with sounds of their voices and laughter. The hell ship waited out the risk of submarine attacks in the open waters for ten days, at which time the original route had been scrapped. It had been decided, Hank learned later, that the men probably wouldn't survive a trip to Japan and they needed to be disembarked and put to work somewhere else in the interim. The rusting tub finally weighed anchor on October 21, cleared the Hong Kong harbor, and joined its convoy motoring out in the early morning. It was foggy.

Japanese guards and their American prisoners alike were uneasy. Talk centered on submarine attacks and their little ship seemed like a slow-moving target for the American Navy. As he reclined in his hammock near the waterline, Hank prayed that if they were torpedoed, it would be a good hit. "After surviving for so many years it seemed that I would never see home again." He was grateful for this makeshift hammock, uncomfortable as it was against the steel side of the ship, and the access to fluid by wiping moisture from the steel wall. As one sweltering day passed into the next, several men seemed to go out of their head, crazed by the heat and lack of water. One man accused his neighbor of stealing a sip from his canteen while he slept. The accuser used that canteen to smash the head of the accused so relentlessly and with such fury that he fractured his skull. The man died that night. Hank lay suspended in the hold with this misery, holding his face with his hands, no longer able to transport himself to another place or time. Memories of Cathy and life at home failed him now. "When will this madness end?"

As the ship churned onward the Japanese made a few concessions for those who died. They allowed the prisoners to weigh down the bodies—after they had been delivered out of the hold—with sacks of coal to sink them. Still, religious services were forbidden.

There was some relief from the misery though. As the sun rose on another day Hank noticed it did not burn as hot, and in the dark of night he sensed a cooling in the hold. They were finally in cooler waters. For Hank this meant less sweating, but he could collect less moisture from the ship sides to rehydrate himself.

They reached the Port of Takao, Formosa, on October 25 without any more submarine harassment. No one but the cooks had been allowed up on deck for two days. Even after the anchor was dropped, they sat. And sat for forty-eight hours more, breathing the dust and gas and bodily stench. By this time thirty-nine men had died.

Finally, the hatch was yanked open and a voice called ordering them to disembark. For some this would be impossible. While the men below stirred into action, collecting their bags and attempting to stand, Hank untied his hammock and joined the movement toward the ladder. The climb proved to be so much struggle for some that the rate at which they moved felt interminable. As the guards became agitated, shouting at the men to hurry, it was apparent that many weren't going to make it up that ladder. Eventually about half of the prisoners remained in the hold, helpless to free themselves.

The Japanese threw a rope down into the hold, and a few able-bodied men who'd stayed with the weakest tied a knotted loop that they wrapped under the arms of the first man who lay nearly unconscious near the ladder. A tug on the rope signaled those in the deck to hoist him up. This was the same method they had used to lift dead bodies out of the hold, and as

Hank remained behind to help, he watched the men hoisted up through the hatch and thought they showed little sign of life.

Once he had climbed onto the deck himself, Hank looked around him at their new home port. Formosa had been occupied by Japan for decades and the Takao Harbor served as a Japanese naval base on Formosa's southwest shore. He gazed out at the city along the water's edge where warehouses and factories served industrial purposes for the Japanese. The air was cooler than Hong Kong but smoky from burning coal.

By the time Hank set his feet on firm land he knew things were different. He was not the same man he had been when he boarded that ship. He was one of the hardened survivors who had witnessed the violence and the despair, and who knew the darkest hopelessness where no one could trust or rely on anyone else. What struck him most was how the guards could have put them through it. "I will never understand the meanness and the madness. It was and still is unimaginable. How can anyone treat someone like that?" Hank recalled, not for the first time.

So as Hank set off marching, his legs shot with pain, he found that for the first time he didn't care about his fellow prisoners, and he could see from the cold gazes of those around him, that they felt the same way. But he still motioned to Boucher and the two put one of the weakest of the men between them, dragging him along until another truck came and loaded up the man with all the other most ailing prisoners.

19

NOVEMBER 1944

FORMOSA

The march to a nearby train station began their short journey to the Toroku Taiwan POW camp in what was formerly a primary school.[1] It was a mystery what would become of those sickest POWs who had been loaded in trucks. Hank knew it was just as likely they were going to be killed as be delivered safely to their destination. He didn't keep track. In the meantime, Hank and the other prisoners each took an arm of those who still showed some life, and they began coaxing, supporting, and even carrying those men down a dirt road toward the train station. If even one fell behind, it could mean punishment for the entire group.

Hank knew little about Formosa. He'd interacted with Japanese-trained, Formosan guards at Cabanatuan, and they were all bastards, as far as he could tell. The dirt road the men were marched down was filled with civilians on bicycles, carts pulled by draft animals, cars, wagons, and pedestrians moving in every direction. The guards shooed the onlookers out of the way, but these people seemed reluctant to yield to the prisoners. Hank saw loathing in their stares. The march couldn't contrast more with the walk they had taken through Manila. Although they gathered to watch, just as the Filipinos had done, no one was flashing the victory sign to the prisoners now. Instead, the jeering started as soon as the men were within close range. Hank kept his gaze fixed ahead of him and shut out the angry shouts. It was in a foreign tongue so he could ignore the curses, threats, or insults hurdled in his direction. Then he felt a glob of spit hit his cheek. His eyes glanced in the direction of a young woman glaring in his direction. Several children came with rocks in their hands and started throwing. Within seconds a stone struck Hank's left temple. It had been a strong throw. The pain was so sharp that he dropped his grip on the man he was helping to carry, the two both stumbled, nearly hitting the ground while Boucher tugged on the man's other arm. "Come on, get your footing. Damn, Hank, they got you good," Boucher regarded the blood pouring from the gash on Hank's temple. With one hand Hank brushed the blood out of his eyes, while he reached for his charge with his right hand, pulling him back up onto his toothpick legs, and the three continued. Hank tossed his head to the side occasionally to shake the blood out of his eyes. The civilians laughed at their struggles.

The prisoners were clearly in Japanese territory now. Not only were a large percentage of the Formosan people of Japanese descent, they had been occupied by that empire for the entirety of the twentieth century, so far, only the elderly would clearly remember a time without Japanese rule. And in the past year they had suffered multiple bombings by American planes, destroying homes, village centers, killing families. Americans were clearly and unquestionably the enemy.

Although the walk was only about a mile's march from the port, and they were being beaten and berated by guards for their slow pace, it still took the men more than an hour to get to the station.

The guards pushed and kicked the men onto a passenger train that provided some sitting space and in surprise, Hank sat down on a comfortable seat. For several hours they headed north in the Formosan countryside, and the train then screeched to a stop at a much smaller station, in a village, where they were told the marching would begin again.

New guards were waiting for them here, a combination of Japanese and Formosans. The train had provided some respite, and Hank had even been able to collect his strength and drink some water the guards had provided. The bleeding on his forehead stopped and his headache lessened. As they stepped out of the train, more of the men were able to walk without support.

The Toroku POW camp that awaited them was fashioned out of a school building and playground. It was unlike the school where the POWs had been held in the Philippines several years before, though. While the previous school was filthy from the thousands of Filipino POWs who had suffered there before their arrival, this Formosan school was recently constructed of clapboard, still fairly clean, while students were nowhere in sight.

A total of about five hundred POWs would be housed in the school, sleeping in classrooms. They received adequate water and several servings of brown rice per day, a similar sticky ball to the ones they ate in the Philippines. Now the rice was higher quality and reasonably clean. Hank was gratified to see no dirt or glass.

The first challenge for medics and doctors was to attend to the sickest. Once prisoners were directed into the school, Dr. Gaskill started issuing orders to Hank and the handful of medics who were with them, "Get the sickest into the back of that room," he instructed. "Anyone with dysentery needs to be outside for now. Let's get some water into this group first." Hank heaved a sigh. He was back to work as a medic, granting less time to think about being a prisoner. It was a role he was familiar with.

They retrieved rice for the ailing patients and spooned it into their dry, chapped mouths. One Formosan guard watched from the door, rifle over his shoulder. When Hank looked up at the man, he was surprised to see him smile. The guard called Hank over to him with a Japanese phrase and motioned with his hand. The medic glanced around him first, but everyone around him was otherwise occupied. Reluctantly Hank stood, walked to the man, who handed him something soft and meaty, closing his hand around the gift. He gestured to the ailing prisoner who Hank had been spoon-feeding and then walked away. When Hank opened his hand he saw a morsel of fish.

He returned to his patient and enjoyed the expression of surprise and sheer pleasure as the man tasted the white meat Hank held to his mouth.

In a matter of days, as his health improved, Hank considered his new situation and ran his fingers through his pockets, pulling out dandelion seeds that had traveled with him from the Philippines. He wandered around the schoolyard—mostly a concrete-defined play area, surrounded by long grass and nothing looked edible. The cook was set up at the corner of the building with a cauldron and fire, but it seemed that they would be subsisting on rice, just as they had in Cabanatuan. Several trees were growing around the school, and Hank picked up a small branch, using it to dig holes. Several of the medics already knew of Hank's previous garden and they laughed to see their friend dropping seeds into the ground, tamping down the soil over them.

Over the following two weeks he watched the garden, which sprouted dandelions as quickly as they had grown at the previous camp. At times he saw the guards watching him as he weeded around them, but they made no effort at interfering.

With two balls of rice and a watery bowl of soup daily, rest, and abundant water from afternoon deluges, the men were seeing some improvement in their health. A cemetery had been established next to the camp, but no one died for days, then weeks. The reduction in mosquitoes meant that malaria was eased as well. But the men were not at this site to recuperate, but to work. Work details were organized early, with men assigned to labor at the neighboring sugar mill, or in the sugarcane fields that fed the mill.

Within about a week at his new compound, Hank was assigned to harvesting sugarcane. With machete-style tools over their shoulders—several guards holding rifles at the ready—the group hiked about a half mile to the field where crowded rows of sugar cane grew over their heads. The cane was ready for cutting and destined for processing at the neighboring sugar plant. They walked into the field, sharp leaves scratched at their bare legs and shoulders while the sun seared their skin and heads relentlessly. Several good hard swings with a machete would cut through the cane, but the men had little strength, and their progress was frustratingly slow.

As Hank got to work swinging at the cane, the sun beating on his bare shoulders, he heard the familiar drone of American planes. Looking up he watched them soar in from the south, sweeping low enough to strafe at buildings or directly into the fields. Hank dropped to the ground while the guards scrambled for cover under low-growth trees. When the planes had passed Hank rose to his feet and looked at the POW standing in the next row over. They silently grinned and held up their thumbs in quiet triumph.

During the march back to the camp, one of the wooden clogs he'd carved himself in the Philippines split and his foot twisted on the bare earth. He had worn this pair of shoes for over a year and now he needed to carve another pair. It was the biggest setback of his day. He went to work the next day in bare feet, cutting his calloused soles on the cane that fell in the fields. By the next evening he had scavenged a chunk of wood and carved his replacement, but the shoe was useless without a support over the top of his foot. He needed a nail to hold the string in place that he could slide over the top of his foot. He was surprised when he found one of the prisoners was carrying a railroad-style spike that he had snatched at some point in the journey to and from the fields. Hank borrowed the spike to worry several nails out of the school siding and created the shoes that would carry him for the rest of the war.

Hunger was still Hank's relentless challenge. The rice filled the men's stomachs but offered little nutrition that they would need to beat back beriberi or many of the ailments they had brought with them from the hell ship. On one morning hike to the sugarcane fields, the prisoners crossed paths with a Formosan farmer passing accompanied by a large hog. The farmer carried a switch and swung it casually at the animal's haunches to coax it along. The prisoners stared in fascination. Hank felt his mouth watering.

"What I wouldn't do to get my hands on that pork," one man said.

"We got to get that pig." The entire group gathered, ogling the swine as it walked away and out of their lives.

"If I could butcher that pig we could be eating all week. I could strangle it with my bare hands." The others laughed.

"You couldn't strangle nothin. Anyway, how would you cook something that size?"

"I would eat that beauty just the way it is, raw, every piece of it."

"Oh yeah? What would you do with the blood?"

"I could make blood sausage out of it."

The musings could go on for an hour or more, imagining the meals that pig could provide and the strange and exotic recipes they concocted to eat every organ.

They passed the same farmer and big, delicious-looking pig in maddening regularity until Hank approached one of the guards, a Formosan who spoke some English and rarely doled out punishments.

"Where is that man taking the pig every day?"

The guard was happy to tell him what he knew. He was a Formosan with no apparent military background, and he bore little hostility. "Daddy pig, making babies," he said.

So the men continued to watch the boar being studded out to local farmers. The payment for successfully impregnating a sow, Hank learned, might be one or two piglets. For the POWs, pork was an unfulfilled fantasy. They were rarely served any kind of meat, but conditions at Toroku were undeniably better than anything they had experienced in several years.

20

LATE 1944

FORMOSA

Within weeks of their arrival, the dandelion farm was in full operation, yellow blooms opening in the hot sun where children had played in the schoolyard months before. Hank and a team of medics cared for the plants, plucking away leaves. As the blooms turned to seeds that could have floated away in the Formosan breeze, the prisoners never let that happen. Instead each new seed was collected and planted. A brief poke into the earth with a twig, placing the seed, and tapping down the earth were accomplished in seconds. And just as he had done in Cabanatuan, Hank distributed the leaves among those in the worst health. Now though, he did it with some reluctance. Hard feelings from the hell ship journey served as a callous when he saw his fellow prisoners suffering. Instincts told him he was in a fight for his life. Gaskill congratulated Hank's efforts though, and he fell back into the role of medic, coaxing the sick and injured back to health.

At night the men slept on bamboo mats spread across the floor of the schoolhouse and in the mornings they lined up at the straddle latrine. Hank still woke with a headache, weak and nauseous. His vision was blurred and his eyes burned in strong light. None of his illnesses abated. But he felt a little stronger, injuries from beatings were healing. His broken hand now allowed him to squeeze his fingers into a loose fist.

He found himself repeating a few of the old mantras that kept him going. When it came to maggots, "You might just as well eat them. Its apt to be the only protein you're going to get." And other food that he wouldn't even consider touching before the war years? "Whatever makes a turd," answered that question. Gaskill's solution for most problems was to forgo the trappings of traditional medicine and be creative. "Might as well give it a try," he'd tell his medics if they innovated some homemade concoction. Hank still knew there were some foods to avoid and he was always on the watch for other prisoners making the mistake of eating something that was more toxin than food.

While working in the fields he avoided the temptation to chew on the sugarcane. The men slashed through the stalks, snapping them off the plant, lugging them to the edge of the field to pile up for transportation. At the end of the day the stalks were stacked so high in a two-wheeled cart that when Hank and another prisoner were instructed to push it they couldn't see over the pile.

"Kura, kura, hurry, go fast!" The guard urged but didn't belabor the point. The Formosan guards' tones were not as urgent or enraged, and Hank felt his tension ease, just slightly. They wheeled the cart to the factory, a quarter-mile from the field where the cane was offloaded by other prisoners tasked with factory work. After Hank had returned to their camp, the men from the factory appeared shortly behind him, triumphant. Boucher had handfuls of coarse brown processed sugar in his pockets. "The guard let me have it," he said. Other prisoners had seen that transaction, and that, Hank gathered, was the reason Boucher was sharing. The field-hand group each took a pinch of sugar, then another, from Boucher's stash, and Hank savored the taste, if not the texture—it reminded him of eating sand.

That night he woke with abdominal pains. He curled up and clutched his hands around his gut, willing the pain to pass. "Damn that, Boucher!" But Boucher couldn't have known the sugar would cause stomach upset. Now Hank willed himself not to vomit and lose what few calories he'd ingested the night before along with the sugar. After a long miserable night, he was roused by the guards and he found his stomach had settled. Another insult to his digestive system had been survived.

The following week Hank's job was to transport bags of processed sugar to trucks destined for the harbor. The burlap bags were fat with the brown granular material Boucher had brought them to eat earlier and each weighed at least fifty pounds. The men were given little instruction but they didn't need to pick up a bag to know it would be too heavy to carry in their condition. Instead two men carried each bag, like a load of rocks. They struggled, rested, and continued, until they reached the truck, dropped the bag with relief, then returned for another.

At some point Hank moved too fast. Before his friend and fellow medic Louis could secure his side of the bag it slipped out of his hands and hit the dirt floor, the sealed seam breaking open and sugar bursting out in every direction. "Oh shit!" Louis and Hank stared at the mess before them and Hank braced himself when the guard ran in his direction, a wooden club held directly over his head. He brought it down square on Hank's back, knocking him into the loose sugar. Several more blows came down on his back and then shoulders as he rose from the ground.

Amidst the angry Japanese, he recognized an English phrase, "You pick up!" and he reached for the broken burlap bag. He received a kick in the chest, but he continued, pulling the sack up with him and reaching for a handful of sugar, then dropped it into the bag. Satisfied, the guard strode away. Louis reached to help him and as fast as they could move they took the sugar in two-handed scoops, shoveling it back in the open bag. Hank started pulling in rocks, gravel, and dirt with the sugar and watching it pour into the bag with some satisfaction. Louis began scraping up refuse with the sugar as well; sticks, pebbles, and any detritus went in with the sugar. With a flourish, Hank tied the bag closed and the two friends carried it to the truck.

The next morning Hank was sent out on a new project, in a vegetable garden planting seeds in one part of the field, then gently tending to each seedling that had popped up in another, pressing a spoonful of human waste from the latrine around each stem. He no longer questioned the work he was tasked with. The men got through the day, ate their rice, lay down for a fitful short night of sleep, and went through the process again. His next job was digging up the roots of daikon—large starchy white turnip-like vegetables that made his mouth water. He handled them quickly, throwing each harvested root into a bucket, and willing himself not to smell it, or worse yet—taste it.

One night Hank heard another drone of plane engines over the camp and then the concussion of a bomb landing on a structure—maybe the nearby sugar factory, he thought. Hopefully the little schoolhouse made no impression on the American pilots and would be passed over. While fires broke out and sirens blared, the prisoners remained where they lay, thinking that just maybe, it meant the war was inching closer to its conclusion.

It was clear though that they would not be staying in this place indefinitely. The guard told them as much one day as they walked back from the farm, their muscles aching, their skin burned. "You go to Japan," a guard told him as they walked back from farmwork at the end of the day.

"When?" Hank asked,

The guard only raised his shoulders and hands in a universal gesture—he didn't know.

Days later new guards arrived to escort the men out of the camp. It was January 13, 1945, and Hank and 563 of his fellow POWs were mobilizing. It had been a miserable existence there, but better than Cabanatuan and Hank felt a familiar uneasiness about his future. He would do anything not to get back into a hell ship.

IV

MINING IN JAPAN

21

JANUARY 1945

MOJI, JAPAN

Hank and 564 men climbed onboard an empty passenger train des-tined for the port of Keelung where the next hell ship awaited: the *Enoshima Maru*. Bitterly, Hank took a deep breath of fresh air before climb-ing down into the ship's hold. It was a bitter descent down the ladder, and as if the Japanese guards sensed his reluctance, one of them shoved a rifle butt between his shoulder blades to hurry him down. His foot slipped and cuffed the head of the man below him, "Sorry for that," he called down.

At the floor of the hold, his foot met grassy carpeting, and he looked down at what was a load of hemp. There was no way to know what was ahead—would it be another thirty-nine-day journey? Would they be fired on by American subs again? Would this ship hold be their grave following a torpedo, or worse, from thirst or hunger? But suffering is a matter of scale and in comparison to the thirty-nine-day ordeal between the Philippines and Formosa, this trip would be almost unremarkable. There were no lengthy delays this time, and they set sail on January 25, 1945.

He put his hand on his waist to feel for the rope he kept there, know-ing the blanket in his musette bag could serve him again. The same ribbing of stanchions striped the hold's interior, so he started planning the best position for his hammock.

The ship departed in a convoy escorted by a destroyer and mine-sweeper. This fleet of vessels held nine hundred prisoners.

From his hammock, Hank only dimly noticed the chatter, muttering, and groaning of the men on the hold floor as he dozed on and off, day-dreamed about food and about Cathy at home. Every man on board had already survived another hell ship voyage. Those who were with him now

175

were the ones with the most forbearance, and so the crying and complaining were noticeably less than they had been in the *Hokusen Maru*. There was another relief the men experienced once the ship set sail—the temperature was not rising to the unimaginable levels it had reached in the Philippines and Hong Kong. And it was becoming more temperate by the day.

They arrived at their destination on January 30, just five days after they had departed. As the men climbed out of the hold, this time, all were able to manage the ladder.

Before they disembarked, each POW had to endure one indignity, however, that seemed both pointless and cruel. Japanese soldiers announced that they would be collecting rectal smears, apparently to test the health of the prisoners. Hank let out a sigh and rolled his eyes, without speaking his thoughts. Each and every one of them was suffering from diarrhea and a variety of diet-related diseases as well as malaria. Most likely the Japanese were determining who was carrying amoebic dysentery, a disease the Japanese did not want to introduce into their country.

The rectal smears were taken from men one at a time as they stood queued up. Japanese medics inserted a pencil-sized glass rod into the rectum of each prisoner and smeared the material on a petri dish with the prisoner's ID number. The same rod was then inserted into the next prisoner. To hell with contamination. "These guys have no idea what they're doing," Hank thought, knowing they were not only ruining each sample by reusing the glass sample rod. They were also transmitting disease from one man to the next. Years later he speculated they were either working with no clear instructions, or they just didn't care.

When the ordeal was over, the prisoners walked down the gangplank. Both the landscape and climate that met them contrasted with that of the Philippines and Formosa. It wasn't just cooler, it was actually cold. Hank hadn't felt anything like it since he left Washington state. The breeze cut through him, raising goosebumps as he wrapped his arms around his bare shoulders and shivered. In front of him snow-peaked mountains rose in the distance. On the harbor front, Japanese port workers bustled around the ships, some glancing at the prisoners with contempt. Most ignored them.

"Where the hell are we now?" he asked one of the Navy prisoners. They could be relied on to have Asian geographic knowledge the rest of the men lacked. "It's Moji. Welcome to Japan boys," was his ironic response.

"I noticed as soon as we got off the ship in Japan that the guards were different," Hank recalled years later. They were younger, wore cleaner uniforms, and seemed freshly bathed, and they didn't have the hardened look of combat veterans. Hank didn't see signs they'd had any battle training.

"Some of those kids didn't act like they had more than a couple of weeks of training."

The group marched from the ship into the city of Moji, again with an audience—gathering on either side of the road they marched down—this time the least friendly one yet. Japanese citizens, hungry from years of war, and suffering from relentless American bombings could now lay their eyes on their enemy in person, and they were ready for revenge. Children lined both sides of the narrow road they marched along, hurling insults, as well as debris and rocks at them. The men ducked and dodged their way down the street, while the Japanese guards shooed the people away. They came to a stop before a warehouse that would serve as their quarters for the night.

When the group collected in front of the entrance they were motioned to wait. The sky was darkening, the sun retreated behind the horizon, and the temperature was dropping. The POWs wrapped their hands around their bony shoulders and huddled close together for warmth. Even if some of the guards spoke a little English, they weren't talking to the prisoners. Chamberlain had no idea what to expect next. Nearly three years without any control over his fate had made him chronically anxious. An interpreter arrived to stand before them, delivering their next order: to strip bare for delousing. Hank looked around the group and saw no sign of replacement clothing. It would be suicide to take off the last scraps of their clothing in this weather, to sleep in an unheated warehouse without clothes. Hank still had his blanket in his musette bag. He looked at Louis standing beside him who had nothing. As men slowly undressed, Hank stood motionless refusing to remove his flimsy shirt and shorts. The blow to his lower back came from a wooden club delivered with such force he was thrown to the ground. He struggled to stand, fearing a longer beating but it didn't come. And despite planting his hands on the ground and bracing himself he couldn't stand.

He felt arms scoop under his armpits, and he was delivered inside the warehouse by American hands and left slumped against the wall. His relief and gratitude were overwhelming but fleeting. He didn't know who had helped him, but he knew now he had to regain the use of his back and legs.

Several Japanese guards returned them their uniforms, to the prisoners' relief, and provided what Hank recalled as a paper overcoat to put over them. As he tried to pull the coat on, Hank realized he now had the worst injury of his war experience. The men would be mobilizing soon for their next leg on their journey and Hank knew he wouldn't be able to march. He couldn't sit up enough to drink or to even raise a cup to his mouth. This, he thought, may be the way he died. He looked around him at the bare warehouse interior, breathing the dust and metallic smell of the place, and regretted that he would end his life in this hated country. Even more he regretted that his mother would probably never know what had happened to him.

But Louis put a hand behind his shoulders and tugged until Hank was angled forty-five degrees and then put a cup against his lips. Chamberlain drank in relief. Dr. Gaskill, still part of Hank's party and the only doctor in the group, felt Hank's spine and announced it was intact, if badly bruised. Several medics then each shared a few spoonfuls of rice, feeding him by hand. It was hard to believe this same group of men, who had been fighting to the death for food and quiet in the hold of that ship, were now gently feeding him one spoonful at a time.

Fortunately for Hank the prisoners spent several days in Moji before the next march began again, and now he was sitting up, through searing pain, strong enough to stand and walk a few feet. He would later lose all memory of how he accomplished that march to the station where men climbed into a small train and traveled into the mountains. The pain in his back would plague him for the rest of his life.

Once on the train the men were able to sit. They had a passenger car to themselves. Their first instruction was to lower the blinds. They obeyed, with no idea why.

When the train reached Yokohama and Tokyo, several concussions told them that Americans were bombing the area. The train jerked so violently on its tracks, even as it still moved, that several of the shades were knocked open and Hank gazed out at the wreckage of a major city. The train rattled past demolition, ruins of what had been large buildings, and entire blocks of homes flattened like sandcastles. Hank watched, mesmerized, as American bombers passed over, and he saw the sticks of bombs fall from the bellies of the planes, followed by more explosions.

Hank felt the familiar dread and euphoria course through him. "Good for you boys!" he thought, and several POWs started whooping in celebration, even as they worried their train might be hit. The guards shouted at the men for quiet, and the train continued into the countryside.

Hank now better understood the animosity of those civilians who had harassed them in Moji. "It was understandable," he would note. Moji hadn't been spared the bombings either.

After seeing the destruction Hank knew the war would surely be over soon. It wouldn't be long now. That hope gave him courage.

For many, the journey from Formosa had taken a deadly toll though. Due to their illnesses or various injuries, about a dozen men were removed from the train in the Osaka area. Hank was relieved not to be among them. They continued north into colder territory and then came to a stop in the city of Sendai. From this location they were reloaded into a narrow gauge train that powered slowly, ever higher, into the mountains. When they reached the Uguisusawa Railroad Station, the men were required to walk the last few miles to their compound. They would march through several feet of snow.

They arrived at their new home—Sendai #3-B compound—on January 28, 1945, known as the Hosokura Branch Camp, established as Tokyo No. 3 Branch Camp at Uguisuzawa (now known as the city of Kurihara) on December 1, 1944. Altogether the camp housed 281 POWs (234 American, 45 British, and 2 Dutch), at least that was the number of souls still living there by the end of the war. Where the rest of the five-hundred-plus men had gone, Hank was unclear.

Their new compound consisted of a thirty-six-mile-long series of underground tunnels where the Mitsubishi Mining Company was extracting lead and zinc. A coal heated smelter burned next to the mine, and on a hillside above that mine stood the men's new barracks. They were miners now, with all the profits of their labor going to Mitsubishi. Not all POWs would be working in the mine, however. Several were appointed kitchen duty. Some would clean the Japanese barracks.

Once the hike delivered the men to their barracks, the Japanese guards lined them up. The prisoners shuffled on their feet, blowing on their hands and warming them under their armpits. But when the commander arrived, they were ordered to stand at attention. Their new leader looked at them with disdain. He did not welcome them to their new home. Instead, he announced, "You are the enemies of Japan and you will be treated as such." He indicated, through an interpreter, "You will work hard in the mine. Those who don't will be punished." He added that the food ration of rice, along with soup when available, was all they would be receiving, and they should express gratitude for it. Those who claimed to be too sick or weak to work would be tested and would have to prove it before they could avoid manual labor.[1]

There were several barracks but the largest one would be home to the Americans. A second, smaller space would be used by British POWs. The POWs from the United Kingdom had survived several harrowing years in captivity themselves, captured in Singapore, forced to provide railroad labor in Thailand and Burma. They too had traveled to Japan in a hell ship. There would be little interaction between the British and Americans, however.

Inside his barracks, Hank noticed the air was as cold as it was outside. There were several windows to the barracks, with no glass, and covered with loose-fitting shutters. Swinging them open provided daylight but also subfreezing temperatures. Even when closed, light and cold air worked through the spaces. The barrack had two stoves, which seemed encouraging, but he would soon learn that fuel for the stoves would be a rarity. A row of three levels of wooden plank bunks lined both sides of the room. Henry found himself a bunk on the middle level, about chest high. He couldn't even imagine how men could reach the top bunks in their weak conditions.

That night with several handfuls of coal the men stoked the two stoves as best they could and climbed into their bunks. Those on top required lifting. Even the middle bunk required a heaving tug to swing so high from the floor. Each man had two blankets or pieces of a blanket for sleeping— one on top for warmth and one underneath to soften the hard plank that pressed into their skinny hips, ribs, and shoulders. These blankets were a combination of what they brought with them, with some issued in Japan.

Often it was snowing at night and the men piled the paltry ration of coal in the stove and coaxed out a flame, blowing on their hands to bring feeling into their chilled fingers. Some men brought chunks of coal back in their pockets, which that they had been able to pilfer, and that provided just that much more warmth. Occasionally the Japanese brought logs onsite and the men chopped firewood out of them. But no matter what the fuel, the fires were short, and the temperature dropped below freezing inside during the night—turning water to ice by morning.

The prisoners were allotted a baseball-sized ball of rice, twice a day unless they occupied the sickbay; those who were unable to work had to survive on one.

Work began at the mine the next day. Around 5 a.m. the men were called to line up. They marched down the hill on a dirt path, worked ten to twelve hours, then hiked back up. From the first day, however, several were too weak to work, and Gaskill set up a small hospital area and asked that Hank remain behind to help treat the patients. The guards agreed to let the medic remain behind each day. This was a gift for Chamberlain that allowed him to heal the bruising in his lower back. Earning the right to miss work due to illness was no easy endeavor. Once the Japanese made the process clear, many prisoners opted to march down to the mine for a day's work whether sick or not. First a prisoner had to meet with a Japanese doctor onsite to seek permission to remain in the little hospital. This required removing all their clothes, standing at attention often for hours, and receiving a slap in the face for their efforts. More often than not, they were turned away and sent to the mine.[2]

From the first day in the hospital, the greatest challenge was to get nourishment into the ill. Men suffered from pneumonia as well as other malnourishment diseases.

In the hospital he had no way of dealing with an impacted gut. Men took to eating the coal tar that was smeared on the walls as insulation from the cold. "We started telling people not to swallow that stuff," Hank recalled.

The men all suffered from diarrhea, including Louis who told Hank when he returned from his work there that there were times they just let it dribble down their legs and onto the mine floor.

In the hospital Gaskill, Hank, and several other medics treated Americans and British. Almost immediately several men returned to the barracks with mining injuries, especially as they were first learning the work. Sometimes they managed to splint them if there was a broken bone. Or if a patient suffered a deep bleeding wound, they would try to staunch the bleeding and to clean it. But just as in Cabanatuan, the only way to clean a wound was water, and there was still no soap.

There were tricks Hank had learned in the Philippines, though, and he applied them in Japan, under the guidance of Gaskill. When one POW came in with infected sores on his legs, Hank returned to an age-old method. He boiled mud which then served as an abrasive for cleaning. By sterilizing mud over the fireplace, they could then press it onto dirty or infected wounds and rub away scabs or dirt. It worked to clean the wound, and then they would wash the mud off. Often, he heard the doctor comment, "let's try this" and another new remedy was put to the test. Sometimes Hank had suggestions. "What the hell, give it a try," was Gaskill's response.

Hank kept busy in the hospital during the day—it was notably smaller than the one in Cabanatuan and the variety of ailments was less. He could stitch up cuts, bandage abrasions, and clean and massage those who were too sick to take care of themselves. Sometimes that was enough. Very few men recovered from their ailments, but they improved enough to leave the little hospital, take up a shovel or pick, and spend the day working in the mine. Any recovery was considered miraculous and Hank devoted his day to achieving miracles.

If a mine injury or broken skin from a beating grew red, swollen, and painful, if it smelled, and pus oozed from it, Hank focused on constant cleaning. If they seemed to have given up hope, Hank talked to them about his childhood and how he planned to return to Omaha one day. He talked about how he scrounged enough food to eat, even when it required a day's labor to earn an apple from a fruit stand. He talked about the St. Bernard that got him through an especially cold Nebraska night when he had nowhere to sleep.

The stories often caught their attention and the men would share their own. That's when Hank dared hope that they might survive the night, the day, maybe the week or more.

22

SPRING 1945

SENDAI, JAPAN

Just how Henry Chamberlain infuriated the Japanese enough that he was banished from serving the little hospital, he later would not remember. There were many ways to get on the wrong side of the guards, and that included not listening to orders, failing to show respect (bowing, saluting, and keeping facial expressions respectful were among the requirements), or simply not following or misunderstanding an order. It wasn't an act of defiance like the one at Bilibid prison that had led to his beating and torture, but instead, something he never fully understood. Whatever he did wrong, he found himself one morning being ordered to join the rest of the men who hiked down the hill with a pick, pan, and carbide lantern in hand to accomplish a twelve-hour day's work.

One of the POWs, an infantryman named Tony gave Hank a sympathetic look as he lined up with them for roll call. "Welcome to our party," he mouthed as the guard strode in front of them, counting.

Once the numbers were approved, the command came, "Wakare! (Fall out)" and they began their trudge down the hill. It was a grim affair. Hank hadn't left the camp for weeks, and his wooden clogs provided little support from the slushy wet ground as they made their way. They all had crafted some kind of foot covering, whether they simply wrapped their bare feet or used a makeshift boot. Hank wrapped his feet and stuffed them in the wooden clogs he had carved in the Philippines, and for the most part was able to keep up with the marching, without getting his feet wet or frozen. His back still hurt when lying down as well as when walking, but he was able to keep up despite that.

As they marched, they carried their tools of trade—shovels or pick-axes, slung over their shoulders. Nearly all the prisoners were barefoot. The Japanese commander stated that the issuance of shoes to the prisoners would be bad for the morale of the civilians who worked in the mines. Leather shoes furnished by the Red Cross were in the warehouse throughout the POWs internment, but the commander would not allow them to be issued. At different intervals, the Japanese commander would order most prisoners to stand at attention from one hour to three hours in the cold for violations such as a prisoner turning his head away at the moment or failing to bow.[1]

For the first time Hank was seeing the conditions of the Japanese living around them. Most remained far from the road or stepped away as the parade of prisoners approached. The guards shouted warnings at the people to step away.

One elderly man and boy disregarded those warnings and stood watching as they approached. The guard reached for his rifle and the man stepped away, shaking his head. The boy followed his grandfather but turned back to stare at the men from a position safely out of reach. American POWs made a strong impression with their scrawny frames, inadequate bathing, and fierce expressions. To settle their empty stomachs, many had taken up the habit of chewing on coal tar, and the tar's dark juices blackened their teeth. One of the prisoners looked at the boy and spit out a chunk of the coal tar that they all had taken to chewing. Hank wasn't sure if the guards were keeping them separate for the safety of the civilians or the prisoners.

Most of the civilians had lost family members or homes to the war and were ready for revenge. For Hank the worst outrage was the way several middle-aged women looked at the prisoners; disgust on their faces, with handkerchiefs pressed to their noses to fend off the bad smell of the POWs.

Past the village and on toward the mine, the trees swayed in a breeze above them, cold enough to rack the men's bodies with shivers. "It's warmer in the mine," his companion said, walking beside him, lantern swinging in his hand.

When they reached the entrance to the underground tunnel system, Hank looked up where a large, portly figure sat mounted above the mine's entrance. The guard ordered for them to halt, and he then bowed to the figure above the mine. Hank looked around him, as his fellow prisoners bowed their heads with the same deep fold, the same formality, but some making their exclamations, "Screw your mother, Mine God." The guards didn't understand the English and ignored the comments, but watched.

"That's the Mine God, better bow low," Tony warned, and before Hank could react, he felt a blow above his ear. "Bow!" He dropped at the waist, his head spinning. The mine god smiled over their heads, unperturbed by the human condition in front of the mine. Hank noted its round cheeks, heavy brows, and bald head. Most prominent was his big round belly, bare, with a navel the size of a half-dollar. "Up yours you freaky bastard," Hank said, and tossed a quick grin at Tony.

The mine god was a benevolent presence aimed at keeping the mine and its miners safe, according to local tradition. This mountainous country was plagued with earthquakes so for protection, the miners were spiritually fortified by the mine god statue above the opening, also referred to locally as the "mountain god." The Americans didn't feel or exhibit the reverence that the Japanese did toward this figure, but they did bow on cue.

Hosokuru mine was one of the largest mines in Japan, in the Ōu Mountains of northeastern Honshu with the village of Uguisuzawa next door. Civilian miners and Japanese workers worked in the vicinity of the POWs but entered through a different entrance. And there was another distinction: they were free to come and go.

Upon entering, a foreman instructed the men to light their lanterns. Hank followed Tony into the mine's black maw and breathed the dark dusty air. He could hear the lumbering carts rolling in and out on tracks, empty going in and full on the way out. One man was expected to push several loaded carts out by himself, Hank would learn.

Both American and British prisoners were at work inside, chipping at rock with their picks, collecting the loose material in pans that they dumped in the cart. It was Hank's first interaction with the British and he didn't care for them. From the beginning he found the British and Americans found ways to needle and irritate each other, as if they were not allies in the war against the common enemy of the Japanese.

Hank didn't have any time to consider the dynamics between prisoners or between civilians though. He had missed any training period and his life depended on keeping up. He'd learned fast plenty of times in the past three years though, and he got to work chipping at the rock wall in the cacophony of falling rocks, the clang of pick striking rock, the shouting of voices in Japanese, and the occasional thud of weapon on flesh. Rarely did anyone cry out in response. It was a chamber of miseries, for the prisoners.

When they came out in the afternoon for a brief break, they were handed each a ball of rice, and Hank sat to eat, taking his time, despite the sour taste of the dirt and insects. It was the best part of his day. He saw now where the minerals were going. As lead and zinc were removed from the shafts, they were wheeled on carts up a ramp over a giant chimney-like smelter where a coal fire kept the heat high enough to liquidize the metals and smoke rolled up into the sky.

Hank worried about some of the men who sat looking at their rice with less enthusiasm. Everyone had sagging skin, and they looked decades older than they were. He noticed Louis's sunken, bloodshot eyes, darkened teeth, prominent bones in his shoulders. As Boucher leaned forward Hank could have counted his ribs through his thin shirt. Still they managed to feed themselves, exchange some jokes, and then lift their lantern and pick to return to five more hours of work. But some had taken the descent toward death one step ahead of the others. Several looked to Hank as if they weren't going to last more than a few more days. They were the unhealthiest people he had ever seen.

"We had been starving for a long time. Starvation does things to you that you would not imagine," Hank recalled. "You do everything you possibly could to scratch up something to eat. I'd eat my shoelaces if I thought they'd been edible." He didn't have any shoelaces though.

At the end of the day Hank walked beside his friend Louis, the two exchanging some jokes about the limping gait of their commandant when Hank noticed they were passing a crematorium, distinguishable by a pile of human bones, white in the cold drizzle that fell around them. He stared and one of the prisoners answered his unspoken questions. "The crematorium doesn't burn through the bones, so they just shovel them out into the pile." Hank wondered if any of those bones were American. He could imagine there would be some American bones there soon if things didn't change.

When they reached the barracks they were then assigned to bathing. This would be Hank's first formal bath since his capture. The first since the saltwater spray on the hell ships or the showers pouring off rafters in Cabanatuan under the tropical rainstorms.

The tub nearly filled the small shed the prisoners entered, warmed by the steam of the heated water, the rain and breeze rattling on the metal rooftop. The water was not as warm as Hank at first believed though. It has already served numerous guards and other prisoners by the time Hank stripped and stepped into its lukewarm embrace.

He had about five minutes. He knew what to do now. He watched a few prisoners standing listlessly in the water. "Start scrubbing fellows, this may be a chance to get rid of some of those damn sores." The POWs started scrubbing each other's backs, some armed with a small scrap of cloth. The water wasn't clean, but in the dim light it was hard to tell just how dirty it might be, and Hank was certain it was better than nothing.

Still, if a man defecated in the water, there it stayed. If anyone had open wounds, the bacteria in the water was sure to cause more irritation. The water smelled slightly sulfuric, but despite that, Hank stepped out feeling better. It was a daily ritual that he would appreciate. They remained in the water until they were ordered out—just how soon depended on how urgently the guards wanted to end their day and get home.

After his first night in the mine, Hank eased his sore body down on his bunk and took several painful deep breaths. This would be his life now. He wondered how much more war they had to endure. He could hear the men above him talking, laughing, and he'd had enough of that. "Hey you bastards, quit your damn yammering" It had been a long enough day already.

When they fell silent he could almost drop off to sleep, then came the loud, longwinded fart of a man nearby.

"You feel better now?" someone remarked and the barracks erupted into laughter.

"Hey next time just whistle Dixie would you?"

"Shut up, assholes," someone else finally shouted again. This time it wasn't Hank. Eventually the group of two hundred dozed fitfully. Several times during the night a man would suffer from stomach cramps and rise from his bunk. If he was on the top, he'd wake those below him for help down. Then he would relieve himself noisily at a bucket that would be emptied into the latrine in the morning. The smell got fouler as the night went on.

As the days continued through January and into February, the men often woke to a new layer of snow. The barracks stoves offered lackluster warmth, with fires fueled by scraps of wood, or a handful of coal. The barracks often froze at night and Hank woke to frost on his blanket, and the water in his canteen turned to ice.

Men were not allowed to go out except to use the latrine behind the buildings. The latrine was a stinking pit with planks over the top of it that carried an odor Hank said he could still smell the rest of his life. Next to their American barracks, with its several hundred men, stood a smaller barracks for the British POWs. While they worked alongside each other, bathed in the same tub, and ate the same rice, there was little communication between them.

The Americans outnumbered the British, four to one, but both groups were large enough to form their communities and it became clear early on that they didn't get along. They found more in contrast than in common.

To the British, the Americans seemed loud, uncooperative, and disruptive. As a matter of policy, and as a way to fight the war, the Americans were unruly and didn't follow orders. On the other hand, the British seemed arrogant to the Americans, not to mention they were too accommodating with the Japanese. Although they were allies at war, at times they were competitors in captivity.

As part of a policy of harassing the Japanese, the Americans shirked their responsibility at every possible turn in the mines. They began developing some tricks to stymy the Japanese.

One of their tricks employed the head and crab lice that afflicted every prisoner. For years each man fell victim to a colony of lice—both head and crab versions—crawling over them and itching incessantly, despite the delousing exercise they had gone through in Moji. To reduce their numbers, the prisoners used the carbide lamps in the mines, running them along the seams of their clothes, popping the lice from the heat.

Like the others, Hank spent much of his time scratching at the critters. Part of the war effort, they decided, would have to be sharing their misery with the Japanese guards. At times Hank was kept behind to clean the commandant's barracks. At the prompting of the other POWs, he gathered up lice and fleas, wrapped them in a piece of cloth. and shoved them into his pocket. When he reported to the Japanese barracks to clean, he was sent directly inside. There he unwrapped the parasites and shook them over the pillow and into the sheets of their commander.

When he left his work, the guards searched him but there was nothing to find. On the other hand, no one had searched him coming in.

The POWs similarly "seeded" many of the town residents the same way, pulling lice from their heads, and then dropping them over a miner's neck or shoulders when the opportunity arose. It didn't accomplish anything more than discomfort, but the men took satisfaction in seeing the townspeople scratching.

The British prisoners were not participating in these practices. So each group worked, ate, and lived separately, eyeing each other and complaining about their behavior when they had the chance.

One afternoon, seated on the ground before the mine entrance, with his ball of rice clutched in his good hand, Hank's eyes wandered to a group of civilian miners huddled together in the wet yard, their meals in their laps. They didn't have much more than the prisoners. He saw them spoon rice into their mouths, some ate the tops of vegetables, probably grown in their gardens.

But one civilian was different. He pulled something much more interesting out of his pocket: a duck's egg. As the man began peeling it, Hank watched in fascination. Bits of shell scattered around the dirt and Hank wondered how he could get his hands on that shell. There was sure to be enough calcium and protein in it to nourish him for days, and maybe he'd share some. The Japanese were tidy, however, picking up the remnants of their meals and discarding them in bins. Maybe the man felt Hank's eyes on him then because he looked up, abruptly, and caught his stare. Before Hank could look away the man smiled at him and offered a surprisingly friendly wave, unconcerned with being watched. Hank flashed a smile in response and was then ordered back to his work.

Later that week after their day's work, the men were all called out in front of the barracks, Americans and British alike. The commandant Lt. Katsuo Ishizawa stood before them, his hands clasped behind his back, his booted feet spread apart and his face angry. He had learned that some of the tools had gone missing recently and had reason to believe someone among the prisoners had deliberately lost a shovel. "Who will tell me that they are responsible for this crime?" he demanded through an interpreter.

The men were silent, so he spoke again. "The criminal is afraid to admit what he did, I see. Someone else will have to be the hero and tell me what happened. I expect someone to tell a guard who lost or destroyed the shovel that belongs to the Mitsubishi Mine. They will be properly rewarded for their information."

The group looked among each other and were sent back to their barracks. The Americans all knew it was Boucher, but it could have been any of them. They had all done it whenever they had a chance, and they would never turn against each other. The wall of silence was secure.

The next day after returning to the barracks and bathing in the communal tub, they were called again before the commandant. This time their despised leader was smiling. One of the guards handed an British POW a large bowl of steaming rice. "One honorable man can now be rewarded for his good choice," the commandant said, then he turned his eyes on Boucher. "You! Step out of the line," he said. Two guards flanked the prisoner before he had taken more than a single step, and he was dragged away for his beating. He wasn't one to cry out, but the Americans felt every blow anyway and knew the pain he was enduring. Hank's own back ached sympathetically. He vowed to keep the tool destruction efforts going as soon as the next day.

As Boucher suffered his beating, the recipient of the rice bowl slunk quietly away. Hank and many of the Americans turned to watch him go.

They knew his face, his name, and now they just needed to wait for their opportunity for revenge. It came after dark when men were permitted out one at a time to use the latrine.

One of the American POWs stood watch at the door until he recognized the figure who slunk past toward the sprawling stinking latrine. "Okay, look alive, men," the POW called out. Hank stood from his bunk and joined the group ready to pounce.

When their prey was on his way back from the latrine, several prisoners leaped out of the barracks and dragged him inside. Surprise can be the best weapon, especially when men are weakened from years of malnutrition and illness. He didn't have a chance to react, and they pushed him down the length of the barracks, with every American taking a swing with their scrawny fists.

When they pushed him back out the door he slammed into the Japanese guard doing his final evening rounds. This second shock had even more dire consequences. The guard was knocked to the ground, and he then leaped back to his feet, shoving and cursing at the hapless POW, while other guards came running. Not only had the man knocked him down, he was breaking a strict rule, no venturing out of the barracks at night.

Somehow it escaped their captors' attention that the POW was a victim of the Americans, and they focused their wrath on the individual rather than the group. The Englishman was tied to a post and American and British POWs alike gathered to see the man's misery, before being chased back to their barracks. A mixture of elation, rage, indifference, and empathy flowed through Hank from second to second.

In the morning the victim was still there, blue from the cold. As the miners gathered for their morning march to the mine, the guards brought out a whip and went to work on the British POW, one strike after another until he slumped in his confines. By the end of the day he had been taken down. That incident inflamed the bad feelings between the Yanks and Brits. The friction was constant. There were fights in the mine. The British and Americans shove and struck at each other when the opportunity arose. The Japanese didn't care.

At times these guards though had to protect the POWs from the Japanese people who stood watching the prisoners march to and from work with bitter contempt. Bereaved family members of the war dead and those who had become the victims of air raids shouted one morning at the men as they trudged down the hill to their work. "You killed my family!" The moods were darkening among guards and civilians alike. People protested over truckloads of food carried into the POW camps, which consisted mostly of large bags of rice. Some miners showed their opposition to what they felt were "special meals" given to the POWs by their employers.

The POWs were getting little of the food the civilians may have seen, however. The Ministry of War had instructed guards and mine management just how little compassion the prisoners deserved, and therefore how little food. Only a small portion of the provisions the Japanese had access to were saved for the POWs. And if a POW exhibited defiance, the Japanese were instructed to carry out "hijo sochi," which meant "killing" or "wounding" of the prisoners, without delay.[2]

When water was low, the men had to find their source as well. As spring approached, water was often running off the walls of the mine and Hank managed to collect water in a pan throughout the day.

Hank had come to hate the sight of the commandant, Ishizawa, who appeared at worksites or the POW barracks at unexpected times, at least once each day, and watched the men work. Hank could feel the man's eyes on him and worked as lively as he could until he was out of sight. Often Ishizawa's eyes would fall on a prisoner who may have struck him as lazy, slow, or otherwise shirking his duties. He would then call a few soldiers or guards to his side and speak to them. A guard nodded, hurried to that prisoner, already raising a cane or rifle over his shoulder to bring a blow down with full force on the man's back or head. The commandant smiled with pleasure at the sight.

Women and children sometimes reported to work at the mine as well to sweep, carry loads, and deliver meals. The mine was a hive of activity. Hank avoided everyone. But one day at the end of the afternoon he felt eyes on him and couldn't ignore it. He looked up to see someone he recognized. It was the man who had been peeling the egg and who had waved to him almost in a friendly way a few weeks before. Now this Japanese civilian—a middle-aged man—was trying to catch Hank's eye. Once their eyes met, the man strode to him quickly and held out one hand. When he opened his palm Hank saw an egg and furtively he reached out for it.

The man spoke to him in Japanese, but he didn't understand. Among the unfamiliar words were numbers, Hank recognized that much. Later he took Louis aside and showed him what he had been gifted. The round duck's egg was still warm from his pocket.

"A Jap gave you this? Why?"

"I didn't understand him. But he did say a number."

"What number?" Hank thought about it. After years of Bongo, hearing men's numbers spat out at high volume, he had learned many Japanese numerals. "It was 19 and 23."

"What do you think that is?" Hank shrugged his shoulder, he had no idea. But Louis seized on a theory. "What if 19 and 23 was a year? 1923?" Hank now peeled the egg. The delicious scent was heady, but he didn't eat it right away. He carefully stashed each shell in his pocket and then took his knife to the golfball-sized, fully boiled egg and cut it down the middle. He handed half to his friend.

"What happened in 1923?" Several days passed before Hank got an answer to his question. Speaking with an older American POW with more Japanese knowledge, he discovered 1923 was the year of an earthquake in Japan that had been devastating.

"What's that got to do with my egg?" Hank wondered.

"America probably sent some aid at the time."

Hank took to smiling at the man when he saw him, if no one's eyes were on him. He spoke too: "Origatu Gozaimasu." Thank you, and the man, who was middle-aged or more, grinned back at him.

Although he didn't receive any more eggs, he did grind the eggshell into a fine powder and stash it back in his pocket. Every day or two he would slip a pinch of that powder into his mouth and swallow hard. The rest he turned over to Gaskill to share where it was needed most.

23

MARCH 1945

SENDAI, JAPAN

Even with the misery of war, spring swept across the mountainous communities, and plants began rising from the ground, budding almost
defiantly, while the days lengthened. As the weather warmed, the sky
brightened in the east earlier and eventually one morning a hint of light
accompanied the men to their work. As usual, the guards woke them each
day at five, banged on the sides of the shelves the men slept on, the posts,
the walls, with their clubs. The moods of the Japanese were growing darker
even as the weather improved and today seemed especially black. As they
marched to work, the guards struck at those who lagged toward the back.
When they approached several civilian women, the guards herded the men
off the dirt path to let the ladies pass. They no longer forced the Japanese
out of the way of the POWs. But as the women were adjacent to the group
they stopped, their eyes challenging, and they shouted at the prisoners, first
in Japanese, then "American, go home!" The women spit at them but the
guards kept them moving, and they continued on their way.

He wasn't happy to see one of the more vicious Japanese guards working in the mine that morning. He was slender, a young man, with a bel-
ligerent grin who enjoyed the power and authority to slap the men across
the face, kick their shins, or take a swing at the back of the POWs' legs
with his cane. Sometimes the guard would circle the front of a man and
hit him in the crotch with the cane, for no apparent reason except simply
because he could.

This morning he escorted the men underground, then shoved past
them and the cart they were filling with ore. Hank saw him squeeze the
cart and disappear further into the mine where the shaft plunged further

underground. This wasn't unusual; guards found places to take a leak without having to leave the mine. That was a luxury the prisoners didn't have.

As the guard disappeared into the darkness Hank was about to return to his work when he noticed several of the American prisoners approach the cart. It was as big as and heavy as a car and wide enough to fill the shaft. One of the prisoners moved so fast it was almost imperceptible. He reached out to release the brake, and then several men put their weight into starting its roll down the track, deeper into that mine. Hank saw it gain speed as it hurdled down the hill into the shaft where it was too dark to see what was happening.

He heard the result however: a blood-curdling shriek over all the noise of the mine, just one lung-full and then silence. All activity underway in the mine fell silent as well and Japanese guards began running past Hank, down the shaft where the accident victim needed rescue.

After only minutes, about five men came back into view carrying that guard, the man's arms and legs dangling, his head lolling back. It was too dark to see his face, but Hank knew, by his posture as he was being carried that he was dead. Chamberlain was delighted his tormenter was dead but would haunted by that event later in life. He would ponder how such a terrible thing could be such a relief. For weeks after, those who passed the area of impact could see the wall smeared with dried blood. For the rest of his life Hank would hear that anguished scream.

Around the same time Hank learned of a deadly accident. One of the guards had fallen into a vertical shaft and died instantly. The mine was a deadly place, and the broken body was removed with little fanfare. The deceased was one of the more brutal guards. He learned that night, in the dark of the barracks when men were lying in their beds in the cover of dark, that the death was not an accident. "He got pushed. But his neck was already broken." That a POW had done such a thing—seen an opportunity, walked up behind the man when no one was looking, twisted his neck, and given him a shove—none of it surprised Hank. They had become a hard group and they were fighting a war. Three years had passed since he had declared in his sergeant's office that he wouldn't kill a fellow man. After all the death he had witnessed, all efforts to save lives—so many in vain—that value seemed naïve to him now. Still, he thought, he wouldn't have been one to take such an advantage, war or not.

Occasionally POWs would die in the mine too, although less dramatically than the guards who lost their lives at the hands of their prisoners. Some simply expired, their exhausted bodies slipping into unconsciousness and collapsing where they had been working. Another POW typically spotted it first, and as a medic Hank was often called on to get down on the floor and examine the prisoner. He would then call on the nearest Japanese guard, and he called to them with a single nickname, "honcho," that he heard them use on each other, and announced a death. More than once Hank helped carry a dead POW to the crematorium, accompanied by a guard.

Back at the mine, Hank took part in nonviolent trickery such as following Boucher's practice of eliminating tools. "We were still soldiers and we were still at war, and we did everything possible to stop them from gaining material from that mine," he recalled.

One way of doing that was throwing away the tools, and the smelter offered the perfect opportunity. The mine itself was a busy place and rarely were men not watched. Japanese civilians and Chinese prisoners worked on mining and processing. Women and children lugged tools and equipment back and forth in front. The smelter chugged hot steam in front of the mine entrance.

The process required sleight of hand. Hank first took a hand tool, a wrench, shovel, or pick, and passed it to another prisoner who then shuttled it to the man assigned to feeding the smelter. A wooden ramp wrapped around the giant oven that brought him to the opening. If a cart was pushed up that ramp, the tool was shoved in with the material.

The contents were then dumped fast. Men didn't stay up there long as few could stand the heat more than a few brief moments. Then the prisoner descended from the smelter, the empty cart, and the triumphant expression on his face told the story of one more small blow to the Japanese mining efforts.

24

APRIL 1945

SENDAI, JAPAN

Hank watched the colors brightening on the thawing hillside with a nutritionist's eye. He had already identified some patches of soil where dandelions would be most likely to thrive, and soon he was back to work, gardening in the evenings or on the occasional day off, when no guard came to escort the two hundred men down to the mine.

The prisoners were noticing further changes as the guards that summoned them in the morning were younger and in some cases less violent than those before them. While some slung rifles over their shoulder, others only carried a stick or club to keep discipline. Hank noticed one new middle-aged guard who seemed mentally incapacitated as he herded them into the mine. He stumbled around the prisoners, seemed easily confused between the different POWs, and repeatedly aimed his rifle at them as if he didn't know how to use it. The other guards seemed impatient with the man.

When he unbuttoned his pants to urinate against the wall his aim was as haphazard as his rifle management. The stream piddled onto the leg of another guard. That man looked at his wet pant leg and lashed out with a fist to the face. Hank and Louis exchanged a glance while stifling a smile. Their frustration seemed to typify how the Japanese war effort was going and every irritation for the Japanese felt like good news for the prisoners.

Before the day was over, though, Hank was surprised when the Americans were called out of their work and ordered to line up to be addressed by Lt. Ishizawa. They stood at attention for several minutes. When the commandant appeared before them he immediately waved at them to stand at ease. Now what? Hank no longer had any expectations, every incident, every Bongo could lead to a beating, execution, or nothing. There was no way to predict.

The man knew enough English to speak at times without an interpreter, although Hank strained to understand his accent. "Today a very important man died," he declared. Hank pondered this announcement. Was it their prime minister Tojo? Or the Japanese emperor Hirohito? Were they going to be directed to mourn one of Japan's leaders?

Ishizawa continued, "American president, Franklin Roosevelt." Silence reigned as the men processed this news. A breeze raised the Japanese flag, cooling the men standing below it, and then fell still. The captain didn't wait for a reaction, he raised a hand dismissively, "You go back to barracks." They had been given the entire afternoon off. He turned and strode to his office, climbed the stairs, and shut the door behind him. There had been no gloating over their loss. The guards motioned for the men to start marching, and they began their trek up the hill. Hank was baffled.

"Roosevelt died? How?" He selected the least hostile of the guards marching beside them, one who had an intelligent expression and rarely made use of his club.

"How did Roosevelt die?" he asked, first in English, then in broken Japanese.

"Sick."

"Who is the new president? Henry Wallace?" Wallace was the vice president when Hank went to war, so that should be the appropriate replacement.

"Henry Wallace?" the guard shook his head. "I don't know. Harry Truman?" was the answer.

"Harry Truman? Who the hell is that?" he thought.

The men talked into the night in their cold barracks, seated around the stove that emanated little heat from a small handful of coal. None could remember any such man. Harry Truman had been a senator when the soldiers shipped off to war, a lifetime before. He had been sworn in as vice president just months earlier, while the POWs were digging material out of the Japanese mine and daring to hope that the war's end was coming. The world was changing without them. Truman told the press he felt like a load of hay had fallen on him, while for the prisoners of that barracks it felt like just one more shock, as if they had been trying to dig out of that hay for three years. Would this lead to even more war, more years in captivity? Hank wasn't sure many of the men would survive it.

The death of Roosevelt served to aggravate their already dark moods. They walked to work with snarled faces. Japanese civilians seemed to watch them with more trepidation. One local schoolboy recalled being frightened of these fierce-looking men who wore rags, glowered, and spit wads of coal tar on the side of the road as they marched.

Their march often took them past small, wheeled carts ornately painted and planted with garden vegetables. In the daylight women pushed these carts out into the sunshine, then brought them back to the house as the sun fell. Hank, who had been carving most of his life, admired the beauty and delicacy of the work. It seemed, he noticed, that whenever the Japanese people could embellish something with art, they did. For most prisoners, however, the attraction was not the cart but its contents. No matter how easy it might have been to snatch something by the leaves, and stuff it into a pocket, the men never stole a vegetable, knowing they would have the hell beaten out of them for it. Even so, every time he spotted the leafy tops of root vegetables or shoots of spring onions in those finely carved and painted carts, Hank, too, was tempted to reach for them.

As the guard skillsets declined, their commander Ishizawa was becoming more volatile. One day he was disinterested in the men, another day they were made to stand for hours at his command for no apparent infraction. More than once he came to them seemingly drunk and spitting furious orders to the guards which led to beatings for his entertainment. Ishizawa relished the abuse the guards inflicted, especially when he had instigated it, watching and laughing while prisoners were bludgeoned, kicked, or slapped.

The enlisted Japanese guards were permitted to beat American and British prisoners at any time they chose and with any weapon that they chose but only a few seemed to enjoy themselves and get much pleasure from beating the prisoners.

As the war raged, the mine's labor dynamics changed as well, with families providing heavy labor, and civilians guarding the POWs. After three and a half years of abuse, Hank was hardened, accustomed to his state of anxiety. Leaving the mine one day he paused to drink from his canteen when he heard exclamations from one of these new guards, waving his rifle at Hank to move in the other direction, allowing the Japanese civilians to pass. Hank was finally tasting his first drink of water for the day, a drink he was not going to interrupt. This time, he decided, he couldn't be bothered by this guard, and he wasn't going to be intimidated.

The guard approached until he stood face to face with Hank, six inches smaller, his face smooth and unshaven—he was just a kid with a weapon. The guard swung his rifle back just like so many guards did, every day, and brought the butt down with all his might on Hank's shoulder.

The force knocked Hank back but the prisoner easily steadied himself and the pain didn't register. He regained his footing and stared into the eyes of the young guard. Then he did something he never expected. He laughed.

Momentarily stunned, the guard took another swing, laid a heavier blow on Hank's chest, then rebounded, and circled back with a blow to the side of the head. But each time he did Hank just restored his balance and laughed louder. Prisoners and guards as well as civilians watched the spectacle in fascination and some prisoners may have expected that to be Hank's final moment. But the guard was mystified. He stared at Hank standing there, his canteen still clutched in one hand, bleeding, and laughing; then he dropped the rifle to his side and walked away.

Later Louis asked him what the hell he was thinking. "I wasn't. I don't know what was so funny," he said. Maybe it was the absurdity of being beaten by a boy in his teens. "There was something about this young kid hitting an older guy like me after I had been through all this combat and he hadn't," Chamberlain recalled many years later. "I actually think he was frightened." That was when he realized the war wasn't going well for the Japanese.

By now and maybe especially after Hank's amusement, the guards handled the prisoners with more caution. "Some of them were a little afraid of us," Chamberlain suspected.

25

SUMMER 1945

SENDAI, JAPAN

The weather was turning hot as the long days of summer illuminated the POWs and their work at the Mitsubishi Mine. By July 1945, the mine teemed with such a wide variety of people—young and elderly civilians and children—who seemed out of their elements, that productivity was minimal. Still, the Japanese rising sun flag flapped over Hank's head as he marched into the worksite, and the mine god gazed down at them unperturbed each day as they entered and left.

On one particularly hot evening, the men sat in their barracks ending their day, the sun hugging the horizon and shooting its last rays through their small windows—the shutters flung wide open. They had washed the sweat-soaked grime off their bodies in the communal tub. Now they sat on their bunks. Louis had scrubbed his ragged shirt and it was hanging from a handmade nail driven into the clapboard wall. Not for the first time Hank marveled at the impact years of starvation was having on the prisoners' bodies. He could count the man's ribs and the vertebrae of his back. He was nothing but a bag of bones. Hank knew he was looking at a reflection of himself.

He opened his mouth to speak to Louis but forgot what he was going to say. He heard a deep rumbling sound. It lacked the familiar buzzing pitch of the Japanese planes. Hank, Louis, and several hundred POWs looked up, frozen, listening. The sound approached them, growing louder: airplanes, more than one. And then came the eardrum splitting crash. The explosion rattled their barracks, throwing anyone who had been standing to the floor.

Immediately they were running for the door. The men gathered in the yard, joined by the British prisoners, all trying to make sense of what they were seeing. The smelter that the barracks looked down upon was gone, a tower of smoke rose in its place, into the evening sky. The planes were flying directly over the barracks, then broke to the left and circled, coming back in again. The symbols painted on the plane wings were familiar but not—they were not the star surrounding a circle that Hank had known when he joined the army. They were simply stars, no circle. During his captivity those designs had changed; the red circle had been removed due to the resemblance to the Japanese sun symbol or "flaming asshole" as Hank had come to think of it.

Three planes came at them again, as if circling back for another look at their handiwork, and the POWs stood frozen to their spot, their eyes fixed in the sky. Then the lead plane did something Hank had never seen before: it barrel-rolled 180 degrees and came at them full speed on its head, waggling its wings in a way no highly disciplined Japanese pilot would ever fly. As it approached Hank could see the top was open and the pilot was feeling the full brace of the wind as he barreled toward them, exposed to the elements. He was low, probably one hundred feet above their heads, Hank estimated. And just before the pilot lifted up over their barracks Hank saw him stretch out a gloved hand—a big glove—he recalled, with one thumb stuck up in an unmistakable American gesture of triumph.

Hank's legs found strength he hadn't had five minutes before and he leaped skyward as if he could reach up and touch those planes, pumping his fist back at the pilot even as it disappeared into the horizon. Cheers roared out from the men, these bedraggled POWs—three-quarters dead—were jumping, laughing, hugging, and shouting in ways they hadn't done in years, if ever.

"We're back, Goddamn, we're back!" Hank and Boucher broke into a hug. Americans and the British were for once on the same side. For Hank three years had passed since he and his friend Earl had come out of their barracks at Fort McKinley to be shot at by a Japanese plane signaling the start of the war with Japan. Now the air attack meant rescue was imminent. Hank wished he had Earl with him for this moment. The contrast was thrilling.

The POWs' jubilation went on all night in the barracks and the Japanese were nowhere to be seen. The question that returned all night long consumed them: "How do they know we're here? How the hell did they know we were here?"

The Navy men among the POWs recognized their planes, taken off from aircraft carriers—either Hellcats or Corsair planes. But ultimately, they all agreed, "We're going home, we won the war!"

There were several bombings of the city. In the early morning of July 20, 1945, 123 aircrafts carpet-bombed the densely packed residential center of the city. Thousands of civilians were killed. A five-square kilometer portion of the center of the city was destroyed, with 11,933 residences burned.

The next morning at 5 a.m., just like every other morning, the door slammed open and the guard strode in, banging on the walls, the bunks, the men, with a club, shouting for them to get to work. But Hank knew things were different.

They headed down the hill to work, marched past the wreckage of the smelter, and saw that part of the mining operations and structures had also been demolished, but the mine itself was there, the mine god gazed down at them. They went about their bow and marched inside as usual, offering him a "Fuck you!" before they entered.

The Japanese were as unhappy as the POWs were elated. A few expressed themselves to Hank. Unknown to Hank the city of Sendai had been devastated. "No good B Needja koo [B-29]," one told him.

On August 6, the US B-29s, which the Japanese civilians had come to dread, flew over Japan again but with a much deadlier mission. The planes dropped the devastating atomic bombs that obliterated Hiroshima and then Nagasaki three days later. The POWs knew nothing of it. At the time of their capture, the atomic bomb was entirely unknown by the public. Since his internment, Hank would soon learn that the world had changed in shocking ways. He sensed the change when interacting with the Japanese guards and mines the next day. They stared at him stunned, shook their heads, and often repeated, "No good. So many dead." There was no one at Sendai Camp 3B who could fathom this new weapon and what it had done. People went about their work as if in a daze.

That afternoon the commandant arrived at their barracks and ordered them to line up. He strode back and forth in front of the men, shouting at the top of his lungs. His face turned dark, his voice was slurred, his steps sloppy. Several times he stumbled. The man was drunk again. He swung his club indiscriminately at any American in the lineup, bringing blows on bare heads, shoulders, guts.

He then singled one prisoner to receive his rage, a big man who had been struggling with beriberi and pneumonia. Too many times beatings were doled out so fast it was impossible to understand what had started it. All Hank knew was that Ishizawa was shouting at the guard who strode toward the unfortunate prisoner with determination and gave the man a blow to the head that knocked him unconscious. He slumped to the ground where he was kicked for several minutes. Then the guard walked away, laughing. The beating was too much for the man's malnourished body and within days he had died. Hank and three others used a sled provided by the guards to drag their comrade's body to the crematory. In the days following Hank found himself staring at that guard with naked hatred. He no longer cared if there were repercussions, and he doubted there would be. He wanted revenge.

26

AUGUST 1945

SENDAI, JAPAN

On August 15 Hank and his fellow POWs trudged to work in the mines just as they had every day for the past eight months. There had been no news, no change in activity, only the slow dwindling of competent labor among miners and guards alike. On this day, in the heat of summer, the underground shaft provided a cool reprieve. But the work was depressingly limitless: always more to dig, more carts to roll out, the smelter in the meantime was being rebuilt. They used their carbide lanterns to light their work, casting long shadows on the walls, working close enough to hear the other workers around them, but none of them Japanese on this particular morning. Hank didn't think much of that, and he was relieved for the quiet. Then at noon a voice called for them to come out. It was too early for the midday break. He had learned to measure out the time internally in the number of shovels or pans full of ore, the number of carts rolled away, the number of breaths as they strained their muscles with one strike after another on the shaft walls. Without hesitating, Hank joined the other POWs in picking up their tools, their lamps, and trudging up and toward the sunlight. They lined up in neat rows, turned off the lanterns, and waited for the next instruction.

Only a few minutes passed before Ishizawa stepped out of his office building across the yard carrying a box in one hand. He limped toward them briskly, came to face the group, turned the box over, and climbed on top. Hank had never seen him do such a thing. The man's face was stony, impassive, hard to read, but it always had been. He stood for a length of time that seemed to stretch into minutes, then he opened his mouth to speak. Hank recalls his exact words this way:

"Our Emperor say war over."

They waited, the mine yard was the most silent Hank had ever heard it. "You go home," he added. Hank watched the commandant step down, pick up the box and walk away, to retreat to his small office. Louis and Hank turned to each other, then the others in their group. They looked around them and noted that any civilians who had remained around the mine now had wandered away.[1]

No one seemed to know what to do next. Hank walked toward one of those guards, and the man raised his hand in a salute. When they marched back to the barracks, the guard accompanied them, their rifles drawn, this time watching for civilians as if fearing an ambush. But they passed the village unmolested, the civilians keeping their distance. The guards smiled politely at them when they handed out their ration of rice, this time served with some tea. The clubs, bayonets, and swords were put away, and their behavior was so uncharacteristic that Hank paused before eating the food.

The next morning no one woke the men, and they stepped out of the barracks to see the guards standing in front of the gate, guarding the fenced-in barracks, but not to keep the men inside, rather to protect them from the Japanese.

That day passed slowly, Americans and British alike lounged in front of the barracks, hungry and excited, eagerly talking about home and how they would get there. Two Japanese soldiers climbed on their barracks carrying cans of black paint and large brushes. When they came down they had painted the letters "PW" on the roof.

In less than a day the Americans reappeared in the sky, flying over the camp. They dropped a note for the men that said, simply, "The US has accepted Japan's surrender." The note also instructed them that a package of food would be dropped tomorrow. As promised, planes swung low over the barracks the next day, so low that the parachutes for several of the boxes of food failed to open. The boxes hurdled down the hillside toward the barracks and struck several prisoners before they could dodge them. Two Englishmen and one American—all of whom had survived to witness the end of the war—died in this accident; one more tragedy for men who had come to expect nearly anything.

The Japanese formally surrendered on September 2, 1945, and from that day forward the guards didn't enter the compound. Occasionally Japanese civilians approached the barracks and stood at the fence looking inside, gesturing that they were hungry. One resident, Tadashi Kano, recalled that scene when he had been a boy, when he saw prisoners hand packages of food to the occasional Japanese visitor. His father strictly forbade him from approaching the Americans for such purposes.[2]

When American GIs arrived in several army trucks, the ordeal was finally over. The men were issued clean uniforms, and with gratitude Hank shoved his sore and swollen foot deep into a black leather, American combat boot. Another truck, filled with grinning, well-fed GIs pulled into the camp and called out to them. One of these GIs looked out at the assembly of scrawny prisoners, gathering to gaze at him with weary eyes, and he lifted a crate of apples to the edge of the truck bed. He reached in, palming the red fruit, and then he threw it down to the closest POW. The men had grown so weak that many struggled to catch the fruit. Hank outstretched his hands when an apple soared across the distance between him and that truck and gripped the fruit between his fingers. He held it for a minute, touching the smooth skin, then put it to his mouth, sinking his teeth into the sweet white pulp inside, juice exploding over his tongue.

The taste was so overwhelming he had to stop, then took another bite, noticed it was salty as well as sweet. He was crying, salty tears streaming down his dirt-covered face. Nothing would ever taste as perfect.

The Japanese leadership was taken into custody, and for a few dangerous hours, the guards were in American captivity and freely accessible to the prisoners they had tormented. Hank realized he had an opportunity to settle a score and he walked around the guards' barracks in search of the man who had caused him and others the most torment around the camp—the guard who had carried out the commandant's orders to beat a prisoner just weeks before and who had done it with so much glee. Hank found his mark in the custody of the Americans, and he approached as if the two of them were alone. He punched the man in the face with enough ferocity that he worried he had broken his un-injured hand. The hated guard lurched backward, fell flat on the ground, his legs spread out. Hank acted on instinct: he brought that heavy new combat boot down with all the force he had on the man's groin. POWs gathering around Hank and this guard cheered the one-sided fight until one of the GIs pulled Hank away. "Okay leave him alone, buddy," the man said.

Exhausted from his efforts, Hank sat on the grassy yard near the mine and Louis seated himself beside him. "Happy now, Hank?" Chamberlain looked at his friend with a sigh and smiled.

"I thought I might kill that son of a bitch. He was like every Jap guard that ever beat or killed a prisoner. But I guess I really was right when I joined the army, I don't want to kill anyone."

When he climbed into the back of a truck and sat shoulder to shoulder with his fellow liberated POWs, he noticed yet again what a ragged group they had become. One of the men reached across the truck bed at him with a hand that had been blackened with frostbite a few months ago. "You saved my life in there, Hank, probably more than once, I'll always be grateful for that." Hank nodded and smiled but then shrugged. He didn't like to take singular credit—the Americans were there to help each other, that's all.

The trucks took them away from their camp, and Hank didn't look back, just breathed the cool air that blew around them, wondering if this was just a dream. At the first stop each prisoner was handed a ration that included canned goods, condensed milk, dried meat, chocolate, and coffee. Hank held it tight in his lap as he sat in the back of a troop truck. He watched Japan pass by through the canopy opening. When the truck paused at an intersection in a city unknown to him, Hank had time to consider the devastation.

The whole country seemed scorched to the ground, and the suffering was palpable. The smell of smoke was everywhere, burned wood, anything that had made a life in Japan was gone. People quietly sifted through the rubble, looking for anything familiar. He shook his head at the futility of it all.

Hank's eyes locked on one skeletally thin woman who sat at the side of the road, her face dejected, watching Japan's enemy triumphantly passing through her town, now idly stopped at an intersection. She held a baby, he saw, a scrawny child that was motionless, exhausted by hunger.

Hank called out to her, beckoning. She hesitated and he motioned again. He almost gave up, as the truck driver was releasing the brakes, preparing to roll back into motion, when she walked over. Hank handed her his rations. He pointed to the baby then pantomimed eating and pointed again. She nodded, smiled, and stepped away as the truck pulled off. "I don't know if the kid got any," he recalled later. As the truck rolled on, Hank wondered, "What good could a few cans of food do for someone who was starving? What would they eat tomorrow?"

Hank was routed to a Japanese hospital for examination. Later he joined the other prisoners on an American Naval ship where they could be fed and questioned. Hank weighed in at just ninety-eight pounds. Onboard the ship, the former prisoners lined up at the mess hall table and were served steak and potatoes. Just the smell was intoxicating. Hank ate with abandon and then stood.

"Where you going?" Louis asked as Hank broke out in a sprint. He reached the ship rail just in time to vomit the steak into the churning waters of the Pacific. He stood there, catching his breath and considering how much his fortune had changed, then he went back to the mess hall and grinned at his friend.

"It came back up, I'd better try again." Hank asked for another steak. He was almost finished before he had to race back to the ship rail. The third steak stayed down.

In the coming months and years, hundreds of Japanese officials and guards would pay a price for the inhumane treatment of POWs. Lt. Katsuo Ishizawa of Sendai Camp 3B and Lt. Col Masao Mori of Cabanatuan each received a life sentence in a Tokyo courtroom. But the greatest suffering was felt by the civilians who lost their homes and lives in a war that had, in the end, provided them only heartache. America's retribution took up to 240,000 lives in the atomic bombings alone. Japan's cities, along with Manila—which lost more than one hundred thousand of its population—and so many others around the world, began the process of healing.

27

SEPTEMBER 1945

MANILA, PHILIPPINES

When Hank Chamberlain arrived in Manila he planned to spend some time there regaining some health and putting on weight. Shortly after his arrival, he walked through the streets of wreckage that had been the city of Manila, the former "Pearl of the Orient." Gone were the stately buildings, Spanish era resorts, hotels, parks, and theaters. Death hung over the city, as tragically pungent as anywhere he had been during the war.

Stationed within an American military zone, he was stronger, better fed, and recovering from his illnesses. He was looking forward to returning home. As he negotiated a busy street, crowded with GIs he wheeled his head when he heard a familiar name. "Hey Schneeweis!" Schneeweis, his old friend, the fourth member of the group of medics who had come into the war together. He couldn't count the nights he'd wondered what had happened to his friend after the rest of them were sent to Cabanatuan. Now he whipped around to look into a sea of unfamiliar faces.

"Yeah?" The man responding to that name sounded like his old friend, but the face was completely changed.

"Sneezy?" The man turned to stare at him. The two searched each other's features for anything they could recall from their earlier lives. "It's me, Hank," Chamberland said, and when Sneezy smiled, Hank finally saw something he recognized. He had the right man. The two fell into a hug, crying, laughing, shaking hands, and pounding each other on the back. Wiping tears off his face Hank declared, "You look like hell, my friend!"

"What about Bill? What about Earl? Have you seen Dr. Brown?" Hank had only bad news for his friend.

"Bill didn't make it, he's buried at Cabanatuan. I haven't seen Earl or Brown in nearly a year."

Sneezy had been sent to Japan and the hardship was evident on his gaunt face and bony body. Now the two were determined to put the experiences behind them and they became inseparable. They agreed that they were in no condition to show up in America and shock their families. Chamberlain feared Cathy would take one look at him and end their four-year romance. He still had no idea that his mother and girlfriend believed him dead.

Hank was delighted to see his old friend Harry Brown in the Philippines, too, who was looking forward to returning home, to resume his medical practice, and to be with his wife.

Eventually Hank found Earl's name on a list of survivors from Bilibid prison, where he had finished out the war. From there it was easy to track down his old friend, and then he reintroduced Sneezy and Earl. The two old friends fell into an embrace, tears rolling down their cheeks. Sneezy and Hank spent several weeks of unrestrained eating and drinking, rarely talking about their ordeal. At quiet times, such as late at night, though Hank remembered the ones who wouldn't be going home, especially Bill who had helped him through those dark early days of prison camp.

One afternoon while walking through the demolished city of Manila, Hank came upon a jarring sight. He was in the American military zone where the remaining fighters of the war were being confined and shipped away or held. He saw a Japanese man seated in a wire mesh pen, staring blankly out at him. The man was stripped to his underwear, seated like livestock waiting for the slaughterhouse. He was Japanese. In an instant a raw rage returned to Chamberlain—every indignity and cruelty he'd endured seemed to replay before him. He thought of the beatings and executions he'd witnessed, the men he'd tried to nurse back to life, only to see them cut down by Japanese gunfire. He thought of how the Japanese laughed at suffering and death. Now here was the embodiment of all that hate, and he couldn't look away.

He stopped directly in front of this demoralized symbol of the Japanese Empire, as the man warily watched him, waiting to see what Hank would do. Hank pointed to himself and said, "POW," the man's eyes flashed with recognition. Hank then pointed at him, "Now you. POW." He raised his hands and began clapping, slowly, dramatically, applauding the way it had all ended. Then he walked away.

The ship that ushered them home was old, worn, and disheartening—dedicated to POWs but without the luxuries the Navy had provided in Japan. But Hank's focus was on the destination. He couldn't wait to get home. For monotonous days he stood on the ship's deck, inhaling the fresh sea air that he had so desperately longed for while on the hell ship. He was finally leaving the war behind him, and he considered what kind of a soldier, and what kind of a medic he'd been. True to the convictions he'd had at eighteen years old, he'd killed no one. He'd never considered how many people he might save, and now, looking back on the thousands of soldiers and even civilians, Americans and Filipinos, who had passed through his care, he had no idea how many might of benefited from his care. Two hands and water make paltry tools or medicine.

After days at sea the men learned they were approaching Seattle and the former prisoners lined the deck railing to gaze on US soil, smelling the fir trees and sea air of the Northwest coast. The forested hills seemed to rise as they approached. Then they spotted the structures of a Coast Guard station. The POWs were awestruck by what they saw at the shoreline in front of that station. There stood a line of Coast Guard reserves, standing at attention, saluting them as they passed. "There's no description for that kind of happiness and elation," Hank recalled. "That was one of the best moments of the war. One of the best moments of my life."

28

FALL 1945

AFTER THE WAR

When Hank called his mother in California, he learned what her personal hell had consisted of. For several years she had believed her only son was dead. Just weeks ago she had learned from the US Army that the news had been wrong and Hank was still alive. As he stood at the payphone saying the words, "Hello Mom? It's me, Hank," he heard her break into sobs. They spoke briefly about his health, his plans, and he promised to come see her within the week.

Then he headed to Spokane to see Cathy. Did she know he was alive? He didn't know, but he didn't want to waste another hour without seeing her. He made the familiar trip to her family home, first by train, then bus. When he reached her parents' home, a small child sat playing on the porch and the toddler stood to watch him approach. Before he could knock on the door Cathy, older but unchanged, stepped out that front door and scooped up the child. She looked at Hank and in her expression he realized the Japanese misinformation had ended his relationship. Thinking him dead, Cathy had moved on, married, and started a new life. Before the conversation could go to his dashed hopes or her regrets, he waved goodbye. He wished her well and walked away. Around the same time, Harry Brown, Hank's friend and mentor had a painful and parallel reunion with his former wife. She had waited for him, but then learned he had died, and she had remarried. It was one tragedy too many, Brown had sustained himself on thoughts of his wife. Within days he took his own life.

Hank spent the following twelve months in a California hospital, fighting back the diseases he had contracted in the POWs camps. His mandatory visits with military doctors and psychotherapists ended badly.

Psychotherapy for post traumatic stress disorder was still in its infancy, and the military, and American society, was utterly unequipped to handle these POWs and the unprecedented trauma they had experienced.

Whether he was being debriefed or a therapist was trying to judge any disorders, Hank found that his stories fell on deaf ears. They just were not believable. He, like many of the prisoners, was questioned about the honesty or accuracy of his memories. No one would do the things they were describing. "What's not to believe?" Hank stood when he was scolded by a therapist for not being forthcoming. He stared at the skeptical face of a man who had no idea what people could do to each other. "You dumb shit," Hank walked out, letting the door slam behind him.

Hank took a job at a local hospital but couldn't comprehend the insubstantial role he was given, the inconsequential conditions he was treating, the absurd hierarchy he had to adhere to. As he helped prep surgeries for minor conditions, he pondered his future there. The people he had to answer to couldn't possibly comprehend what sickness, pain, and mental anguish he had already treated for four years. When he went home at night, his mother couldn't understand his surly mood.

"You think the war was hard for you?" she asked. "We suffered too, there were times we had no butter, even no sugar if you can imagine that." Hank walked to his bedroom to start packing. He regretted now that he had spared her from seeing his condition when he was liberated. She would never know what he had been through and there was no way to explain it.

Hank joined the newly formed independent military branch, the US Air Force, went through paramedic training, and shipped out to Greenland for a year at Thule Air Base providing medical support to troops there. He stepped into the coldest and quietest place he had ever seen. "Even when I was a little boy I wanted to see the North Pole," he recalled, and now he was as close as he was going to get. The silence gave him a chance to think. It was there that he met with a chaplain.

"I am so filled with rage over what happened, over what the Japs did to Bill, over all those men," he told the minister, a military man who had not served in the war and could only imagine the experience that had caused so much anger. "I've seen so much gore, so much death," Hank shook his head. "There is no way to ever move on without seeing that right in front of me."

They sat in silence and Hank started to stand. There was nothing more to be said. But the chaplain cleared his throat and spoke.

"Are you a church-going man?"

"No I'm not, but I pray every night. I used to pray that the war would end, now I pray it will end in my mind."

"Well Hank, I don't know if the war will end for you, but I do know if you can't forgive you'll never be able to truly move on. Can you forgive what was done out there? To your friends and to you?"

Hank shook his head, "I don't know." From that day, however, he resolved to try to do just that. And seventy years later he could say with conviction, "I forgive them all, even Ishizawa. I had to forgive them. I wanted to live my life right." He was stationed at Fort George Wright when he met his future wife Dorothy Wunnenberg, a surgical technician herself with the Women's Army Corps in Spokane. She carried her burdens, too. Her fiancée had been killed in the war, and Hank appreciated that they had both suffered profound losses. They married in 1947 and she was the love of his life.

He returned to Asia, serving as medic and senior master sergeant in Okinawa. In the 1960s Hank and Dorothy took their family of seven children to live in the Philippines where Hank found Manila strikingly changed: still gritty but rebuilt, crowded, and seemingly recovered in just two decades. He was taken by surprise one day when he and Dorothy received a dinner invitation from Philippine President Ferdinand Marcos and his wife Imelda. Marcos, a former POW of the Japanese, and now leader of the Philippines, wanted the camaraderie of fellow prisoners from the war. After the small group dined in the Marcos' palatial home, Imelda gave Dorothy a tour, while the president spoke privately with Hank and several other former American POWs. He asked for their stories and shared some of his own. Time has erased the memories of those stories Marcos shared at the time, but Hank did recall one thing, "He suffered the same thing we did, he was beaten and tortured like the rest of us." One point that Hank did notice was the resentment Marcos still harbored toward the Japanese, resentment that was as thick as the walls around his mansion. He had not let go of his anger.

Chamberlain took his son Mike to visit the site where he once treated desperate patients in Bataan's Hospital 2, but the jungle had reclaimed the space and its memories. Although a memorial has been built at the Cabanatuan Camp, he could never bring himself to go to that place. "World War II is never over for me, or for anyone who was affected by it. It always continues," Hank says. It comes to him in his sleep, it ambushes him on the Fourth of July, and each anniversary is as hard as the one before it. "You never forget the death or the gore, every day you think about it."

He has gained an appreciation of the Japanese culture and cuisine and he has always loved rice. "Rice is a beautiful food. I think it must feed 90 percent of the world," he says. And while he has forgiven the guards he once hated, he carries the burden of knowing the darkest side to human nature. "I think that's part of being human unfortunately, that's what we are all capable of, and it's what can happen when your anger gets away. It's something people need to watch for."

In 2017 the Japanese Ministry of Foreign Affairs invited a party of former POWs and their family members through the American Defenders of Bataan and Corregidor Memorial Society to return to the site of their captivity as a guest. It was part of a conciliation effort between Japan and those who had been their prisoners.

Hank weighed the option for some time. Traveling wasn't out of the question. He was steady on his feet, but walked with a cane, a piece of twisted willow he carved and polished for himself—with the kinds of bends and imperfections that life can deliver. It supported his slow, steady stride. At ninety-five years old he had outlived his wife Dorothy and most of the POWs he'd shared his war experience with. He'd survived open-heart surgery the year before. He enjoyed his family: six daughters and a son, all within driving distance. There was no reason to go far from home now, on a mission into his past.

He learned he was the last and only living POW from the mine, not even a living former guard could be found. He was obliged to share his story, to help a new generation of the Japanese and Americans, to under-stand what happened in that place. He went to that place, flying first class with his daughter Rebecca for support, escorted by private car directly to the mine, now owned by the Hosokura Metal Industry Corp. The portion where he had worked seventy years before was long closed.

Everything seemed unfamiliar. Where were the thatched roof houses on the road to the mine? The mine's entrance was blocked with an iron fence. Henry walked to that fence, slowly, leaning heavily on his cane, and peered inside, then froze. His body suddenly stiffened, recalled Yoshiko Tamura, his escort to the site and to his past. "Mr. Chamberlain's body didn't move even an inch." She recounted. "We heard the raindrops hit-ting our umbrella and the sound of the eternal flow of the stream of the wastewater from the mine." That's when the small party felt the full impact of what had happened at that site, "Silence and intensity surrounded us."

They brought Hank to the mine's Memorial Monument—erected on the hill across the road from the entrance—that commemorates the POW labor provided at that site. "Mr. Chamberlain took a long time in reading the whole of the epitaph of the memorial, then he turned to the others and expressed his gratitude in a clear tone," Tamura said. He spoke the following: "I thank you for having built this Memorial Monument."

Later, as the group escorted him by wheelchair into a section of the mine known as Mine Park, open to the public, Hank was overcome by a recording of the sound of dynamite, recreated for tourists, but so immediate for him that his face contorted with pain and sorrow. Later the group surrounded a diorama of the mine in the public gallery, and it triggered a memory. Hank had a vivid recollection of one of the worst events that took place at that site: the time the POW sergeant shoved a Japanese guard down a vertical shaft to his death. He knew he had to share what he was thinking, this might be the only time the story was told. "He twisted his neck and pushed him off, downward. I think he died instantly," he told the group. It was a homicide, a death, among so many lives lost in the war, that had gone unaccounted for so many years. Those listening were momentarily stunned. For the Japanese, "It was too sudden and horrible a story," Yoshiko remembered. They were taken aback by the almost casual violence of the act, and the unprompted retelling of it. Had anyone ever heard that story before? "Mr. Chamberlain might have wanted to let us know the painful and miserable circumstance in those days through this one example." Mitsubishi Material personnel provided an apology for the suffering caused to Hank so many years before and Hank accepted that apology on behalf of his friends, as much as for himself. For those Japanese members of the party, it was an opportunity to face the past, and to reconcile that history with the evolution of Japan's and America's amicable relationship. "After that, we were on our way back with the father and daughter, who were perfectly serene feeling," Yoshiko recalled. Hank, however, said he was in turmoil, remembering the past, reliving what he had tried to put aside.

Once returned to his home in Edmonds, Washington, Hank considered the experience with the benefit of some time and geographic distance. "It was a melancholy trip for me," he said, "I'm so grateful I had the opportunity to revisit Japan and to see how beautifully Tokyo has been rebuilt from the rubble of the bombed out city that I remembered." Yet he acutely felt the pain of all those men who had been there, and the restive sense of spirits not yet at peace disturbed him.

For Japanese and Americans alike, the visit provided some acknowledgment to the wasted lives, the rage that caused so many deaths. A dark cloud hanging further over this somber occasion was the memory of two atomic bombs that took as many as 226,000 Japanese lives in a matter of days, with many more Japanese civilians killed in the firebombing of Tokyo and other cities. The rebuilding of Asia began in 1945 and Hank was gratified to see what had resulted.

Today he says, he hopes to never see unchecked rage seize a society again or see a government sanction or sponsor that rage. For Hank, his memories start with the most recent ones in Japan. "I was treated with such respect and honor," he mused. Still, the POW experience lives on in him and in those who hear his stories. "I do believe that this was a healing trip, although there will never be closure." For Hank, like most war veterans, the sounds and sights and anguish of those years in combat, or captivity, never fully leave him. He summarizes it this way: "War never ends."

NOTES

CHAPTER 5

1. Department of Defense, nurse interview, Geneva Jenkins.

CHAPTER 6

1. John R. Bumgarner, *Parade of the Dead* (McFarland, 1995), 58.
2. Bumgarner, *Parade of the Dead*, 58.

CHAPTER 7

1. https://history.army.mil/books/wwii/5-2/5-2_21.htm, 380.

CHAPTER 8

1. The AMEDD Historian history newsletter, Spring 2018.
2. John R. Bumgarner, *Parade of the Dead* (McFarland, 1995), 66.
3. Bumgarner, *Parade of the Dead*, 66.
4. https://history.army.mil/books/wwii/5-2/5-2_21.htm, 380.
5. https://history.army.mil/books/wwii/5-2/5-2_21.htm, 380.
6. "US Army in World War II," edited by Kent Roberts Greenfield, *The Fall of the Philippines*, 444.
7. Bumgarner, *Parade of the Dead*, 71.
8. AMEDD Historian history newsletter, Spring 2018.

CHAPTER 9

1. POW, Julien M. Goodman, M.D.
2. POW, Julien M. Goodman, M.D., 3.
3. Mansell.com Lt. Col Jack William Schwartz Affidavit.
4. http://www.us-japandialogueonpows.org/Nelson.htm.
5. Col. Masanobu Tsuji was at least partially responsible for many Japanese atrocities including the Bataan Death March. To avoid prosecution for war crimes when the war ended he went into hiding in Thailand. (*The Pacific War Online Encyclopedia*, Tsuji Masanobu [1901–1961?]).

CHAPTER 11

1. Bob Wodnik, *Captured Honor: POW Survival in the Philippines and Japan* (Washington State University Press, 2003), 62.

CHAPTER 12

1. Gordon Rottman, *The Cabanatuan Prison Raid: The Philippines 1945* (Osprey Publishing, 2009).
2. John R. Bumgarner, *Parade of the Dead* (McFarland, 1995).
3. Bumgarner, *Parade of the Dead.*
4. This story is blazed into the memory of Henry Chamberlain and not officially listed in the execution records for Cabanatuan. Whether time has altered his recollections of this experience, or it was simply another undocumented incident from the war, we may never know.

CHAPTER 13

1. https://bataanproject.com/proviso-students/beecher-lt-col-curtis-t/
2. William R. Evans, *Soochow and the 4th Marines* (Atwood Publishing, 1987), 101.
3. http://www.mansell.com/pow_resources/camplists/philippines/Cabanatuan/schwarz_jack_l_affidavit.html
4. https://bataanproject.com/proviso-students/beecher-lt-col-curtis-t/

CHAPTER 14

1. E. Bartlett Kerr, *Surrender and Survival* (William Morrow, 1985), 150.
2. Lt. Col Jack William Schwartz Affidavit regarding Bataan Hospital 2, Cabanatuan, Bilibid, Oryoku Maru sequence: Moji, Fukuoka 1 and Jinsen.
3. Alfred A. Weinstein, *Barbed Wire Surgeon* (Macmillan, 1948), 2444.
4. Bill's remains were recovered after the war and buried at a Philippine American war cemetery.

CHAPTER 15

1. This incident does not appear to be included in available documentation. The best confirmation is Chamberlain's recollections and consensus among historians that the event could have reasonably occurred based on similar instances in this time and place.

CHAPTER 16

1. Alfred A. Weinstein, *Barbed Wire Surgeon* (Macmillan, 1948).
2. A. V. H. Hartendorp, *The Japanese Occupation of the Philippines* (Bookmark, 1967), 142.
3. Hartendorp, *The Japanese Occupation of the Philippines*, 142.

CHAPTER 17

1. https://ww2vetsstory.wordpress.com/2011/11/15/chapter-2-cabanatuan-prison-camp/
2. http://www.ibiblio.org/pha/comms/1944-09.html

CHAPTER 19

1. http://www.mansell.com/pow_resources/camplists/china_hk/toroku_roster.html

CHAPTER 21

1. http://www.mansell.com/pow_resources/camplists/sendai/sendai_3_hosokura/meridith_2.html
2. https://bataanproject.com/provisional-tank-group/whittinghill-pvt-grover-d/

CHAPTER 22

1. According to the recollections of Alonzo C. Meredith, State of Texas, County of Palo Pinto.

2. http://www.powresearch.jp/en/pdf_e/archive/pows_e.pdf

CHAPTER 26

1. According to another account Ishizawa was more effusive when the war ended. Speaking in broken English the message this prisoner received was "Now you will be soon returning to your homes and loved ones. I want you take great care and look after your health." It's possible that there were several such speeches made among the various prisoners. In both cases though, the shock was the common theme, the following silence, the sound of throats clearing, the confusion. And then the joy.

2. Based on "Research of the Homeland Kurihara," a 1973 interview with Mr. Tadashi Kano.

BIBLIOGRAPHY

Ashton, Paul, Capt. *Bataan Diary*, 1984.

Blazich, Frank. *O Say Can you See, When the Dandelions Went to War, An American Prisoner of War's Story*. National Museum of American History, 2019.

Bumgardner, John R., MD. *Parade of the Dead*. McFarland & Co., 1995.

Daws, Gavan. *Prisoners of the Japanese*. Quill William Morrow, 1998.

Evans, William R. *Soochow and the 4th Marines*. Atwood Publishing, 1987.

Franz, Harry, M. B. E. *Bamboo Treadmill*. http://www.orpheusweb.co.uk/ynnad/.

Goodman, Julien M., MD. *MD POW*. Vantage Press, 1972.

Hartendorp, A. V. H. *The Japanese Occupation of the Philippines*, 1967.

Ind, Lt. Col. Allison. *Bataan: The Judgement Seat*. MacMillan, 1944.

Jacobs Eugene C. *Blood Brothers: A Medic's Sketch Book*. Carlton Press, 1985.

Kerr, E. Bartlett. *Surrender and Survival: The Experience of American POWs in the Pacific 1941–1945*. William Morrow, 1985.

Knox, Donald. *Death March: The Survivors of Bataan*. Harcourt Brace Jovanovich, 1981.

Marshall, Peter B. *1368 Days: An American POW in WWII Japan*. Luminare Press, 2017.

Miller, J. Michael. *From Shanghai to Corregidor: Marines in the Defense of the Philippines*. Marines In World War II Commemorative Series, https://www.nps.gov/parkhistory/online_books/npswapa/extContent/usmc/pcn-190-003140-00/sec1.htm

Morton, Louis. *The Fall of the Philippines: US Army in World War II*. Center of Military History, United States Army, 1953.

Norman, Elizabeth M. *We Band of Angels*. Random House, 1999.

Scott, James M. *Rampage, MacArthur, Yamashita and the Battle of Manila*. W.W. Norton, 2018.

Utinsky, Margaret, *Miss U: Angel of the Underground*, Arcadia Press 2019.

Weinstein, Alfred A. *Barbed Wire Surgeon, A Prisoner of War in Japan*. Macmillan, 1948.

Wodnik, Bob. *Captured Honor*. Washington State University Press, 2003. http://www.mansell.com/pow_resources/camplists/philippines/bilibid/POW_Camp_Information_RG389Bx2206A.pdf

West-point.org/family/Japanese-pow

INDEX

Photo insert pages are indicated by *p1–p15*.